Subtext

Subtext invites and encourages personal and blatantly subjective responses to photographs and analyzes the drivers behind them. During decades of participating in critiques as both student and teacher, André Ruesch has become convinced that it is the personal response to work that connects us in the most visceral and meaningful way. This book aims to encourage and educate viewers how to read and understand photographs on a deeper level, honoring and validating their responses to photographs. This book seeks to vitalize students in the photography classroom. Rather than a dense tome of theory, this is an accessible guide to taking individual ownership of—and enjoying—the visual experience.

To be visually literate is comparable to being linguistically literate. Such literacy is necessary to engender a deeper understanding and valuation of culture: both types of literacy create, enrich, define and historically document the expression of one individual to be shared by all.

André Ruesch has been an active photographer for over thirty years. After receiving a BA in photographic studies at Edinburgh Napier University, Scotland, he moved to Albuquerque to receive his MA and MFA for graduate studies in photography at the University of New Mexico. While there, his main mentors were Patrick Nagatani, Betty Hahn, and Eugenia Parry.

Ruesch's work has been internationally exhibited in museums and galleries and published in the *British Journal of Photography*, *Art in America*, and *Asian Art News* among others.

He lives in Massachusetts, where he is a Professor of Photography at the Lesley University College of Art and Design.

Subtext

Critiquing Individual Photographs within a Collective Consciousness

André Ruesch

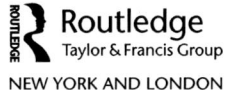
Routledge
Taylor & Francis Group
NEW YORK AND LONDON

First published 2018
by Routledge
711 Third Avenue, New York, NY 10017

and by Routledge
2 Park Square, Milton Park, Abingdon, Oxon OX14 4RN

Routledge is an imprint of the Taylor & Francis Group, an informa business

© 2018 Taylor & Francis

The right of André Ruesch to be identified as the author of this work has been asserted by him in accordance with sections 77 and 78 of the Copyright, Designs and Patents Act 1988.

All rights reserved. No part of this book may be reprinted or reproduced or utilised in any form or by any electronic, mechanical, or other means, now known or hereafter invented, including photocopying and recording, or in any information storage or retrieval system, without permission in writing from the publishers.

Trademark notice: Product or corporate names may be trademarks or registered trademarks, and are used only for identification and explanation without intent to infringe.

Library of Congress Cataloging in Publication Data
A catalog record for this book has been requested

ISBN: 978-1-138-88606-3 (hbk)
ISBN: 978-1-138-88607-0 (pbk)
ISBN: 978-1-315-71485-1 (ebk)

Typeset in Times New Roman and Helvetica
by Florence Production Ltd, Stoodleigh, Devon, UK

Printed in Canada

I

Dedication

For Kristine, Max, Evan, and Isabelle
In memory of Lilian and Sam

11
Quotes

The problem with conformity in education is that people are not standardized to begin with.
Sir Ken Robinson

. . . Also, why did you feel the need to write it? You're an inspiring, highly intelligent teacher. And anyway, one never learns photo or anything worth doing from BOOKS. Take yourself as the best example of that!
Eugenia Parry, writer on photography

Contents

I	*Dedication*	v
II	*Quotes*	vi
III	*Contents*	vii
IV	*Foreword: An Interview with Patrick Nagatani by Ryoichi*	xi
V	*Acknowledgments*	xv
VI	*Introduction: For Whom This Book is Meant and How to Use It*	xvii
VII	*Prologue: The Periodic Table*	xxi
1	The Velvet Hammer: The Potency of Elements	1
2	The Personal Galaxy: The Symbol	7
3	Just Fashion: A Question of Identity	13
4	Nike and the Butterfly: The Reversed Stereotype	19
5	Staying in Line: Conductivity	23
6	Politics: The Metaphoric Landscape	29
7	Henry's Tale: The Photographic Fable	35
8	Moment by Moment: Elapsed Time—Eadweard Muybridge Revisited	41

9	The Drowned Gun: Time as Poetry	46
10	Split Again: The Reversed Connection	53
11	The Other Half: Water and Air	57
12	The Original: Please Touch the Art	61
13	The Tyranny of Borders: The Fractured Elements	69
14	The Holy Rosary: Belonging	75
15	A Conversation with God: The White Elephant in the Room	79
16	Superstructure: Conflation	85
17	Lady Like: Body Language	89
18	Recycling: The Image Ecology Approach	93
19	Appropriation: Reinterpretation	101
20	Dad: Titled versus Untitled	107
21	Speed and Stoicism: The Nature of the Elements	111
22	Reflection: The Literally and the Figuratively	117
23	Sky View: Upside Down	121
24	Blood is Blood: Assumption	127
25	Hypnagogia: Viewpoint	131
26	Harmonia: Rendering the Invisible	137
27	Snap: Breaking Point	143
28	Recognition: The Need for Invisibility	149
29	Big and Small: How We Give Thanks	155
30	Ammo and a Happy Meal: Be Theatrical	159
31	The Spider and the Net: Catch and Caught	165
32	Dirty Jobs: A Deceptive Comedy of Errors	173

33	What is to Come: Dreaming	177
34	The Angel and the Wasp: The Order of the Elements	183
35	In the End: Censorship	191
VIII	*If Lost or Lonely: Get Your Work Out There*	*199*
IX	*Epilogue: Florence +The Machine*	*203*
X	*Quick Reference: Featured Artists in Alphabetical Order*	*205*

Foreword
An Interview with Patrick Nagatani by Ryoichi

The following interview took place on August 6, 2016, the 71st Memorial Anniversary of the dropping of the Atom Bomb on Hiroshima, Japan, by the United States of America. The interviewer, Ryoichi, is a longtime friend of Patrick Nagatani. Ryoichi has relatives in a farming community outside of Hiroshima. He earned his M.F.A. degree from the University of California Los Angeles in 1980.

Ryoichi: Both of us have read many chapters in André Ruesch's book and I am interested in how you were chosen by André to write the foreword. Can you elaborate on this?

Nagatani: Certainly. I taught in the visual arts and primarily in photography for 38 years. Twelve years at Hamilton High School in Los Angeles, and at various junior colleges and Fairfax High School adult classes. I ran the photography program at Loyola Marymount University in Los Angeles, taught for a semester as a visiting artist at The School of the Art Institute Chicago, and did two stints as a visiting artist at The University of Hawaii and the University of Nevada Las Vegas and for 20 years I taught photography as a Regent's Professor at the University of New Mexico. In addition I did numerous short visiting artist gigs nationally. At all of the institutions I met with graduates and undergraduates and "critiqued" their work. I served on several national art-granting committees, most notably the California Arts Council and the last National Endowment for the Arts Individual Artist's grants. I am retired now but still meet with graduate and past students about their work.

I chaired André Ruesch's graduate committees while he earned his MA and MFA from the University of New Mexico. He challenged me with his brilliant work and writing throughout his studies. We remain as friends and colleagues to this day. He has graciously written a chapter in my upcoming novel, *The Race—Magic in the Sky*. I have read many parts of his book and am honored to write this Foreword.

Well it does seem that you have done a lot of critiques in your career and your closeness to André's life and work makes you a good choice to write this introduction. I am curious as to what value you generally and personally see in a book of this nature?

For over 40 years of reading everything I could concerning photography, which included reviews of work in all the mass media art venues, and critiques of student work, I am and have been terribly disappointed with the regular jargon of "art words" that at times can easily fit into anyone's work. Feedback is usually rushed, formalistic, mediated, and derivative. It is also often safe, yes encouraging and compassionate, but sometimes without rigorous analysis. I remember the last review in my MFA program where the entire faculty walked through looking at my work. A famous faculty artist, whom better remain nameless, had not said a word about my work in 4 years of reviews. This last time, after looking at what I put up, he turned around at the door and said, "Make them bigger." So much for critical feedback.

There are not a lot of good critique books written for educators and writers. André's writing and critiques fill a huge gap in the nature of feedback that young and old educators and writers should read and benefit from. I do want to get back to this question at the end of this interview.

What specifically is unique in André's critique and writing thoughts in this book?

A college friend once told André that he was more of an intellectual than an academic. I disagree in that I believe André is an intellectual multicultural educator as well as an artist. In this book he puts all of his strengths together in critique analysis. He has the ability to provide a perspective from different cultural viewpoints and he applies this in his open critique of images. Most important is the fact that he is so well read. His knowledge of photography, history, religion, socio-political issues, and various cultural gender issues is applied in connecting thoughts. His critique weaves together ideas in honest and risk taking analysis.

I have been living with Stage 4 Metastatic Colorectal cancer for over 3 years and have received over 58 chemotherapy treatments. Cancer patients will tell you that chemotherapy affects the brain. This has been true for me. I call it chemo emo. My intuitive and dreaming qualities have been enhanced with the loss of the ability to multi-task and think technically. More importantly though is the fact that I desire things that move me and are inspirational. I've got no time for nonsense and shallow thoughts and dialogue. For this reason I have been so excited by this book and André's giving critiques. I believe his intellectual knowledge is coupled with his dreaming ability. André is a dreamer. He also loves music as he writes about in the epilogue. The lyrics of Supertramp's song *Dreamer* seem to fit.

Before I leave the dreamer in André, there are two things that impress me further. In his critique he often talks about the flow of liquid and being under water. It is often said that being under water is like being in another world. André has visited this world in his art and in his thoughts. He transverses other worlds and brings this into his interpretations of student work. And then there is the intuitive, compassionate, and visual connection he makes with animals. I have an old doggie that tells me things through her eyes and behavior. In all the years that I have known André, I realized his connection with animals. This connection comes out in his response to student work that has animals in the compositions.

Finally and possibly most importantly, is André's visual connection and analysis of all the details in an image. After his emotional and intellectual response to the images, he takes the time to look at all the details within the frame. Everything is important and as he points out, it should be to the image-maker as well. André will break down the environment and background as a ground for directing the image. From red string to other directed props in the images, he responds to meaning and constructed dialogues that are implicit in the image-maker's thoughts and his responses. It seems to me that all educators should look at student work with this kind of intensity and feedback. The visual arts classroom should be a place where it is exciting and where anything can happen. I constantly smiled at the suggested assignments after each critique that provided challenging ways to further explore image creation. Hopefully with this book the reader will be anchored in thinking about the reciprocity between the global and personal and how perspective changes depending from where you are looking and reading. And I say this for the students as well as the educators.

In answering your question Ryoichi, I have tried to point out the attributes and talents that André brings to his critiques, and writing and offers his students. André is a unique educator that his students obviously benefit from in various ways.

You obviously have a lot of respect for André and this book. In closing this interview, you spoke about the value of this book to educators and students earlier. Can you be specific now?

Yes, on the longtime respect for André as intellectual, academic, teacher, and artist. I think this book is long overdue as it provides uplifting and original ways to look at, think about, and critique student work. It should contribute to the field of visual arts education in a magnificent manner.

I feel that every educator can't possibly critique work as André has done. I certainly couldn't. But every educator comes with personal history, their own aspect of intellect and reading that has probably entered their own art making, as well as an understanding of the visual arts and a sensitivity to their students. Otherwise they wouldn't be educators. I think it is up to the educator to pull these things out and give to the students the best that they can.

I attempted to write specifically on this but backed off of my words in finding a text of André's that did it so eloquently. I am sure the reader won't mind reading this twice.

> The journey into the heart of images should be an adventure for both maker and viewer. Each time we set sail we can't know where it will lead us. Like most adventures this can be perilous and enchanting and probably both. As we set sail to shores unknown at the beginning of a semester or whenever we pick up the tools of our trade and engage the process, the reciprocal dynamic of impulse and feedback,

intuition and rationalization will be different for each person, each cohort, and each viewer. Really all that is required is an open mind and heart. This is the currency that makes life worth living; it is what gives life its true meaning. But unfortunately, to protect ourselves, we shut it off more often than not. When art teachers tell their students to take a risk that can mean many things. For me it is the willingness to take that risk, which makes you vulnerable. That is the price. A leap of faith, which, at times can be painful, is essential to pursue. If the passion and courage of the images we have explored throughout this text have taught you anything, it should be that the alternative of not taking a risk is worse. Sometimes, it is worth crying over spilled milk and then to make art about it.

Acknowledgments

It is with immense gratitude to my wonderful students, whose encouragement that I write down my critiques about their extraordinary work has led me to embark on this project. I am grateful for their willingness to contribute their inspiring, often-courageous photographs, too few of which are represented in this book. Nobody works in a vacuum. Let me also acknowledge all the others who have supported and helped these artists.

Contributing Artists: Anni Abbruzzese, Chai Anstett, Henry Aragoncillo, Elaine Carson, Christine Delay, Jennifer Edwards, Liz Ellenwood, D. Robertson Fay, Jordan Fleckenstein, Johan Jansson, Andrea Jones, Anouk Jutta, Rigby Kelly, Elliott Kravits, Vanessa Leroy, Tyla Levesque, Jon Lewis, Paul Lewis, Max Maez, Hannah Mainhart, Sara Plum, Eleanor Rappe, Jackson Reeves-Henning, Adriana Reyes-Newell, Karen Riley, Thap Saengsouriyheth, Marcos Sanchez, Richard Saunier, Sherry Selavy, Steve Sikora, John Smith, Mark Teiwes, Trang Vu, Megan Whitney, Missy Wolf.

Great thanks to Routledge—Focal Press editors Judith Newlin, Elise Poston, Kimberly Duncan-Mooney, Galen Glaze, Anna Valutkevich, for their trust in giving me this opportunity. Also with much gratitude for their care and creative layout to the production editor, Kristin Susser, editorial team leader, Laurence Paul, project manager, Ellie Jarvis, copy editor Quentin Scott, and editorial intern, Lorna Wilkinson, of Florence Production Ltd. I am equally indebted to Professors Patrick Ryoichi Nagatani and Henry Horenstein for their tireless efforts. Karen Riley's invaluable insights, critical reading, and ongoing editing while I was preparing the manuscript for final submission cannot be overstated and are deeply appreciated. As is Richard Green's careful reading of the final drafts, from the British perspective. Eli Green, a student in his final year at Brandeis University and Megan Eckles, a student in her final year at Lesley University, also read the final version of the manuscript from a student perspective, providing invaluable insight.

Neither can I fully express my thanks to Patrick Ryoichi Nagatani for his generosity in writing the foreword, nor my sadness for his suffering at the hand of cancer that he endures every day with inspirational poise and pragmatism.

My wife, Kristine Kenner Ruesch, and friends Henry Aragoncillo and Paul Lewis, I thank for their unyielding and, eventually, exasperated encouragement, without which this book would certainly never have been written.

Introduction

For Whom This Book Is Meant and How to Use It

From its inception, photography has mirrored our experiences, reflected and contradicted our opinions, inflamed our passions, and otherwise informed and misled us with its uniquely subjective objectivity.

It is not uncommon to have a strong emotional response to an image, to feel a connection to it, but it is not always easy to say why or how that connection came about. In fact, the more intensely we are drawn to or repulsed by an image, the more difficult it can be to say why. Yet, studio artists are expected to speak in eloquent and informed ways about images—both those of their peers and their own.

This book invites and encourages personal and blatantly subjective responses to photographs and analyzes the drivers behind them. During decades of participating in critiques as both student and teacher, I have become convinced that it is the personal response to work that connects us in the most visceral and meaningful way.

That is not to suggest that traditional scholarly approaches are unimportant, quite the opposite in fact. Since, however, as human beings we attempt to balance the individual with the collective in almost everything we experience, it only makes sense to value our responses to photography in the same way. Therefore, I believe the more this is developed the more valuable texts on photographic theory, history, aesthetics, and skills will become.

As we are dealing with the potential enormity of everyone's particular response to every image ever made, it also makes sense to develop a roadmap for navigating these potential encounters. A compromise therefore needs to be found between an overly formulaic approach versus complete disorganization in tackling critique.

Before we discuss ways to analyze and deconstruct these photographs, it is important to understand that no assumption about a right or wrong way to do so will be suggested here. The reader is encouraged to take away what helps hone her or his responses to photographic works.

My preferred method of critiquing is based on what I think of as a *reverse critique*. Rather than several students hanging and discussing their work side by side, I believe it is more helpful to concentrate on one student's image or series of images at a time.

This avoids the dynamics that inevitably occur among different bodies of work. While such dynamics are the lifeblood of great curatorial or editorial efforts, in my experience they tend not to be particularly helpful in a critique. Multiple bodies of work together generate complexity in a way that often distracts from the work at hand, or else creates the illusion of a shared narrative generated by the interaction among simultaneous presentations.

Second, a *reverse critique* requires that the creator of the work not speak until the very end of the critique. This avoids the proverbial leading of the jury and the self-imposed prism through which the work might be viewed. Often myopic perceptions of an image(s)' success or failure, based on the maker's statements at the outset of the critique, are thus avoided and lead to a broader consideration of the work for both viewers and makers.

A *reverse critique* requires students to critique the work cold. A different student is designated to start the critique each time and everyone has to comment. Thus students end up discussing work whether it resonates with them or not. More importantly, the voicing of personal responses to the work introduces avenues of experience and perception that often come as a surprise and great enrichment to the creator of the work. If the work has a specific intention behind it, any feedback referencing this intention will also be more credible because the image-maker will not have had the opportunity to steer the viewer's perceptions in a particular direction.

This approach isn't just rooted in the belief that an image should be able to speak for itself. As a viewer, if you do not respond to an image, its relative historic, cultural, or even monetary value might be informative or educational in valuable ways; nevertheless, your appreciation is not likely to change in terms of feeling personally connected to the image.

To be visually literate is comparable to being linguistically literate. Such literacy is necessary to engender a deeper understanding and valuation of culture: both types of literacy create, enrich, define, and, eventually perhaps, also historically document the expression of one individual, to potentially be shared by all.

To be visually literate requires awareness and responsibility on the part of the creator; not only by understanding how to create photographic narratives but also by being able to gauge his or her own intentionality and motivations. Recognizing the motivation behind your work may take time to become apparent; by letting your work speak back to you and by listening to the experiences of others. What may start off, as an intuitive probing, will begin to take shape as you work, sequence, and see the connections among the images. Often the direction of a series will be revealed by the images themselves.

The power of the photographic image is inevitably entangled with the diverse tolerances that cultures have in relation to photographs and the vast divergence within different cultures as well. We only have to remember the cuts by the US Congress to the National Endowment of the Arts in the mid-1990s as a result of controversy. This was caused by prominent photographers such as Robert Mapplethorpe and Andres Serrano, whose explicit works were foremost examples of intercultural disagreement and divergence.

Photographic images have reflected and shaped culture since the inception of the medium. Critical thinking and creative problem solving are inherent aspects of all rigorous pursuit in artistic expression. Photography is hardly an exception to this, but is fundamentally embraced by many societies as a means to challenge and reinforce cultural values.

To photograph is inextricably linked to personal accountability. Photographers represent a force in relation to our continually changing cultural values, whether by challenging them or reflecting them; photography is co-creating them.

This book is, primarily, meant for students interested in developing their skills: to make and understand photographs; to expand upon their ability to articulate their thoughts; and to broaden their vocabulary during a critique.

To that end, we will be considering images mostly made by art school students at the Lesley University College of Art and Design, in Cambridge, MA and at the School of Art and Design, Santa Fe Community College, in Santa Fe, NM. Photographers who submitted work to LensCulture, for which I write reviews, have made additional contributions, and some work found its way into the pages of this book from Neal Rantoul's photographic critique group as well. As such, this book aims to meet the needs of photography students of various ages and teachers by exploring strategies for how individual experience can be utilized, encouraged, and contribute to discussions during critique and in formulating intentional narratives.

By discussing ways to unravel an image, I hope that each reader further develops the skill and confidence to bring their own increasingly emancipated voice to the encounter of looking at the photographic image.

Herein lies the power of the "subtext." The most successful images have the power to engage the viewer way beyond the subject matter and, even if we can't say why, hold our attention for longer. Like everything else this can be learned, and I hope this book will help you in taking steps to develop these skills for yourself.

Finally, when we make work we are usually asked to present the images along with an artist statement.

Our choice of words will define the work for others. When the image makes its way into the world, we will have intentionally framed and codified it, and we will have attempted to determine a starting point for the viewer—a starting point into the narrative, an entry point, something to guide the experience of the viewer into the journey they are about to embark on.

This is an opportunity to connect with an audience and to avoid "over-directing" them. A short, sparse, and enticing statement is a little like reading the menu in a restaurant; you don't want to describe the meal to death, just enough to make someone want to order it, to experience it.

Books are no exception: they usually rely on the jacket being the guide. By summarizing or codifying the content, we are directing the perception of the work, and how people talk about it, as if we are protecting a hard-won task. The artist or writer has bled and now the verbal forces have been marshaled to protect this effort. When exercising this control we similarly end up directing the experience for our viewers or readers. I understand that I, myself, am also expected to do this here—to provide the context of what this book is about.

However, I encourage you to resist this convention and will instead urge you not to protect your work—to avoid having it pigeonholed: that urge to control something that, in many ways, is inherently uncontrollable anyway. Therefore, to place us on a level playing field, I have to resist that same temptation. If I suggest that you take that risk with your own work, then I must obviously do the same.

In the chapters to come, we will see where that takes us. In one case, we will also examine how strongly even just the title of an image can direct the viewing experience.

It is for this reason that I leave you with this introduction and deliberately vague roadmap, keenly aware that we share a starting point and hopefully multiple individual destinations.

In the spirit of being prepared to take a risk, I believe that no matter how strongly you might feel about what you have created, it can be extremely beneficial to forego revealing those feelings, and your original intentions, in order to provide a non-mediated experience to the reader and the viewer.

As this book finds its way into the world, I hope taking this risk will prove to be effective for you as a reader and an artist.

This is my reason for not contextualizing what follows in the coming chapters. I am going to leave that to you, the reader, whether you are a student or a fellow teacher. As you explore this non-contextualized approach in relation to the images discussed here, I hope I will have made a contribution to promote the importance of visual literacy and helped develop confidence in your own approaches.

Prologue
The Periodic Table

As you may remember from your chemistry classes, the periodic table organizes known elements based on their characteristics. Like chess pieces, some elements are very common and others exceedingly rare. In combination, they create new matter just as components in photography create meaning.

In this book, we will use the periodic table of elements as an ongoing guide—as a metaphor for thinking about images. The elements are "relative" in their appearance: that is to say we experience gold as a solid and water as a liquid. However, by changing the temperature enough one way or the other, gold becomes a liquid and water becomes a solid.

Combining chemical elements together can lead to compounds whose emergent properties bear little relation to the constituent parts—and by altering the ratio of one element to another, even more variability can be introduced. The elements approach, both in terms of making and reading images, therefore does not rely purely on the element(s) but also on the ways in which they can be combined.

Then there is the "chemistry"—and here, I am referring to an altogether more elusive quality that we can feel but can be very hard to pin down, at least at first. Initially, we feel drawn to something, to someone, or to some image—and in those cases that matter to us personally, this experience can be quite intense. In many cases, it doesn't feel right to start analyzing such feelings: we should accept them, enjoy them, work with them. However, I believe that while people should enjoy being attracted to an image, you should also try to understand why. And of course, there will always be the shocking or distressing images to confront; you can feel drawn and repelled in equal measure, but you shouldn't stop looking and questioning.

We'll be exploring the images very closely for how the combination of elements can become greater than the sum of their parts. How it makes you feel; whether your encounter with the image has a lasting effect—one that takes you beyond what is represented and continues to keep you engaged.

This is the subtext.

The best journeys, at least for me, are not preplanned with a particular destination in mind. The most satisfying outcome to me, leads to the discovery of places I hadn't known of and hadn't imagined. Sometimes this will lead to great joy. When you meet what you have always known for the first time. That is how we can find a home in places far away. This is traveling with no map and no destination. This is exciting, hard, even disorientating, and a little dangerous at times. Relying on our own wits to deal with what we discover, is not embarking on a journey with a passport, credit cards, cellphones, and other multiple safety nets. Instead, it is as if you just start hiking, you just set off and surrender to whatever experiences you encounter. As this is unique for each of us, the examples in this book attempt to demonstrate how this can be tackled in thirty-five distinct chapters, even though some have flowing boundaries between them. I hope to slowly build into the deeper narrative and subtext and to invite you along on your own terms.

Any guidance I give is not meant to become the way by which you learn to follow. Rather, I hope that when you are done with this book you won't be looking for guidance in this regard any longer—that in fact you can lead your own exciting expeditions into the visual jungle, confident in knowing that you will always have the skill to read images in your own way.

Let's go to the images and see what we can experience through them.

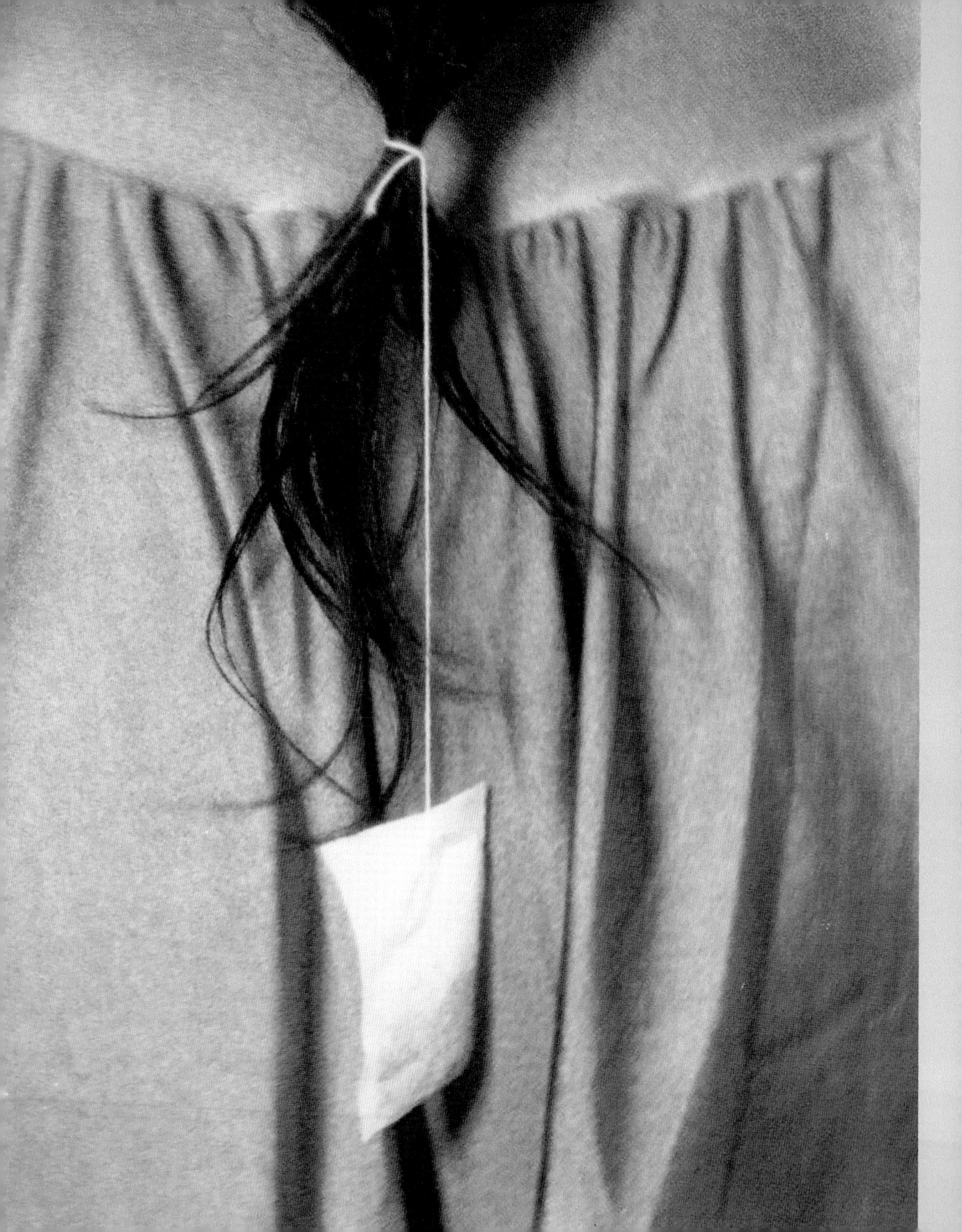

CHAPTER 1

The Velvet Hammer
The Potency of Elements

Featuring work by Rigby Kelly

FIGURE 1.1 Untitled. © Rigby Kelly

CONSIDER THE FIRST IMAGE that we will be exploring here. The takeaway from this image is how the arrangement of the utterly familiar or commonplace can lead to a very powerful and not immediately obvious narrative. The image under consideration contains benign elements—or so it seems at first glance.

What is it? It is a black and white film photograph. Yet, before we take that statement for granted, it is important to remember that many photographs no longer correspond to what we generally assume them to be. They could have been manipulated, composited, or scanned. Digital, postproduction alterations are commonplace and are often very subtle in photography today.

This does not mean that we have to encounter every photograph with distrust, looking for signs that it is not purely mediated through the lens. It simply means we should take into consideration that all images can easily be manipulated. Even the lens-mediated, black and white film photograph, which is largely unaltered relative to other types of photographic images, is, in fact, heavily manipulated.

Every photograph represents the exclusive perspective of its maker and that maker's viewpoint from one very particular position in three-dimensional space—most often during a fraction of a second. Choices made during development and printing further emphasize or de-emphasize elements in the image. Choices are continuously being made by the photographer, some barely conscious, others in a much more considered and deliberate manner, with the result that the viewer's experience can be subtly, and sometimes substantially, altered.

What Are We Looking at?

It appears to be a young woman, photographed from behind who has used a teabag to tie her hair. Many viewers might stop right here. We seem to have an almost "innate" need to understand and to process information. In fact, this is one of our primal survival mechanisms and we bring this same urge to the virtual experience of an image. It appears that we are more adept at rationality as opposed to emotionally processing visual imagery. This is why we don't jump out of the way when we see a ferocious tiger coming toward us in a photograph, yet we can feel deep grief when we see an image of the same desecrated predator, skinned for the beauty of its fur.

It is this empathy that makes the image above so powerful for me and so loaded with meaning. None of us can truly divorce ourselves from our experiences, the time we live in, and our increasing global awareness and collective consciousness. Things that are in the ether exert so much power on us.

Identify the Elements

The image under consideration here consists of only five elements: hair, string, fabric, paper, and tea. Arguably, these elements are benign on their own, but they can become volatile in combination.

Let's be slightly more precise: dark hair, thin string, creased fabric, gossamer paper, and dried tea leaves. The string, the paper, and the tea are collectively known as a "teabag." An entire compendium could be written about tea, its various geographical origins, its leaves and blossoms, its historic and cultural significance and the traditions for serving it from the Japanese tea ceremony to afternoon tea and crumpets. If we get into the symbolism of "reading the tea leaves," the Boston Tea Party and the contemporary "Tea Party" movement, that could be an entire other book.

Contextual Meaning of the Elements

It is quite possible that you are discussing an image similarly charged with historic, contemporary, and global meaning in class and now it is your turn to say something, but all of the above has already been mentioned. Rather than feeling daunted, the elements approach can be used to great effect. After all, there are only five elements and we haven't really dealt with them as such. What is hair? What is string? What is fabric? What is paper? What is tea?

Do they have anything in common? If so, what is it, and frankly does it matter? They all grow and age, they can all be burnt, cut, and boiled. Now you may be understandably concerned about where this is going and just how volatile any possible point can become. The simple way in which this image addresses vulnerability and transience is where the power resides for me.

The hair suggests youth—it is dark and long but it seems slightly unkempt and not recently cut or styled. The teabag has no label and therefore no identity. The fabric is about as nondescript as a crumpled up, monochromatic curtain and seems to be predominantly utilitarian—more along the lines of a hospital gown or drab uniform. Not much to go on, but that is where the image sources all of its power for me. I say "for me" because this process of interrogation also involves you. You may be considering a completely different amalgamation of these elements and this is just as valid and important as any other subjectivity, including my own.

Demonstrating the periodic table approach in this case leaves me with the teabag. It is after all the most complex and processed element in the image. Yes, the gown, if cotton, is also equally processed and if it is an artificial fiber, even more so. And it too has a string, though hidden in the collar of the bunched up fabric. Nevertheless, the teabag is the brightest part of the image and therefore the element the eye is most drawn to.

How Can the Image Be Interpreted?

Based on the approach above, I arrive at this interpretation. What is a teabag then? It is a one-time, one-use product. What could that mean in the context of an anonymous young woman? Sadly, human trafficking is one of the scourges the world is steeped in. The destruction of the individual is as shameful as the lack of resources allocated to this reality. The one-use analogy is intensified by what is most highly prized in that market, virginity. The unlabeled teabag becomes a label in itself. It says only two things: unused and unidentified. It is in this simple statement that the image finds its power and collective condemnation and becomes so powerful.

Chemical elements, if combined in a certain way, can become potentially unstable until their nucleus and orbiting electrons find balance. This quiet image talks about imbalance—morally, ethically, and legally, to say the least. Just as we can't see morals or ethics, or indeed atoms, we know they exist and impact everything in physical existence and possibly more. This image has the audacity to engage this entire discourse by proxy. It works like a velvet hammer. The soft surface makes the blow only more crushing once it is recognized.

Kelly's image speaks very softly in this instance. As many of us have experienced, it is often the quietly spoken word rather than the screaming diatribe that cuts the deepest. The shocking truth is mentioned in an almost casual, yet utterly determined way. Imagine an anti-human-trafficking campaign. How would you address the issue visually?

Conclusion

By selecting a few highly effective elements that say everything necessary without hitting the audience over the head, Kelly allows for expansive interpretations in a very successful way. The grainy quality of the print and lack, in some areas, of depth of focus suggest a possibly surreptitious printing of the image under less than ideal circumstances. This could be a message in a bottle. The nature of the print therefore supports the narrative. Were it a perfect, glitzy studio-generated image, much of the visceral impact would be "sanitized," probably displaced, and, ultimately, lost.

I have found this to be a basic but very effective way to deconstruct any image. Hopefully, this simple deconstruction will help you engage the other images as we move along.

Assignments You May Want to Challenge Yourself With

- Human trafficking
- (Self-) portraiture
- Surprise element
- Melancholy

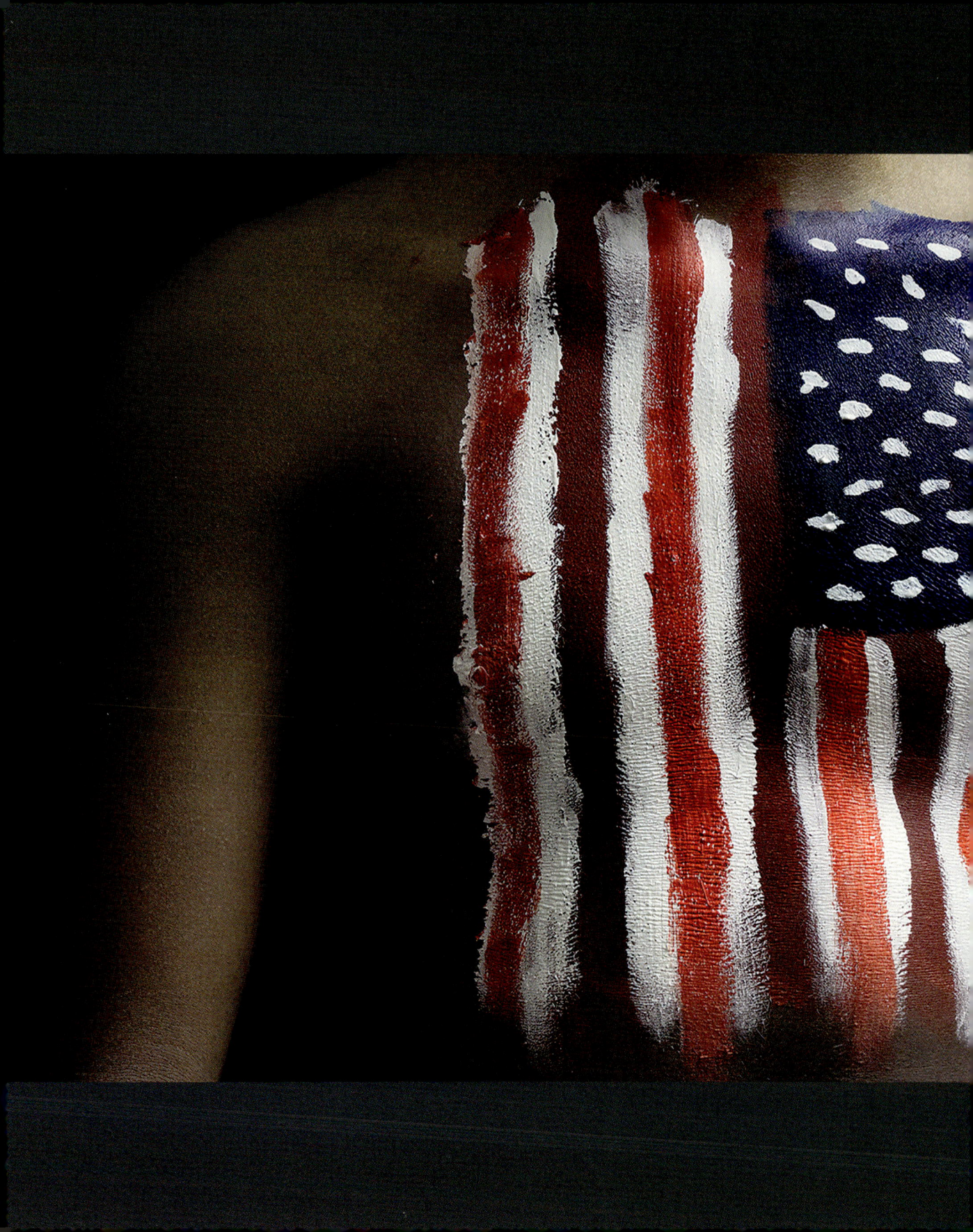

CHAPTER 2

The Personal Galaxy
The Symbol

Featuring work by Vanessa LeRoy

FIGURE 2.1 Untitled. © Vanessa LeRoy

WHAT HAPPENS IF YOU MAKE the image in a studio setting?

What Are We Looking at?

We have moved from black and white into color and the studio. Glitzy and ineffective? I don't think so. I have included this image here to counter my own point in the prior chapter for two simple reasons. First, don't agree too readily with anything anyone says and, second, the proverbial rules can always be broken.

Identify the Elements

This image could also be said to consist of a very few elements: skin, paint, and an impenetrable dark background. For the image to be glitzy the lighting would have to be adjusted to fill in the shadows, to be "brighter"—the flag should be a near perfect replica, and the body would need to stand straighter.

Contextual Meaning of the Elements

Instead, we are confronted with a frayed flag, as if time and the elements have ravaged it. The painted flag immediately unleashes an onslaught of associations: the body has been branded; the stars and stripes, Old Glory; Black Lives Matter, the aftermath of disproportionate police shootings; incarceration, poverty and prejudice; life, liberty and the pursuit of happiness; the first African American president; slavery, stolen lives and displacement, to name but a few.

How Can the Image Be Interpreted?

As in the previous image, this can be thought of as a portrait of an individual or of a culture. It can be thought of as documentation—a photographic genre that used to be well defined. Genres are increasingly morphing, changing, and becoming hybridized as never before. Other than for submission to a contest or juried show such labels seem increasingly irrelevant but are still worth knowing about because of the anthology that has defined photography for so long.

The American flag overwhelmingly labels the black torso. Black skin and the flag, elements around which many people experience great personal and social sensitivity, are simultaneously presented to the viewer. Some may respond by feeling the skin is being desecrated. Some may think it is the flag. Why? The photograph of the young man might merely symbolize support for a favorite sports team in a hot stadium. But the absence of other fans and more importantly body language contradict this notion. The light is somber, the body seems vulnerable, and although we can't see the hands, we know they are in front of the body and are visible. There seems to be more resignation than tension in the body, as if in capitulation. He, possibly, might be cuffed.

Of course we will have differing responses to what we see and the catch-all argument against anything mentioned above is that it is pure speculation or projection. In the face of this image, speculate we must, and projection is what most likely connects us at the deepest level, if we do connect. This starts with the maker and ends with the viewer. The what, why, who, how, and when are already obscured, demanding introspection about the troubled history of our country, in particular with its citizens of color.

We have something to go by: whether we learned it in school, at home or later, the US flag should have its stars on the viewer's left. In this image the stars are to the right and for this reason alone something may seem off, whether we consciously realize it or not. During a politically polarized time, left vs. right is an almost unavoidable discourse asserting itself through the flag's reversal. The only way for the viewer to remedy this experience is by putting herself or himself into the body of the black young man and looking out. Now the flag is correctly displayed and the union stars are over the boy's heart, where we put our hand when we pledge allegiance. By showing us the flag as a mirror, LeRoy not only mirrors the flag for us, the image makes us feel what it might be like to have another body, how we may be looked at differently, and how the experience of the flag may feel different and therefore tell a different story (Figure 2.1).

This too is not snatched out of nowhere but contained in the painted flag itself. Rather than stars, the most recognizable shapes in the fifty white marks look like dolphins, whales, and gulls. The most likely spectators of a departing ship to traverse the ocean from one continent to arrive at another. It is subtle but it is there. And if that is there then tarring and feathering, whipping to the white fat below the skin, mingled in red blood is not far behind. Now the flag is transformed from a symbol identifying a nation into a tapestry of personal and collective history with the kind of pain only the heart can know.

When I see this image that is what is happening for me. The plausible deniability of this interpretation only confirms fear, coded language, and the infinite power the apparently simplest of images can hold. If we stand in this other person's shoes, shoes that were not so recently even available to the other, what would our new perspective be, knowing that we came from somewhere else but often not exactly where on the vast African continent. We might want to rid ourselves of that history, and of the identity lost in the dust of violent abduction that we will never be able to retrace; not to deny it, but to insist on our rightful place at the American table so to speak. We are here now and have been for almost as long as anyone else, except of course, Native Americans.

Native, a word that is key, coded, and stigmatized. In the broadest sense, at worst natives have been colonized and sold. At best they are dismissed as regional, unsophisticated, betrayed by local accents and less than what? Those who have travelled the globe? Those who have shed their localized identity? Those who live everywhere and

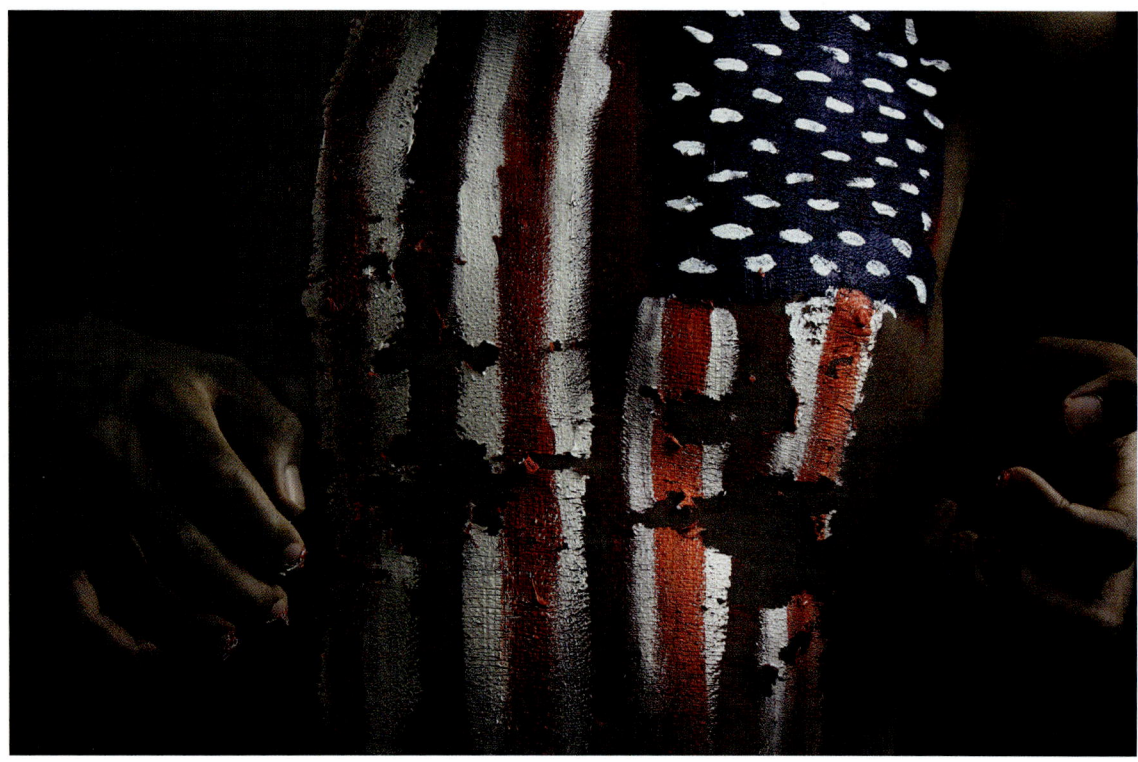

FIGURE 2.2
Untitled.
© Vanessa LeRoy

nowhere? Those who stash their wealth in one country, their children in another, and their ex-spouses yet somewhere else? In other words, broad identities, worldviews, and experience are only valued as a result of wealth and choice rather than the opposite, even if the opposite contains the same base ingredients. A foreign accent can either be a key that opens doors or shuts them in your face. And based on what exactly? This too is referenced in this image. What does it mean to belong in a globalized playground and not in a localized ghetto, self-made or otherwise? Who decides whether you are a rube or a sophisticated person?

I see the engagement of modern-day slavery status as a consistent theme in Leroy's work. The brown skin of the subject therefore becomes code not for something exotic but for something less protected. Whether we are talking about equal opportunity or legal protection, these rights cannot be taken for granted by what must be acknowledged as pervasive white and male privilege, which still dominates much of our culture. One would only have to look at the lack of wage equality, disproportionately harsh sentencing, and more, to know that these are ongoing and serious issues.

The stars are above the heart, suggesting by implication, that it has been pierced by the journey long ago of ancestors whose abduction was also navigated by the stars. We are pointed to the place that pumps our blood throughout our body and where the deepest, most private and never visible pain hurts all of us the most. The broken heart is maybe the most difficult to heal and by directing us visually with the suggestion of "under the skin," we will eventually come to rest there as viewers.

Leroy's exploration of her subject matter continues with the image of the boy tearing at the paint, at the label, at the flag, at his skin. DNA evidence is often found under a victim's fingernails when they have been able to fight during an assault. How others paint us is often wrong and can lead to frustration turned inwards which is associated with depression, lack of confidence, and even self-harm. To develop a positive self-image takes acceptance and support from families, communities, and peers. Many take this for granted and have difficulty imagining anything else. Unfortunately, that is also true in reverse. LeRoy effectively appeals to our collective responsibility to make the American Dream a reality for all (Figure 2.2).

Conclusion

There are as many ways to read photographs as there are people looking at them. I hope to show you a variety of approaches and suggest where they may lead you intuitively—they may even prompt you to undertake some research.

The formula at work here remains concerned with the elements and how they can symbolically direct the viewer. What we have added is the consideration of certain formal, compositional, and organizational elements that effectively work as tools for directing and misdirecting the viewer's journey through the image.

Assignments You May Want to Challenge Yourself With

- Contemporary issues
- Racial identity
- Aspect of US history
- US flag

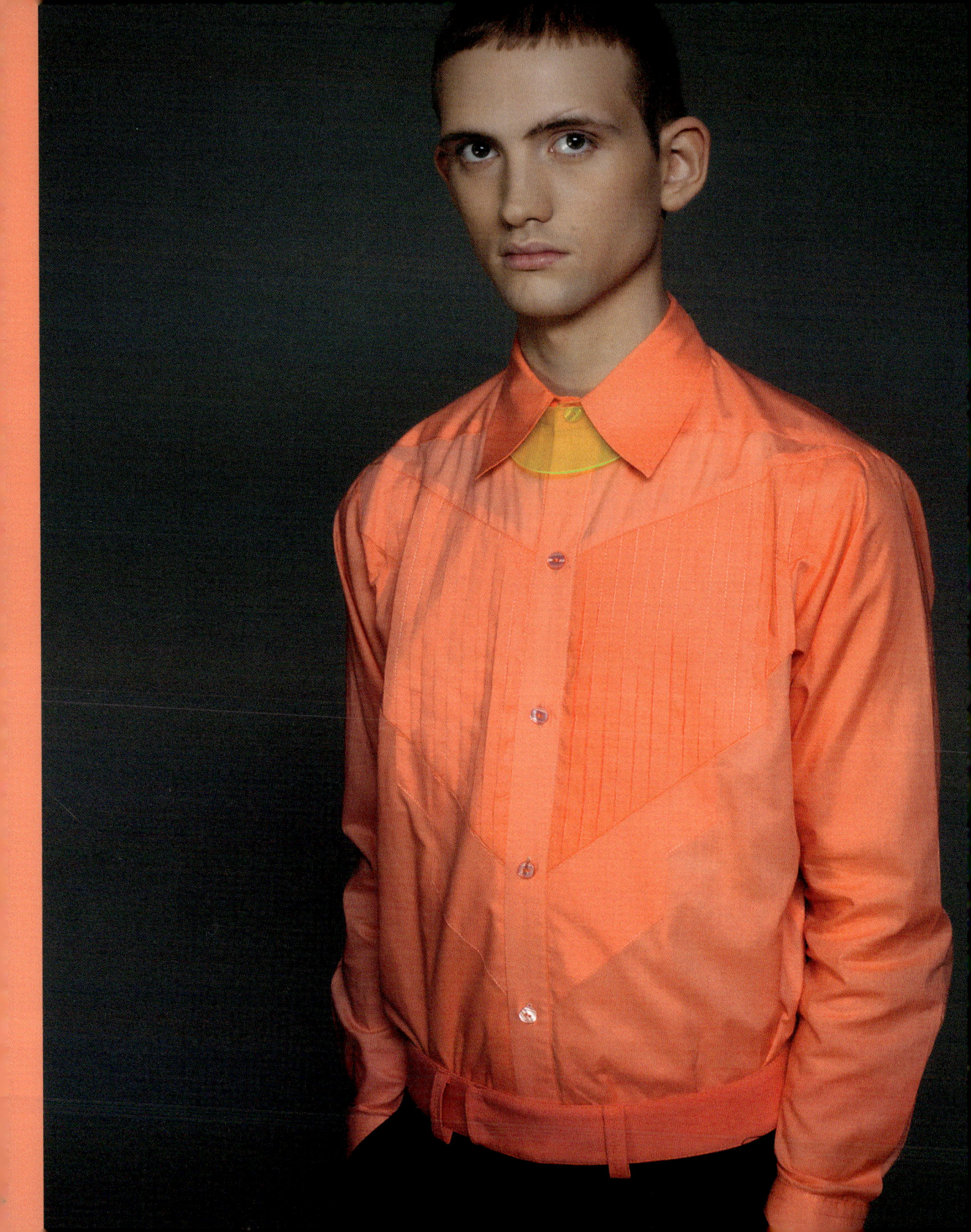

CHAPTER 3

Just Fashion
A Question of Identity

Featuring work by D. Robertson Fay

FIGURE 3.1 D. Robertson Fay photographing Chevalier Homme clothing. ©

WHEN YOU FIRST GET UP and ready yourself to meet the day, part of your morning ritual deals with getting dressed. What to wear today and why? There are of course practical considerations. Is it freezing cold or swelteringly hot? Are you going to a place that has a dress code? Even if you aren't, chances are you have your own dress code. In all likelihood you've chosen most of the clothes you wear on most occasions. You may dress to project a multitude of messages and more or less obvious signals. Do you want to stand out, project power, blend in, conform, or rebel? Paying no heed to any of this is also a message in its own way.

Choosing elements to define an identity is maybe the easiest and most difficult at the same time. In order to project and read identities you have to be open to what you identify with, where you see yourself as belonging, if anywhere, and what prejudice you may harbor among a host of other things. What you can afford comes into play here too. It would be nice to think that we have no prejudice and that none is

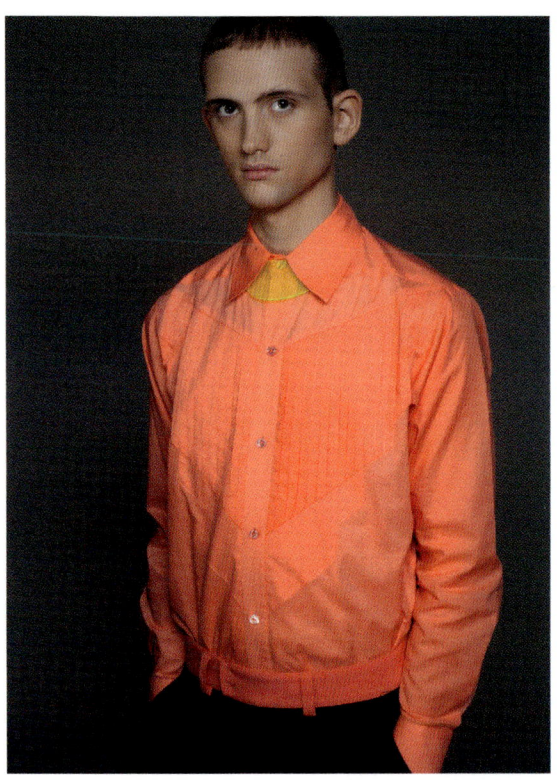

FIGURE 3.1 D. Robertson Fay photographing Chevalier Homme clothing. ©

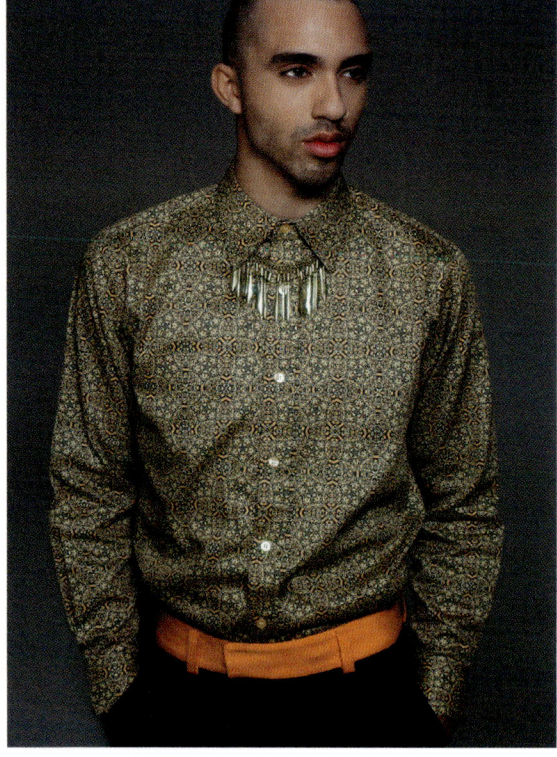

FIGURE 3.2 D. Robertson Fay photographing Chevalier Homme clothing. ©

applied to us because of how we dress, but most of us experience both to various degrees. What may define us most is how we recognize our own reactions in this regard and how we manage them. In order to do that we have to observe ourselves as dispassionately as possible and consider ourselves as if we were the stranger we fear the most.

This is a valuable exercise for both life and photography and since the two are so intertwined, as your outlook on life changes, so will your viewpoint in relation to photography. How we present ourselves can have profound connotations in how we will be seen, categorized and labeled. Therefore, not surprisingly, much of photography deals with just that: clothes, fashion, fashion accessories, and the global conditioning and reinforcement of identity.

What Are We Looking at?

Upon first looking at Fay's fashion photography, the general consensus among the class was that it was well lit, that the models' expressions seemed uncontrived, and that the work presented a cohesive look and identity for the designer, Chevalier Homme. There was some discussion on whether the cropping of the tops of the heads was beneficial to the images or not, yet no consensus was reached.

Next I asked about the narrative in these images. At first the students answered as if responding to a trick question. "These images are meant to sell clothes, they do and that is it. The narrative is about the clothes." But is it? What is the meaning of attire?

Neither the designer, nor the photographer, or the viewer live in a vacuum and are unlikely to have escaped the dominant discourses of the last ten years.

How Can the Images Be Interpreted?

If we look closer it seems these images tell a history at least a decade old. Let's start on the surface: one of the models looks like a choirboy, dressed in vestment colors. The other model looks like a person who could have Middle Eastern origins (dressed in green and orange). The "choirboy's" looks create a connotation of religion, which is reinforced by the collar. The "Middle Eastern-looking" man's shirt is dappled green with connotations relating to camouflage.

Discussion, press, and debate over sexual abuse by clergy and the longest war in US history in the Middle East have become a staple of the content that has pervaded all manners of our lives over the last ten years. These themes are therefore in the ether, the collective consciousness, and the fashion line presented here appears to reference this history quite directly.

How Does This Play on Our Sense of Identity—Does It Affirm or Threaten It?

It could be argued that the Crusades never ended, because it is the "religious" man who makes direct eye contact with the audience and therefore establishes a dominant and suggested relationship. He seems to know his audience and by implication they know him (Figure 3.1).

The other model looks away and therefore avoids eye contact. By implication, he can be more easily dismissed as the one with whom the audience has no relationship. He also wears a green patterned shirt with its association of military fatigues. This is as implicit as in the allusion to religious garments in the other image (Figure 3.2).

Consider the Subtleties

Deeper still is where it becomes really fascinating. The shape of the embroidered section on the orange shirt looks like the outline of a stealth bomber, or even medieval body armor worn over chainmail. The bomber, by extension, becomes an extended shield to protect Western religion. By contrast the camouflage shirt suggests a more individualized representation of the chronicled conflict.

This speaks to the ambiguity of the relationships that inform many of our political associations in the region. Initially the necklace of the "soldier" resembles a round of bullets or miniature bombs. On closer inspection however, they look like miniature machetes or scimitars, a one-bladed weapon. Most striking is the belt. It looks like standard issue Guantánamo Bay. While belts are not allowed in prison, prison orange still insinuates either a future or a past in this notorious holding place.

The designer of this clothing line, Chevalier Homme, seems to very directly engage these narratives of our time, which Fay cleverly staged and further reinforced. By staging both men with their hands in their pockets they both seem passive but at the same time might possibly be hiding something. By cropping their heads or photographically lobotomizing them, Fay does not attack their individuality but rather asks the question of how long it will take for the world to come to its senses.

Turn the Tables on Identity

What if the models were switched? How would the narrative change? Given that many ethnic Middle Easterners call and identify with the West as their home, and given that many beheadings, also alluded to by the sliced heads, are carried out by Westerners who have joined ISIS, the medieval boundaries of the Crusades have become blurred. Fay and Chevalier Homme, it seems, are questioning to what extent conflict today is based on personal choices rather than on ethnic origin. The notion of hybridized identities is thus also evoked.

Conclusion

This brings us to another religion, where the belief system is based on multiple incarnations of an individual soul to learn what it must. Associated with that is the saying, "How other people treat you is their Karma. How you respond is yours." The photographs promote individual identity and distinction through clothing. Seen together they also ask the question of how the wearer identifies himself beyond the gossamer boundaries touching his skin.

Assignments You May Want to Challenge Yourself With

- Fashion
- Political insinuation
- Crusades
- Ethnicity bias

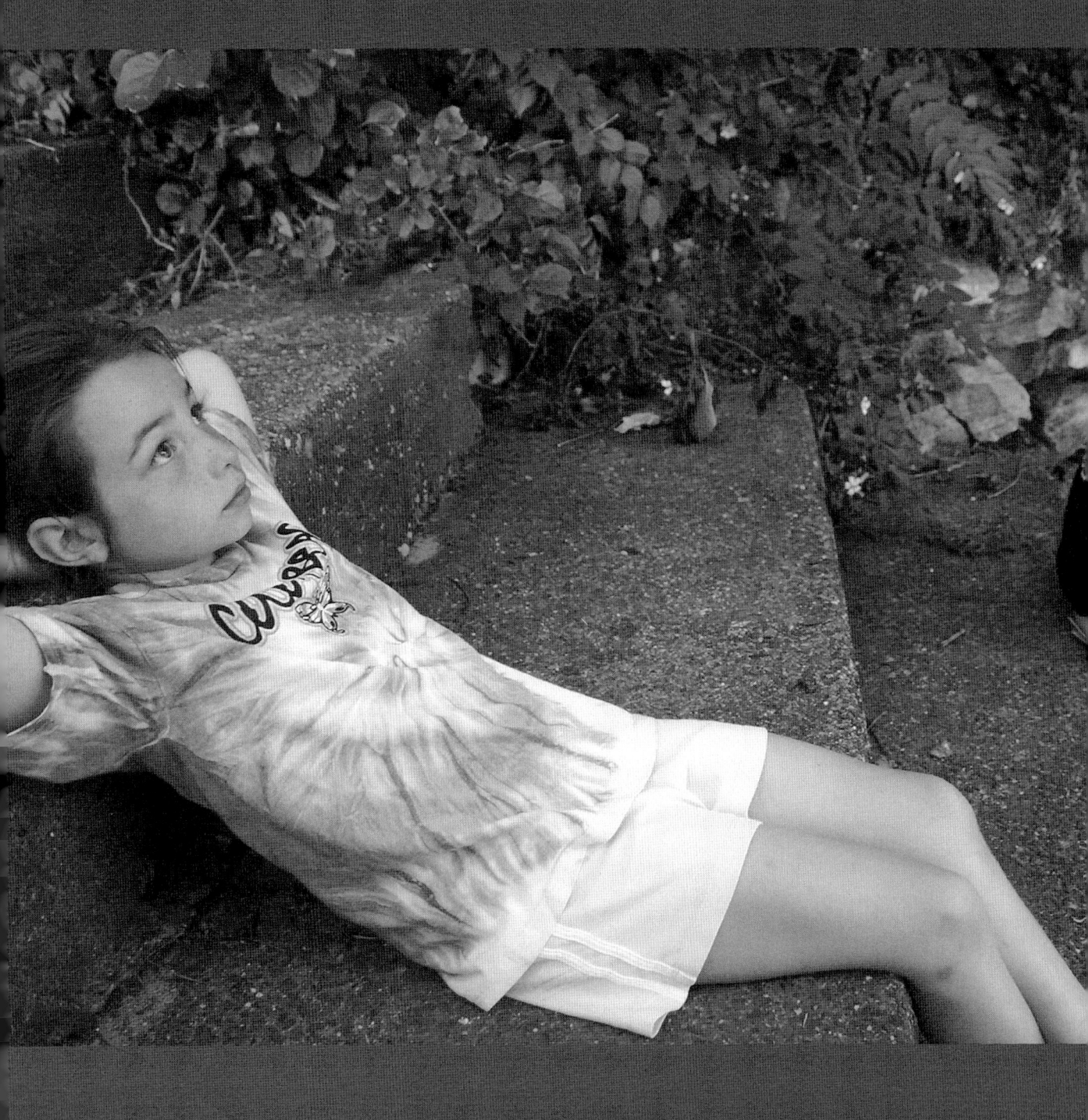

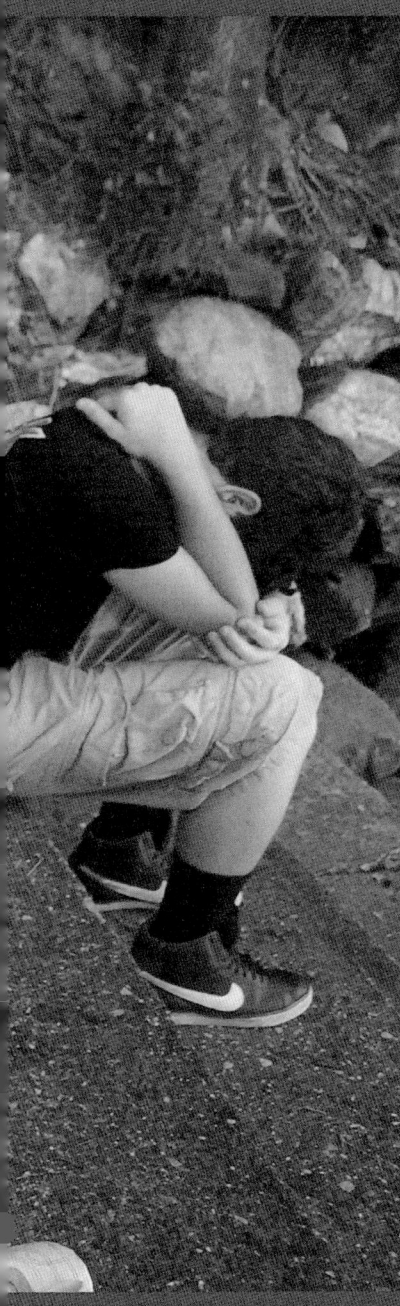

CHAPTER 4

Nike and the Butterfly
The Reversed Stereotype

Featuring work by Anni Abbruzzese

FIGURE 4.1 Untitled. © Anni Abbruzzese

What Are We Looking at?

WHEN WE LOOK at Abbruzzese's image of the girl with the butterfly on her shirt and the boy wearing his Nikes, I think we can recognize immediate association of symbols. From the Greek legends to the butterfly effect we are reminded of actions and consequences, conflict and responsibility, intention and helplessness. Recognition abounds, yet the true dynamic at work remains a mystery. This leaves plenty of room for contemplation and emotional access for the viewer.

The girl seems pragmatic in dealing with her apparent supremacy, though a bit conflicted. She is enigmatic, strong, and supine across multiple steps, claiming space even outside of the frame of the photograph. Her arms folded behind her head suggest that she is here to stay. She will see through whatever problem has arisen with the boy.

The boy is fully covered by the frame. Yet, he seems small and hurt. His body language is the opposite of the girl's. Where she leans back, he leans forward; she reveals her face with an inscrutable nuance while the boy's face, and his likely tears, are hidden from view. Though he appears to favor his right elbow, as if possibly injured, the pain seems to emanate from his whole body suggesting that this is a deeper, emotional, pain.

How Can the Image Be Interpreted?

While he is wearing the brand of shoes that is named after the Greek goddess of victory, Nike, the real Nike is sitting right next to him. Her prone elbows reinforce this image of the winged goddess, as does the butterfly appearing on her chest. In the way the boy's shoes identify her, the butterfly seems to identify the boy—a butterfly with a broken wing.

They are seated on concrete stairs leading the viewer diagonally up and down out of the frame. The girl's head is inclined upward and the boy's downward. We have no idea where either direction leads. We don't know whether this is a public or private place. Nature, or the nature of things, is where each rung disappears in a lush canopy of diverse leafy plants or a natural stone retaining wall next to the boy. In the other direction, the steps flare out towards the viewer. Again, we don't know for how far and whether we are on the steps with these children or beyond them.

Conditioned as we are in the West to read from left to right, the natural progress would be to go down. But the girl's eyes look up, whether out of exasperation or on the basis of a determined wisdom we can't know. Since we are guided most by Nike, it is her and her mythology that we must surrender to. She had three siblings—Zelos (Rivalry), Kratos (Strength), and Bia (Force). Nike and her siblings may be on their way to Mount Olympus to join Zeus in his battle against the Titans. This could be an outtake of her and her brother Zelos (etymology jealous or zeal).

It so happens that I knew that this was an image Abbruzzese took of her siblings, which would make her Bia. Now, I must discover whether there happens to be another brother. If so this would be quite the example of how what we learn in school, what informs our culture, what is emblazoned on our clothes conflates and conspires again and again to tell a variant of the same story.

The above is one way to look at the image. As mentioned in the foreword, this book aims not to suggest the most obvious interpretation, nor to make any claim to a right or wrong way of looking at and experiencing a picture. I encourage you therefore to take a fresh look at this image through your own eyes. The story you bring to this image is as valid as anyone else's. Never forget that. The feminist lens would be important to consider more closely here. In an overt way, the image empowers a girl and disempowers a boy. Until Disney truly catches up to this concept, the image will retain a primary power for blatantly contradicting the still-prevailing stereotype of an empowered boy and disempowered girl.

Conclusion

Allegations of using child labor in sweatshops to produce the famed shoe brand have gained traction in recent years; they have become another inescapable aspect of this photograph, least of all because a sad child is wearing shoes that may have been made by another sad child, albeit their sadness exists for very different reasons. Whether we are considering social justice for women, or children, it is still the mythology of ancient Greece that is the foundation for our contemporary culture's ethical identity.

Assignments You May Want to Challenge Yourself With

- Mythology
- Gender roles
- Environmental portraiture
- Emotional dynamics

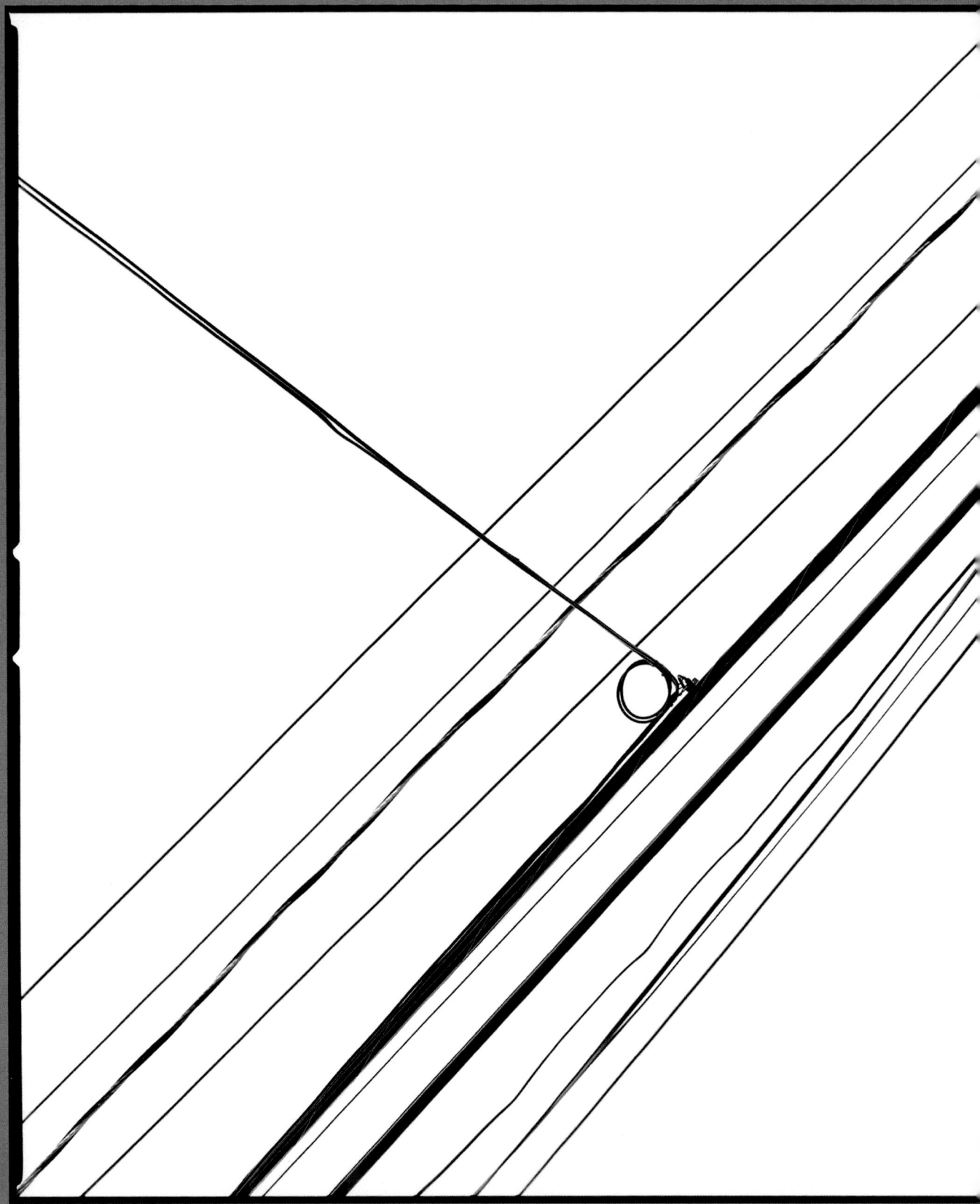

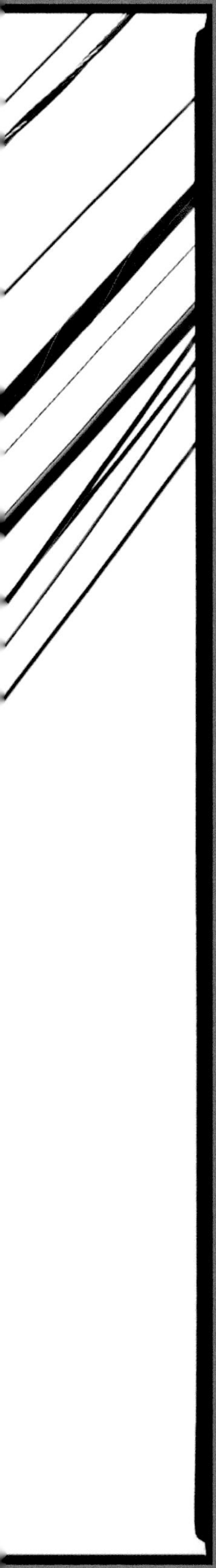

CHAPTER 5

Staying in Line
Conductivity

Featuring work by Liz Ellenwood

FIGURE 5.1 Wire Sketches. © Liz Ellenwood

HAVE YOU EVER FELT that political correctness has gone so far that it feels like the tool of the oppression it is meant to combat? Have you ever seen one bumper sticker too many telling you that there is something wrong with you and how you ought to live your life?

If so, have you ever deliberately left a light on just to prod your hippie-fascist parent's obsession with energy conservation? And to add insult to injury, subsequently felt guilty about it because you don't fundamentally disagree, in fact quite the opposite, but simply can't stand hearing one more "don't forget to turn the lights off dear" before you even had a chance to reach the switch?

Your parents are of course the product of their parents and the apparently limitless growth and consumer generation, which they were rebelling against. The austerity brought by War and The Great Depression, which can be traced back to The Great Crash, informed each preceding generation in turn. Each new generation tries to carve out an existence in response to what had seemingly traumatized them the most at the hands of the previous one. This kneejerk is as predictable as it is important to understand. The inevitable trajectory this causes is not unlike one electron bumping into the next down an electrical line, all the way getting heated and losing energy at the same time.

Identify the Elements

Liz Ellenwood's *Wire Sketches* engage black and white photography at its core— literally in black and white and tonally in true opposition to one another. There are essentially no or few mid-tones in most of her self-described sketches that could have been drawn with a steady hand and black pen on white paper (Figure 5.1).

What Are We Looking at?

Ellenwood has stripped the vaunted richness of gray tones in her gelatin silver prints and reduced her images to their lowest common denominator. No exposure, paper-white, complete exposure and maximum density in the black areas. At first this seems like an almost sacrilegious waste of all the non-exposed silver in her paper. The prints themselves seem to represent a deliberately wasteful and inefficient exploitation of the paper and latent chemistry.

Yet, there is great beauty and truth in her extravagant compositions. Indeed, truth in a photograph, who would have thought? We all know that photographs lie or, at best, are so subjective that what at first appears as unassailably self-evident easily evaporates when the frame is shifted just a little.

How Can the Images Be Interpreted?

The great truth Ellenwood so poetically references is inefficiency itself. For non-photographers it would not be relevant how she initially sets this stage through her process, though it is a great opening line. The inefficiency is the subject matter itself. Transmission wires lack efficiency. Through the process of transmitting power energy is lost. Only rare, highly expensive superconductors can transmit power with virtually no loss.

How this loss is to be mitigated in the future represents research into which many companies are investing substantial R&D resources. This I see as part of Ellenwood's topic. For the purposes of this analysis, inefficiency and loss are quite enough to consider. Ellenwood's vignettes don't show us how the transmitted energy is generated, where it is sent from, or where it ends up. As such she opens up windows on intersection, energy, and the interminable flow of information. This makes our lights work, supplies our entertainment, powers businesses and global industries, and even the NSA depends on this grid (Figure 5.2).

Highways of voltage transmission where one electron bumps into another down the line in a chain reaction of endless invisible movement are not dissimilar from our motorized highways, and like our roads, this infrastructure has to be continuously maintained. Wildfires, falling trees and branches due to storms or heavy snow, and even cars smashing into an electrical poll can black out anything from a few homes to multi-state-wide areas.

The grid is highly vulnerable, visually polluting, or beautiful, depending on your viewpoint, and arguably, a thing of the past. European countries that are highly developed bury their power lines the way we bury our gas, water, and sewer lines. Developing countries that are just starting to provide energy and information choose wireless information distribution and localized energy sources such as solar and geothermal. As such we are looking at another aspect of the divestment in our infrastructure. When the visible distribution grid is going to disappear in the US is anyone's guess, but its vulnerability to weather and even terrorism is as troubling as the many coal-burning or nuclear power plants that supply our massive energy consumption.

Conclusion

Ellenwood's photographs therefore speak, like minimalist Japanese haiku, to sources of power, the nature of information or misinformation traveling on our energy and information highways, and are imbued with a nostalgic simplicity about a realty that is anything but simple. As mentioned, Ellenwood "wastes" most of the silver waiting to be exposed in her paper. Were the images digital, they would use a negligible amount of ink in comparison to other photographs.

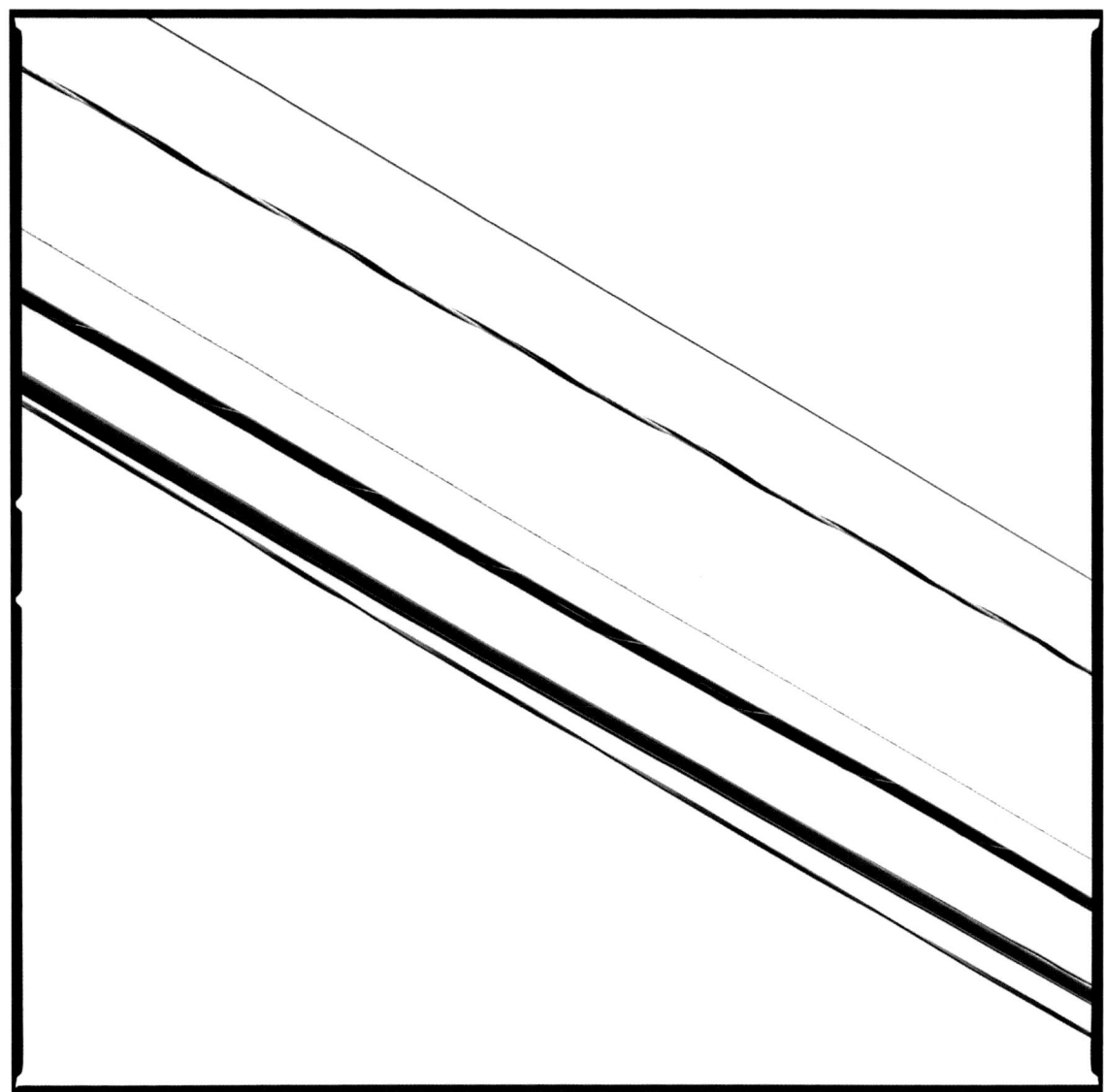

FIGURE 5.2
Wire Sketches.
© Liz Ellenwood

The dawn of widespread individually generated renewable power and its subsequent storage will pit the individual, legislators, and energy corporations against each other in new and unprecedented ways. The scalability of energy, through innovations like the new Tesla home battery, which can draw and store energy, is reflected in her process too. This entanglement of competing interests will be far messier than the wire salad that is currently part of our visual landscape.

Assignments You May Want to Challenge Yourself With

- Energy
- Visual haiku
- Vulnerability
- Infrastructure

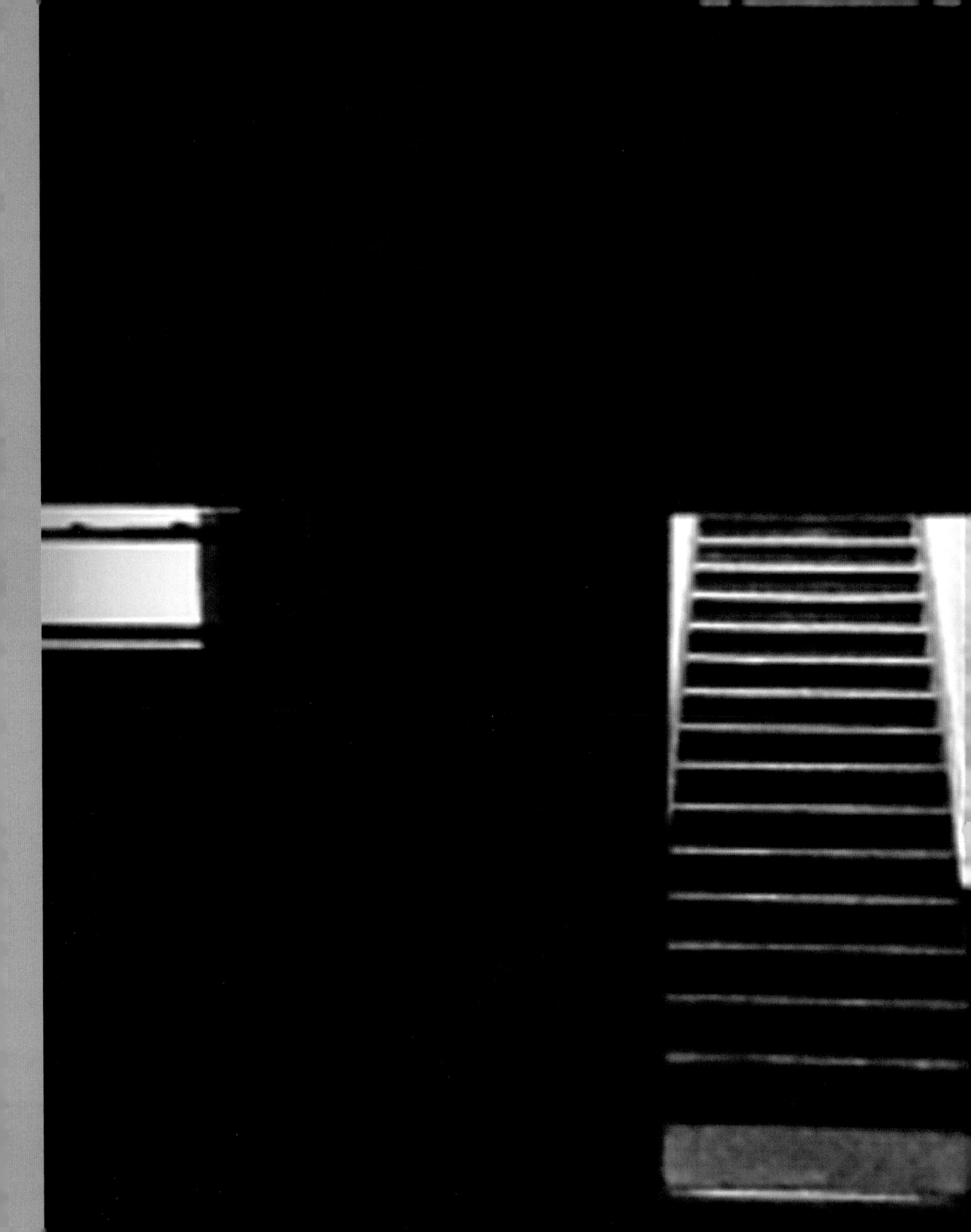

CHAPTER 6

Politics
The Metaphoric Landscape

Featuring work by Karen Riley

FIGURE 6.1 Untitled. © Karen Riley

THIS WORK WAS PRODUCED during a recent election cycle where the increasing divide between the have and have-nots was part of the discourse.

While looking at Riley's work in that context, it is easy to connect it to a landscape, an interior and exterior that continues to assert itself as it has for millennia, though we refer to this erosion of the middle class now as "the new normal."

The images have a sense of unease, even edginess to them. To my eye, they easily

FIGURE 6.2 Untitled. © Karen Riley

relate to the concept of dark recesses, dark backroom deals, a lack of transparency, and a mockery of democracy where corporations are now people, money is free speech, and individual voter rights are rolled back as never before.

What Are We Looking at?

The first image portrays an image of a staircase. In the ever-present context of politics, this can easily lead to associations with upward (or downward) mobility. The set of stairs, seen from within a dark basement space, reinforce the idea of the lights having been turned off in the basement, emphasizing the notion that the sun only shines for those at the top (Figure 6.1).

How Can the Images Be Interpreted?

This contains the next layer of subtext — the new upstairs–downstairs classifications. The US has the highest rate of incarceration of any country, and targets individuals of color, the young, and the poor. Those whose voting rights are being limited most overtly, as previously mentioned, also fall within this classification.

By contrast, the second image seems to mostly consist of a burst of light in the dark. Easily a metaphor for epiphany, the proverbial light bulb is turned on with some serious wattage, implying realization, comprehension, and even shock (to the system). The white light at the moment of death in the electric chair lingers in the context of these images too.

Beneath that, we can find reference to streets that are lit, to manicured lawns, and to sidewalks that can actually be walked upon. In this world things still work as we expect them to and the sun undoubtedly rises there in the morning. The streetlight can thus also be interpreted as a moonscape, a place where the political sun keeps the lights on and makes the area safer at night.

The third image of a lit, empty parking space further references security — a possible work place, a leisure space, or a relatively safe place to walk to one's car,

FIGURE 6.3
Untitled.
© Karen Riley

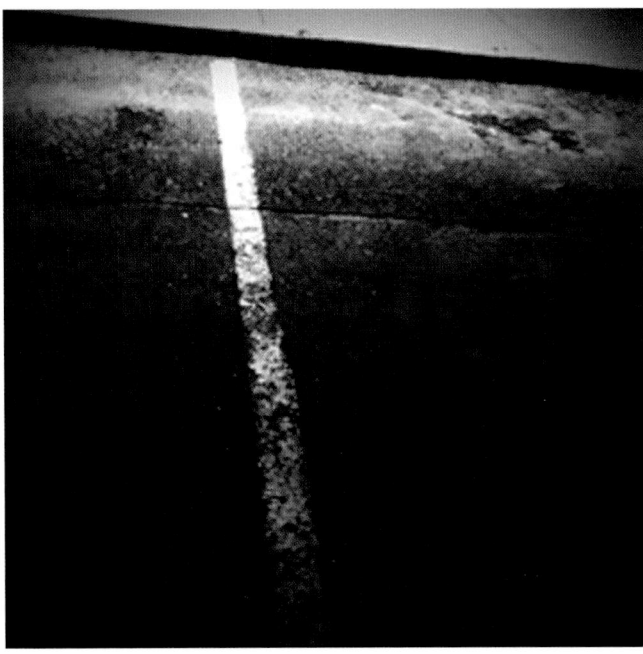

FIGURE 6.4
Untitled.
© Karen Riley

And so we arrive at the fourth image in this square-minded series, which, with its four components, can form another perfect square, when not considered linearly, as we have done (Figure 6.4).

The last image shows a simple line, a very basic graphic and compositional approach, to establish a lasting punctuation mark to this series of photographs.

This image provides no relief but doubles down. The image connects viewers to some of our most basic ways of understanding and describing our world spatially, morally, and politically.

Left or right, right or wrong, good and bad, light and dark, one side or the other, in other words: polarization, blind allegiance, and ideology. Nicely enough this too has a counterpoint: choice.

What Does This Do?

This reminds us of the opposite and vice versa: An empty space or abandoned location also lives in this image as an inevitable counterpoint; job loss, shuttered businesses, repossessed vehicles and homes. This could be a potential place to sleep for someone without anywhere else to go. The image provokes a reinterpretation of even the most basic space designations for personal use in conjunction with available infrastructure as a result of public tax dollars, private or public permits, or "reserved" parking on the basis of status or reward, usually at a business, let alone a safe enough place where you can own one (Figure 6.3).

Conclusion

These images weren't created with black and white film: technology predicated on a negative that physically records the opposite of what we end up seeing. Instead, they were shot with a cell phone camera, the new Polaroid, and the countersurveillance/counternarrative tool of the twenty-first century. Of course the citizenry has to enter into a contract with a corporation to gain access to use these multi-function, multi-communication devices, usually at exorbitant cost. Still, in addition to recording endless breakfasts destined for consumption on Instagram, they have had a significant impact on the political landscape. The power of photography remains, and not only that, its power to change the political landscape now lies in the hands of those who can afford a smartphone and monthly cellular bill. The rest of the English-speaking world refers to cell phones as mobile phones. Even German speakers have borrowed an English word. They call this nifty tool a handy. This easily portable device, serving as a phone, still and video camera, satnav tool, iPod, compass, book, and so much more, is handy indeed. Something that is handy or mobile engenders quite different associations than something that is cellular. It is at this cellular level, at the foundation of life's building blocks, that we found ourselves polarized during this most recent election cycle. Its wide chasm inspired the original photos in previously unimaginable ways.

Will it again be a cell phone that to a large extent determines the outcome of the next election?

Assignments You May Want to Challenge Yourself With

- Income inequality
- Political landscape (in public spaces)
- Urban landscape
- New Polaroid
- Citizen journalism

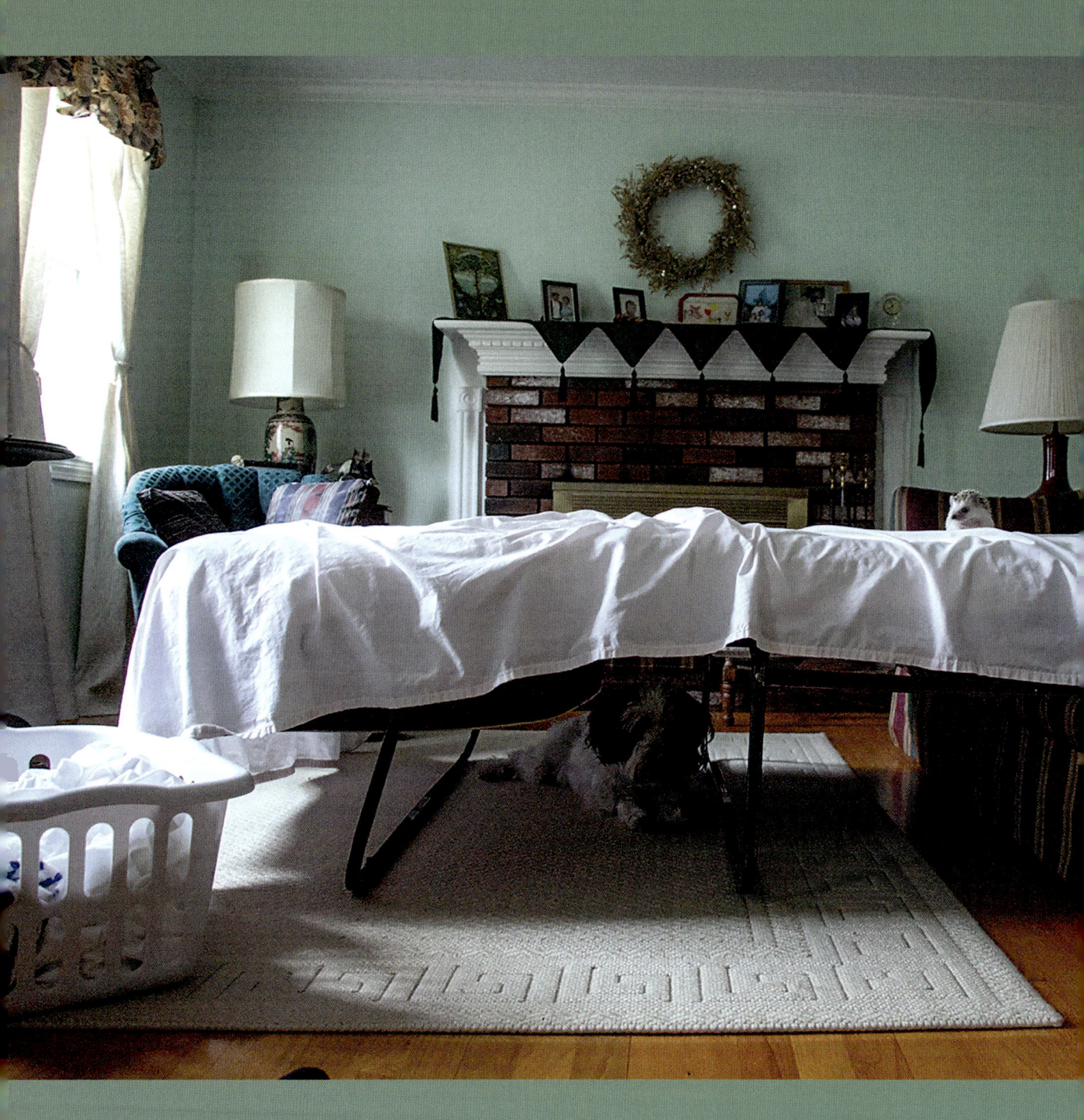

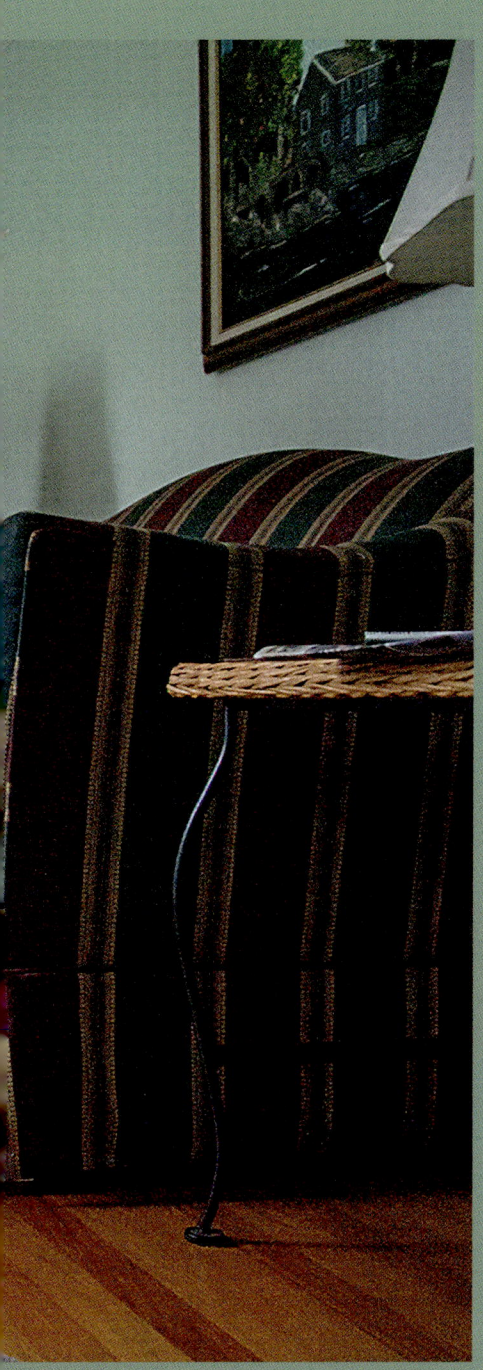

CHAPTER 7

Henry's Tale
The Photographic Fable

Featuring work by Christine Delay

FIGURE 7.1 Untitled. © Christine Delay

THE REASON FABLES OFTEN TEND to feature animals is not coincidental. There have always been times when it was safer to write an innocent story, seemingly about a bunch of critters so as to create an air of plausible deniability and to make it hard to tie the tale to real people or events. There is also something of the court jester in such stories and with that we have the introduction of the element of humor. We will revisit this approach again later in the book when things really get tough, but we are not there yet. Animals have delighted and frightened us with their song or their snarl since the dawn of time. From those depicted in ancient tribal societies all over the planet to the sports mascots of today, animals have been worshipped and recognized for their spirit. Special people and deities were believed to be able, as shape shifters, to transform themselves from one form to the other.

The probing of the inequity, prevalent in every political system was, in the previous chapter, signified by structures and urban landscapes. Here this dynamic is being explored with actual characters, specifically animals photographed in such a way that they convey more than a representation of themselves. This is important. I caution students not to confuse a picture of their pet with an image of an animal which illustrates a point, a narrative beyond itself (Figure 7.1).

What Are We Looking at?

Delay has staged her characters in just such a way. We now move from the public into the private landscape of inequality. The stage is a house where the dog appears not to be allowed on the furniture and appears to be living downstairs, downtrodden and depressed. In fact he hides under the furniture, like a squatter in fear of discovery. By contrast the cats, the aristocracy, live upstairs on and in the beds, the proverbial societal fat cats. The equally proverbial underdog, literately and figuratively, is connected by the unlikely character of the hedgehog. The hedgehog, Henry, easily navigates these two extremes, those of the underdog and the elites. He himself is neither and is so small that at first glance he looks like easy prey for either party. The cats upon their encounter of the interloper certainly appear to think so (Figure 7.2).

How Can the Images Be Interpreted?

Henry is different. Fables anthropomorphize animals, so who is Henry in this tale? He spends time with the lonely dog in the shadows and the entitled cats in their sunny lair. Among these groups his muzzle, fangs, and claws are insignificant, there is no contest and he is no threat. Yet, he is not defenseless and shows no fear. He is not going to be intimidated by any of this lot. He is akin to an aikido master who will use the strength of his enemy against him or her. The harder they hit him, if they do, the deeper their sensitive paws would be impaled on his spiky quills. And so, hit they don't.

In nature, Henry would be prey for badgers and foxes. The beauty of fables is we don't have to be concerned with the real world of the animals but the magical theatre of their performance. In fables animals also talk. Left with only the pictures, we have to extract the clues we are given which are clearly directional. Whether with the apparently benign dog, or with the stalking cat with the puffed-up tail and the one with the flattened ears, we are directed to get the clues from that which is not constant. Henry is the glue that holds the story together, the only character in every image, but he gives very little away. He projects an innate calmness and gestural sparseness. As he interacts across the sociopolitical landscape of the house, he seems to hold his own council and is attentive to the others who, by comparison, appear to be close to hysteria.

The dog's apparent resignation of life itself makes him look forsaken. The wreath above the fireplace reinforces this. The pull-out bed, a temporary shelter for both him and a visitor denotes a holiday, a time well known to trigger depression. The cats' posturing is also associated with holidays when people often have one drink too many to dull the fact that they can't stand each other. They drink and get

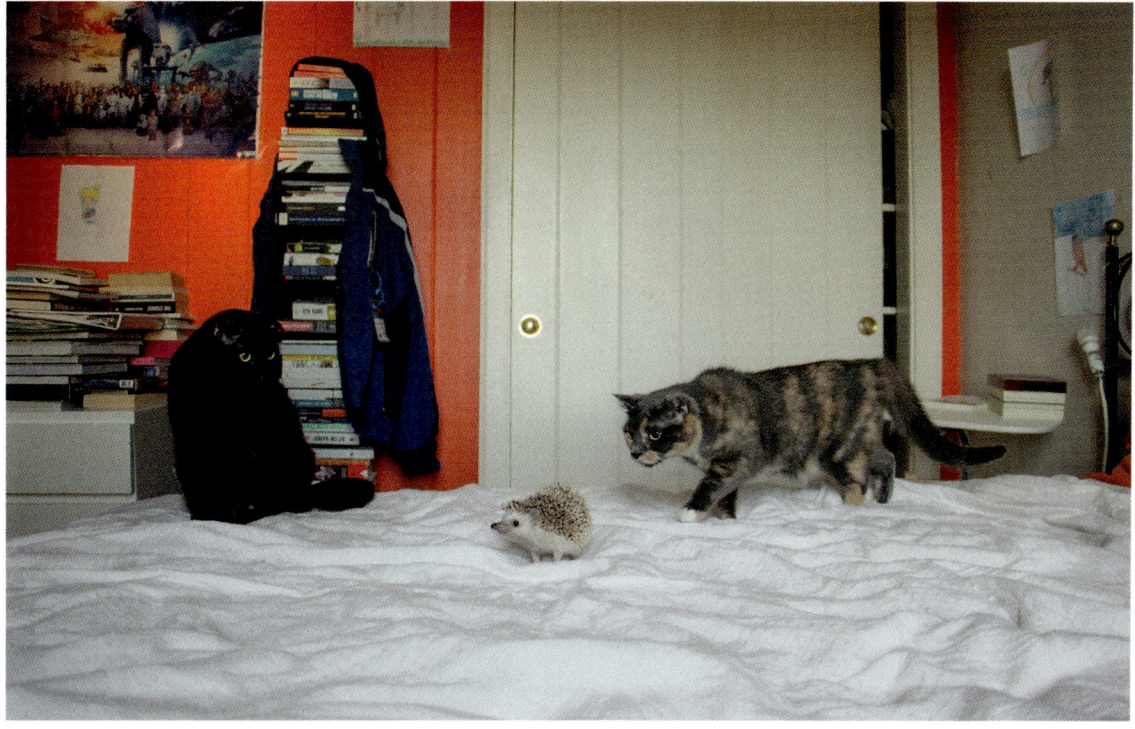

FIGURE 7.2
Untitled.
© Christine Delay

angry, and more often than not, yell at each other over differing political views. The cats seem intent on provoking Henry, to get a rise out of him, though it looks highly unlikely that they will succeed.

One can almost hear Henry saying to the dog, "I can see that you are feeling sad. Would you like to talk about it?" and to the cats, "I can see that you are agitated. Would you like to talk about it?" It is easy to imagine the dog's unintelligible howls about how everything has gone off the rails and the cats spitting frustration for being called out on their rudeness by the temerity of the hedgehog. It is in the contrast between Henry's studied calm and the other protagonists' behavior that we find a spectacle so overdramatic as to be ludicrous. Only Henry shows curiosity, apparent goodwill, and an ease of existence, like an old Zen Master. This only further emphasizes the dog's apparent closeness to a nervous breakdown and need for intervention and the cats' collective need for some serious therapy to help them with their anger management. Maybe Henry knows that the dog and the cats are afflicted by communal pain or worry, and are acting out in their own ways. After all they live in the same house.

The dog appears to have lost his confidence, his self-respect, and probably the belief that things will ever get better. By embracing victimhood the dog may have given up entirely, alienating others even more with his pessimism and self-pity. Maybe he howls in protest over a cause he cares less about than the outlet it provides for his own sense of personal disenfranchisement, and in so doing drives everyone else even more crazy.

By contrast the cats appear to epitomize a sense of entitlement by their reaction to the intrusive presence in their private club. Their hostility may well mask feelings similar to those of the dog, a profound sense of insecurity. In all likelihood they know only too well that their status can be lost, that they too are as vulnerable as all the others, and therefore they simply can't stand any reminder that they are deeply afraid. Deep down they probably suspect that no one deserves to have almost everything when so many barely have anything. From their perch in the window, they may well have seen the rain-soaked stray, sniffing around the garbage cans. They may have even glimpsed a coyote who would not give a second thought to having any of them for breakfast. This type of dog they fear, the dog they learned about in history class, when they studied the French Revolution.

Conclusion

Had Delay or Riley attempted their narratives with actual political figures, positions on the part of the viewer might have hardened as soon as they contemplated the work into agreement or dismissal. Metaphors and fables can be used in a way that is less confrontational, and which is delinked from personalities, and thus speak truth to power without coming across as being partisan. In that light, Henry becomes less of a shrink and

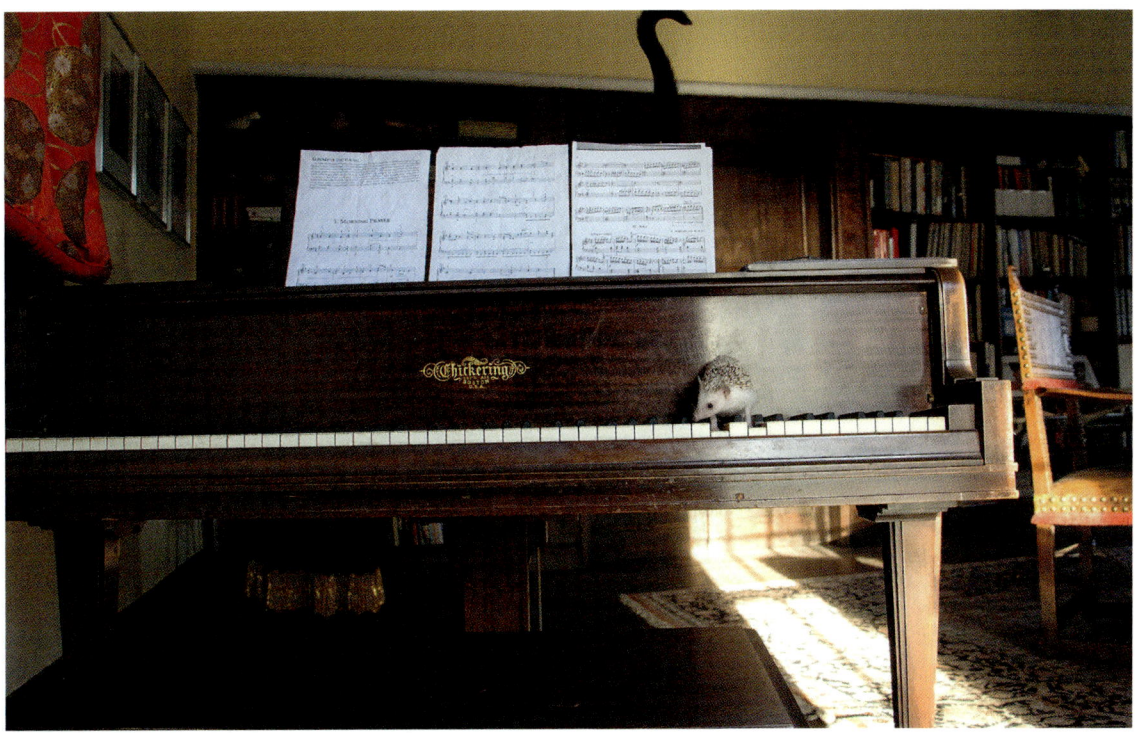

FIGURE 7.3
Untitled.
© Christine Delay

more of a politician with diplomatic skills honed to the point where he can interact with both parties. But how can he bring the respective parties together? (Figure 7.3).

Henry plays the piano in his own magical way. We know his music must be beautiful because some of the partisans have already shown up to listen. A cat is actually on the piano, its tail up and viewed from one side curled into a clef or viewed from the other side, curled into a question mark. With questions come new perspectives that can change long held precepts. Maybe Henry is the teacher that shows up when the students are ready. Maybe we can take solace in that Henry's song is for all of us, and that his generosity is something to be shared. So what is the moral of the story? Make and listen to more music, visual and otherwise.

Assignments You May Want to Challenge Yourself With

- Anthropomorphism
- Social inequality
- Political dysfunction (in private spaces)
- Fable
- Individualism

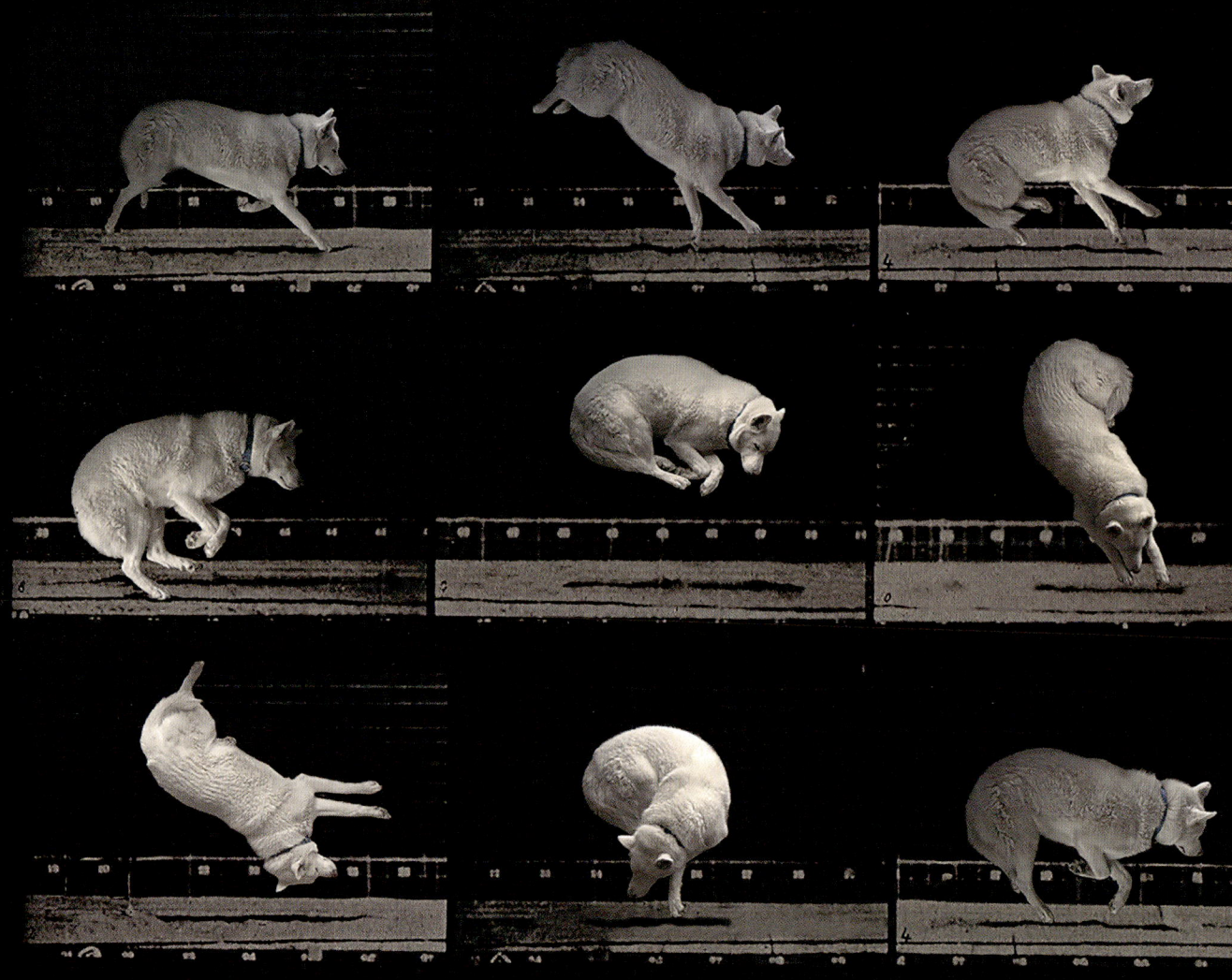

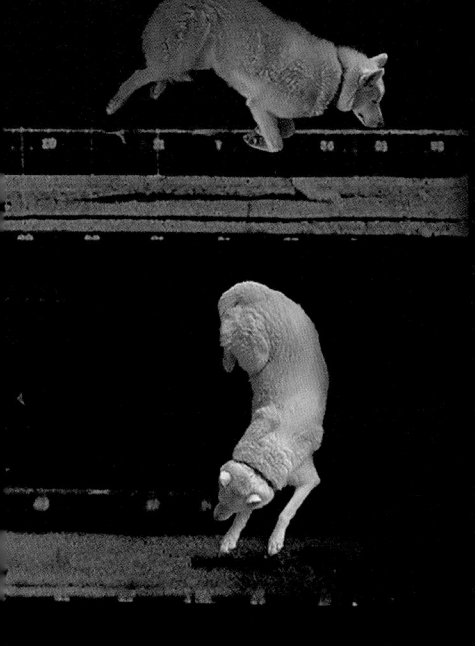
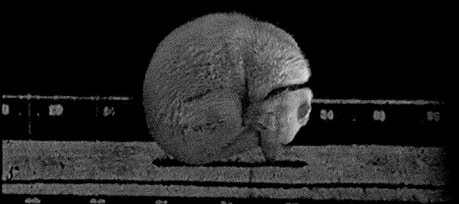

CHAPTER 8

Moment by Moment

Elapsed Time—Eadweard Muybridge Revisited

Featuring work by Andrea Jones

FIGURE 8.1 Lucy. © Andrea Jones

JONES MADE THIS WORK by adopting Eadweard Muybridge's famous grid representations of photographic studies of human and animal locomotion. Muybridge's stop-action images affirmatively settled the question of whether all four hooves of a horse in a gallop were simultaneously airborne. Up until that time, most painters depicted galloping horses with at least one hoof on the ground. These studies and the latter part of the nineteenth century secured photography's viability as an objective scientific means of recording and proving factual information.

What Are We Looking at?

Jones's choice of adopting this visual iconography of repeatable provable fact to document a sleeping dog and dying bug expands the context of both scientific and psychological endeavor. In so doing, she is arguably placing love and suffering within a quantifiable context as well as inviting a dialogue between the old enemies of fact versus conjecture and science versus spirituality.

How Can the Image Be Interpreted?

Lucy, the dog, appears to be asleep. We can make this assumption because her eyes are closed and she looks to be very relaxed and at rest. Sleep is still a state being researched and is not fully understood, but there is no doubt that we all need it to survive and thrive. Even more magical is dreaming. Have you ever woken up utterly elated, or utterly mad at someone because of how they behaved in your dreams? The brain appears to have difficulty in distinguishing between what has actually happened as opposed to what we experience while dreaming. It could also be argued that the brain has difficulty distinguishing between what has actually happened versus what we think or feel happened to us while being awake. Think about widely disparate eyewitness accounts of the same event.

There is great playfulness and maybe a little mischief in appropriating Muybridge's visual ledgers, designed to establish certainty, in order to do the opposite. Well, up to a point. There is certainty that the dog is asleep, although we can't begin to guess where her dreams are actually taking her. Rotating some of the images further erases scientific integrity, even of observation, and moves us further into the photographer's interpretation of her dog's adventures while tumbling through her imagined dreams. Just as some of the dog's saltos are impossible, the joy of the impossible is maybe the greatest dividend of dreams. How often is it not the possible but instead the impossible that sustains us? Daydreaming is maybe the best antidote to perceived reality. I suggest you use this element of imagination and bring it to your work (Figure 8.1).

What Are We Looking at?

While a nightmare technically describes an unpleasant dream, it would seem that most nightmares are experienced awake.

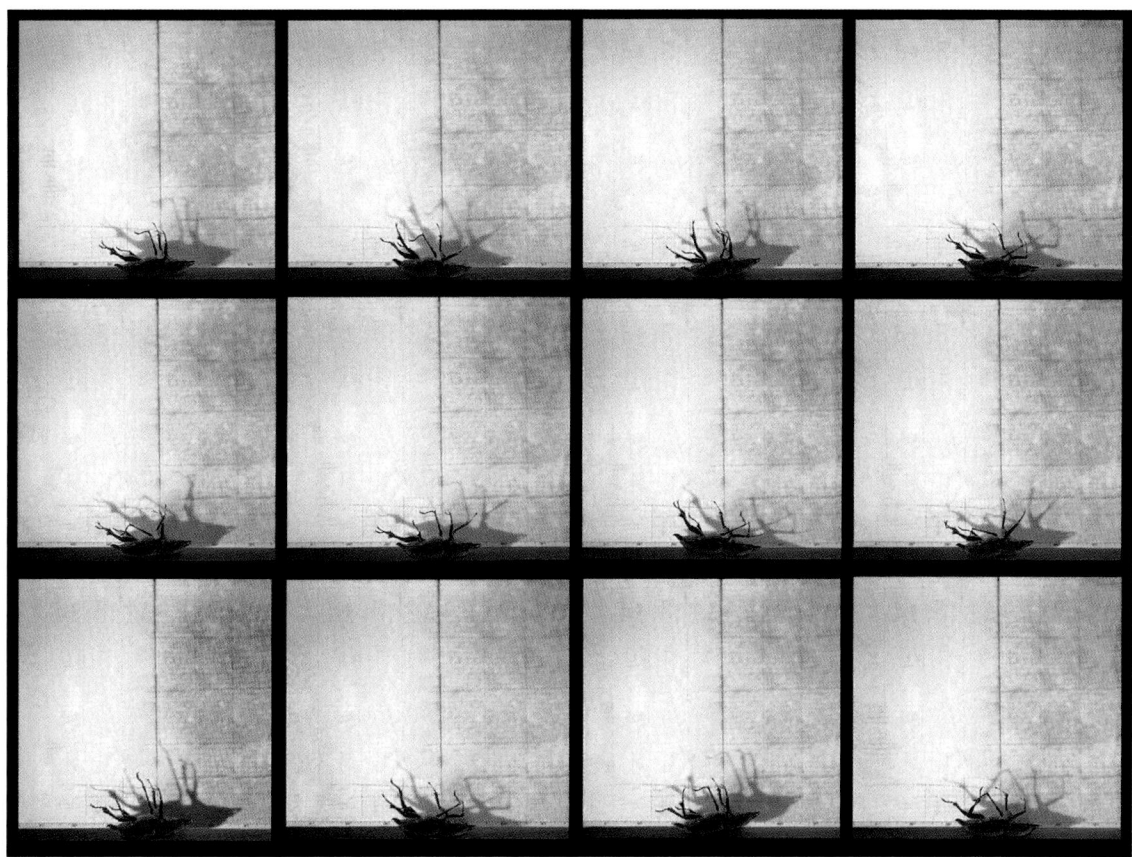

FIGURE 8.2
The image of the suffering beetle.
© Andrea Jones

Yes, we may be suffering in our dreams and experience relief when we finally wake or experience disappointment when true bliss turned out to be just a dream. But true suffering belongs to the fully conscious: the struggle of the dying beetle thus becomes a metaphor for battling both physical and emotional pain (Figure 8.2).

Maybe this little creature just needs a helpful gesture of a finger to turn it over and send it on its merry way. Is it the photographer's job to document or to help? This is an old question that can only be answered in the moment, requiring the full knowledge of the circumstances, and the judgment of the person who is wielding the camera.

How Can the Image Be Interpreted?

I rather suspect that we are looking at a dying beetle: an insect that probably had the misfortune of crossing an undetectable pest control barrier and whose body is now contracting and cramping within its protective exoskeleton that will soon become its tomb. Jones is making us look again and again at its desperate and futile gestures. The twelve frames now become charged in a different way. Given the short lifespan of most insects, is the suffering equivalent to twelve months of a human life? Is Jones alluding to the twelfth station of the cross and many of the other historic, holy, and magical associations the number holds? Whatever the significance of the number, all of us live by its recurrence, twice, each day, once each year, and generally when buying eggs.

If we have a closer look at each image, we can see that the beetle's spasms move it very slowly to the right; past the centrally placed line, the finish line, the line between life and death that each of us must cross one day.

Conclusion

When looking at time-lapse photography, time becomes an overt element. It informs each and every frame. The time taken to compose, to adjust depth of field or to adjust shutter speed is preset; and it constructs its own electromechanical rhythm. The preordained intervals may last for a small eternity for the beetle. However, although the time that elapses between a new encounter with another frame for the viewer may be inconsequential, the image, in its totality, may be resonating in ways that aren't confined to time. A new compassion may prevent the spraying of another poisoned border or the purchase of factory farmed eggs.

Please note. The beetle was already dead and Jones in no way made it suffer. She moved the legs in Photoshop, arguably another layer to using Muybridge's scientific methods, appropriated for emotional affect and provocation. What of all the images that have recorded the most cruel and nefarious experiments conducted in the world? Jones subtly reminds us of this too.

Assignments You May Want to Challenge Yourself With

- Reinterpret the canonized and iconized
- Empathy
- Compartmentalization
- Time-lapse

CHAPTER 9

The Drowned Gun

Time as Poetry

Featuring work by Mark Teiwes

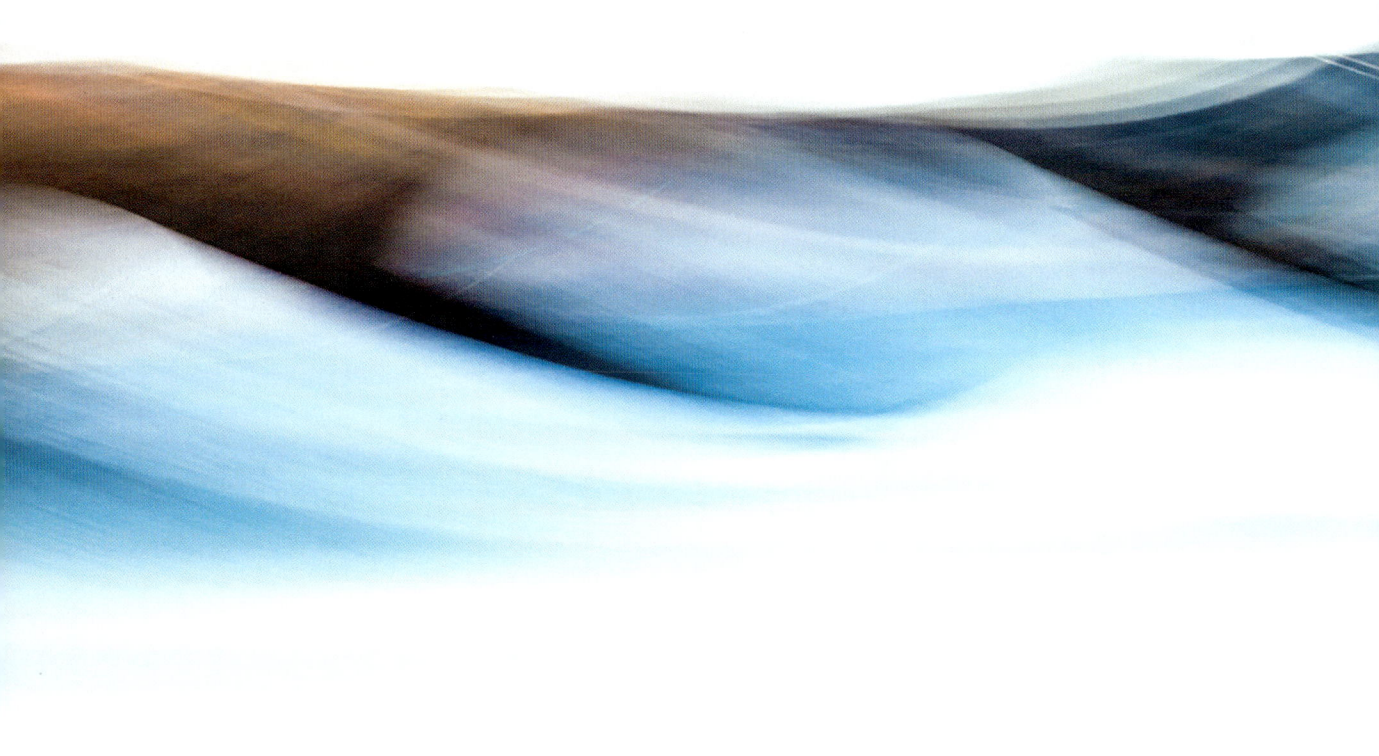

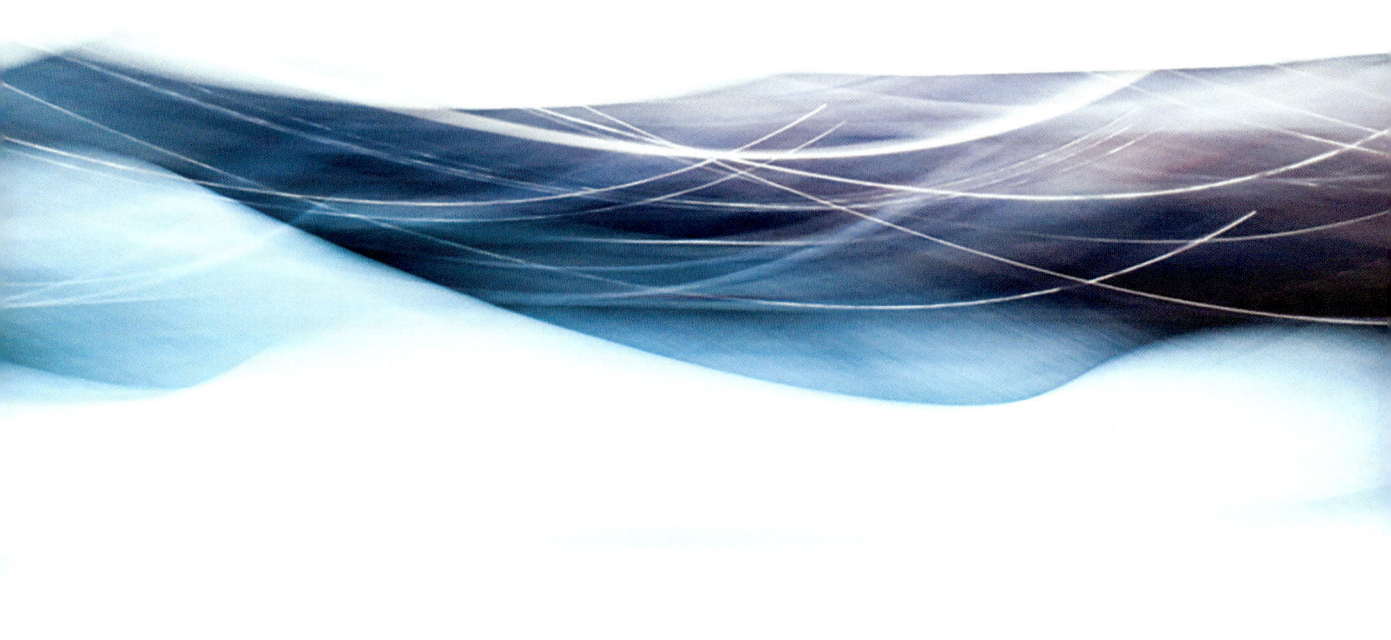
FIGURE 9.1 City Spirit. © Mark Teiwes

What Are We Looking at?

Teiwes' CITY SPIRIT IMAGES do indeed have a spectral quality to them: both in terms of the color spectrum, as well as the capture and notion of spirit as a specter—an old thing whose presence is sensed more than it is glimpsed. Like many cities, his has been built around the river's kiss into the sea. This river has been flowing for millennia, but its lifespan with a city around it is minuscule in geological time. It has been flowing incessantly for so long that the amount of water it has shed into the sea seems incalculable, immeasurably greater than the mere volume of gallons upon gallons. Uncountable are the animals whose thirst it has helped to quench, as are the fish that found their home in its flow. The city now sprawled around it is one of the older ones in the New World and as such, it has carried its quota of inhabitants whose last sense of this world was the river's cold embrace with some of their blood adding to the endless flow into the sea that everything once crawled out of a very, very long time ago.

It is something of all this enormity that eclipses the fraction of the city's existence and of every life that has passed through it that Teiwes has managed to capture with more poetry than tangibility; more feeling that precision, and more surrender than insistence (Figure 9.1).

How Can the Image Be Interpreted?

In this image of one of the many landmark bridges, he allowed his eye to momentarily wander, in order to end up with an image that looks more like the surface of the river than the elegant bridge that spans it. This massive and solid bridge is nothing but a flow of color and waves. It feels almost crazy that we experience the world or photography mostly as frozen moments when indeed everything is fluid and in motion. Even something as colossal as the Himalayan mountains are hurtling through space; not only that, they are unceasingly altering their form, although at a speed of flow that is almost imperceptible—to us they seem to be perfectly still. That is one of the satisfying things about a river: we can see it flowing, hear it rushing, feel it trickle, combat it with an ore or a swim stroke, outwit it with a sail, search for life in its depths with a lure on a hook, launch a paper boat or dispose of evidence in a hurry.

How many spears, arrows, axes, muskets, and more recently, guns, have sunk to the river's depths, dancing in the current on their way down? How many secrets and scraps of evidence are languishing in its waters, slowly decaying, stripped of DNA and fingerprints; even a serial number will eventually deteriorate. And what of the incomplete stories, only half known and those we'll never know? These are not forensic images but they touch upon the many secrets the river eventually tells

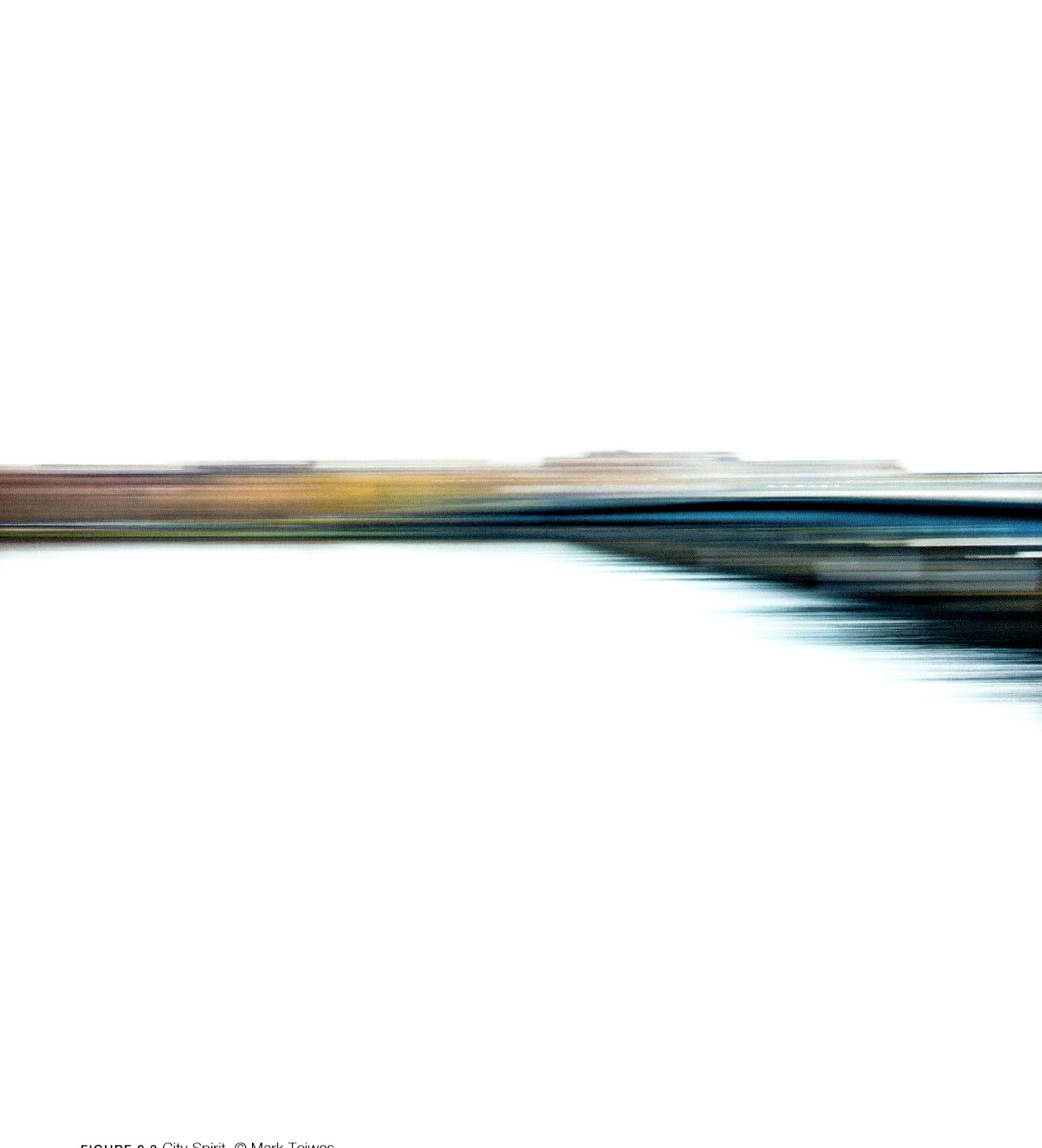

FIGURE 9.2 City Spirit. © Mark Teiwes

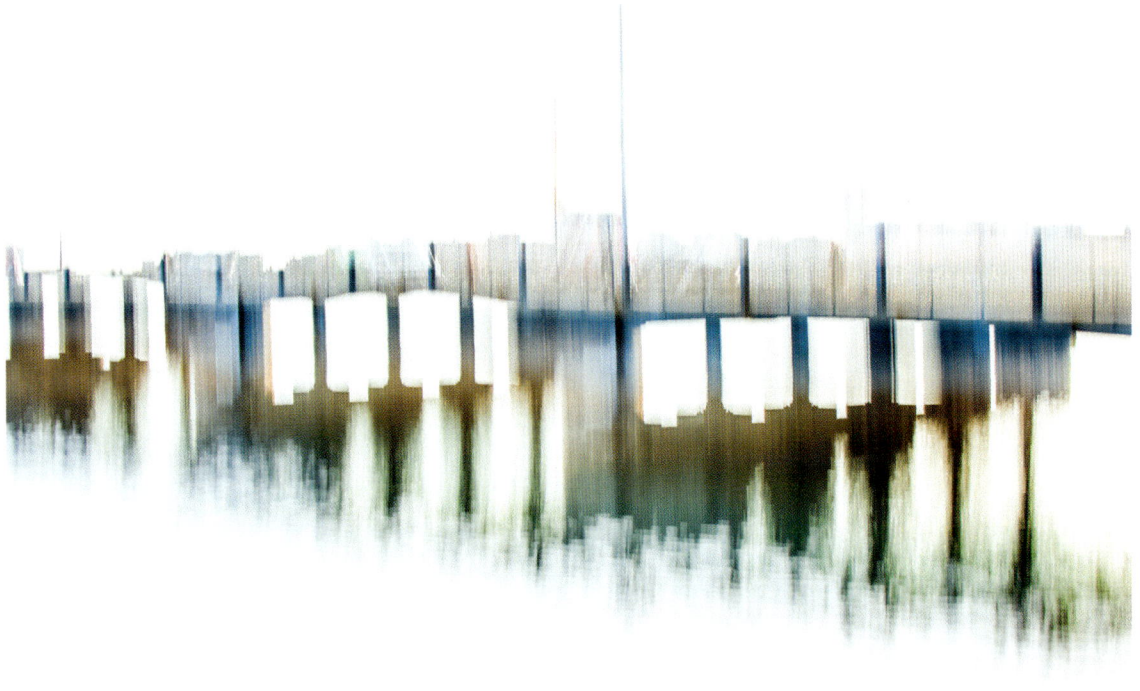

FIGURE 9.3
City Spirit.
© Mark Teiwes

the sea. These are not images that prove the pain or lead to justice. Rather they can be read as a poem to all of these things; a melody that reveals itself in the movement of the camera.

The endless gray winter sky reflected on the river's surface is overexposed and becomes white nothingness as the muted winter colors find themselves stretched into an unlikely radiance. Time has no meaning in these images and yet makes them powerful for that reason alone.
In the image above, the panning of the camera transformed the riverbank into the shape of a rifle. It points against the left to right direction our eyes are used to traveling in, as if attempting to shoot time itself (Figure 9.2).

Conclusion

Yes, the river's name is the Charles and before this name, it will have had many others, and at some point in the distant past, no name at all. Boston is a big city and its history, both before and after its founding, is rich and complicated; so too are all the stories of all the rivers that bisect the that final city or settlement on their way to the vastness of the oceans. They all touch each other at some point, and eventually share the stories each river has told them, maybe just as molecules, a language we do not speak but which, as with whale song, has been spoken for far longer than before we started to communicate.

In this way, Teiwes does not only bend time, but place, even geography itself: for rivers appear sometimes to be willful and just change the direction they want to flow towards; sometimes they just lose their way and dry up; sometimes they are bent to our will, for our convenience or harnessed for power generation.

This then also represents a meditation on photography: misdirection, change in direction and the hold on one moment, inevitably in the past, before the image comes into being. The latent image precedes its appearance on a screen or in the form of a print. This may take an instant or decades. You may also want to consider sequencing when contemplating this work. I presented the images out of sequence based on how they resonated with me. How do they resonate with you and how would you rearrange them?

Assignments You May Want to Challenge Yourself With

- Visual poetry
- Time
- History
- Cityscape

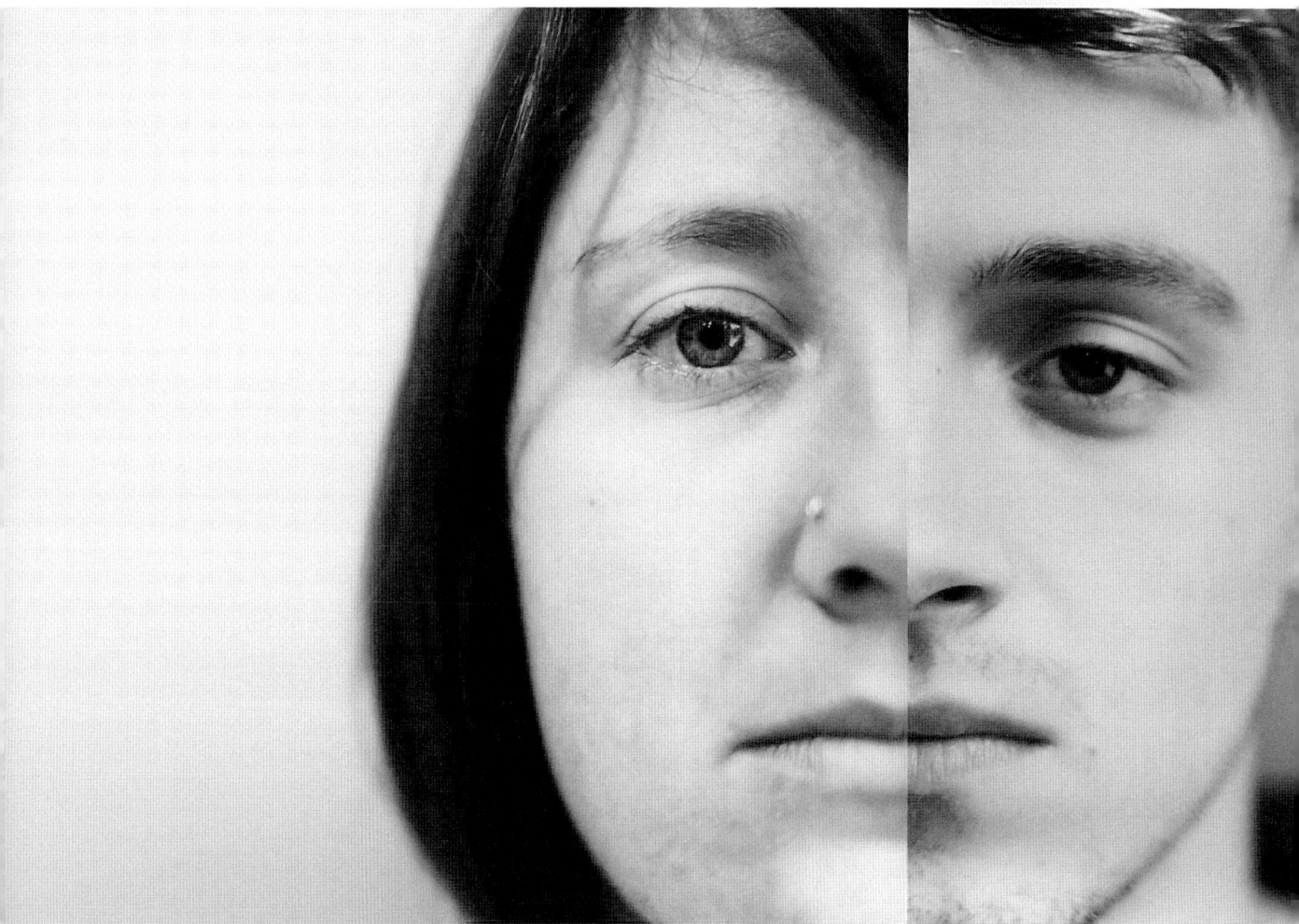

CHAPTER 10

Split Again

The Reversed Connection

**Featuring work
by Megan Whitney**

FIGURE 10.1 Twins. © Megan Whitney

THE WORK OF WHITNEY explores the complex bond that connects most twins and their unique experience of existence. A twin herself, her interest in researching and conveying her experience and that of her brother's, as well as that of other twins, is a challenging and highly personal journey.

Identical twins originate from a single fertilized egg, which splits into two entities that continue to develop. Fraternal twins stem from two fertilized eggs that develop simultaneously. It is this embryonic companionship that appears to be the origin of a lifelong bond that predates their arrival into the world.

What Are We Looking at?

It is this oneness, arguably the closest kind of bond two human beings can have to one another, that never quite gets conveyed when twins are photographed together. Splitting the two to make one again therefore seemed a promising strategy to convey the connection and separateness, the singularity and plurality of their existence and experiences.

How Can the Images Be interpreted?

By splitting and aligning individual portraits of twins, Whitney powerfully conveys this unresolved separateness and togetherness. Depending upon birth order and dominance she shifts the frame of each half portrait out of alignment. The effect reinforces the split between the two halves and provides additional negative space around the actual images.

This space seems important and can be seen as a placeholder for the unseen half of each individual. Indeed, when this space becomes compressed or removed the images lose some of their mystery.

Instead, they start to evoke images of medical research and allude to physically conjoined twins where physical separateness is no longer a choice. This alone makes the surrounding space a crucial component of the composition. Seen as a series, these staggered surroundings form a subtle rhythm of ups and downs that informs even the closest of relationships.

Whitney also incorporates strategies found in many great portraits that use a shallow depth of field. An example is her own (self-) portrait with her brother. This was hard to miss for the class or her teacher because we all knew what she looked like and that she is a twin. Though it is the only image with an even space around it, thus not overtly designating dominance or birth order, she remains the dominant component of the image with her eye in clear focus as opposed to her brother's eye, which is slightly out of focus. When we look someone in the eyes we have to focus on one eye at a time. Our switch of focus from one eye to the other occurs rapidly; if we break eye contact, before it is re-established, during a myriad of other gestures and facial expressions that we process all at once, the switch may go unnoticed. We often experience more intimacy or a more personal connection when looking at portraits where one eye is slightly out of focus than in portraits where both eyes appear sharply in focus.

Though the audience is confronted with a flat piece of paper, this focusing strategy makes Whitney physically appear closer to the audience. This stance with the audience makes her also seem protective of her brother. This is additionally reinforced by the illusion that her gradually less focused strands of hair appear to continue into the other frame. Draped over her brother's shoulder, they are reminiscent of a protective arm or the warming tail of a cat (Figure 10.1).

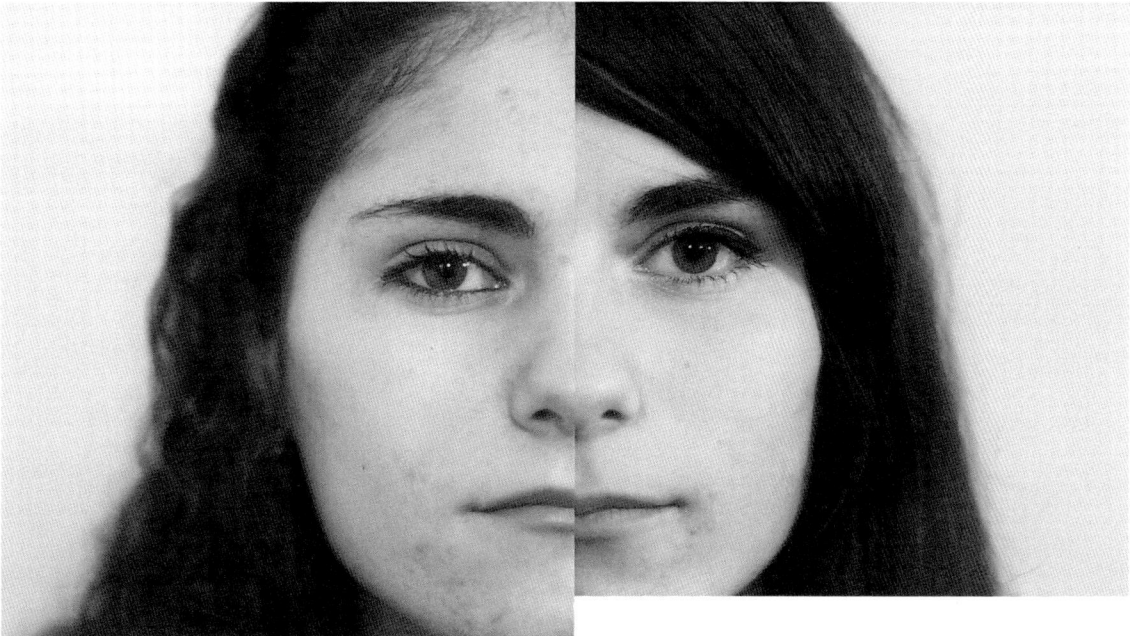

FIGURE 10.2 Twins. © Megan Whitney

By contrast, it is therefore of significance that in the second image under consideration from the series, this distancing is retained by focusing on both eyes simultaneously. The relevance becomes completely clear when we read about the twins in their own words. Below each image she displays a second image of an open notebook where each twin, in her or his handwriting, comments on the experience of having and being a twin mirroring the "open book" photographs of the twins above (Figure 10.2).

Conclusion

In the case of the twins in the second photograph each is blind in one eye, which could be learned from the notebook. The twin on the left in the right eye and the twin on the right in the left eye; the one on the left is left-handed and the one on the right is right-handed. The distancing by having both eyes in focus is therefore apt because in combination we are looking at a blind person. It is not we, the audience, who can't see her/them; it is her/them who can't see us. As non-twins we are likely to only ever have a vague inkling of what being and having a twin really means. Whitney has generously offered us such a glimpse in all of the images in her series but this one seems to make the point most directly.

Assignments You May Want to Challenge Yourself With

- Siblings
- Identity
- Facial composites
- Leveraging negative space

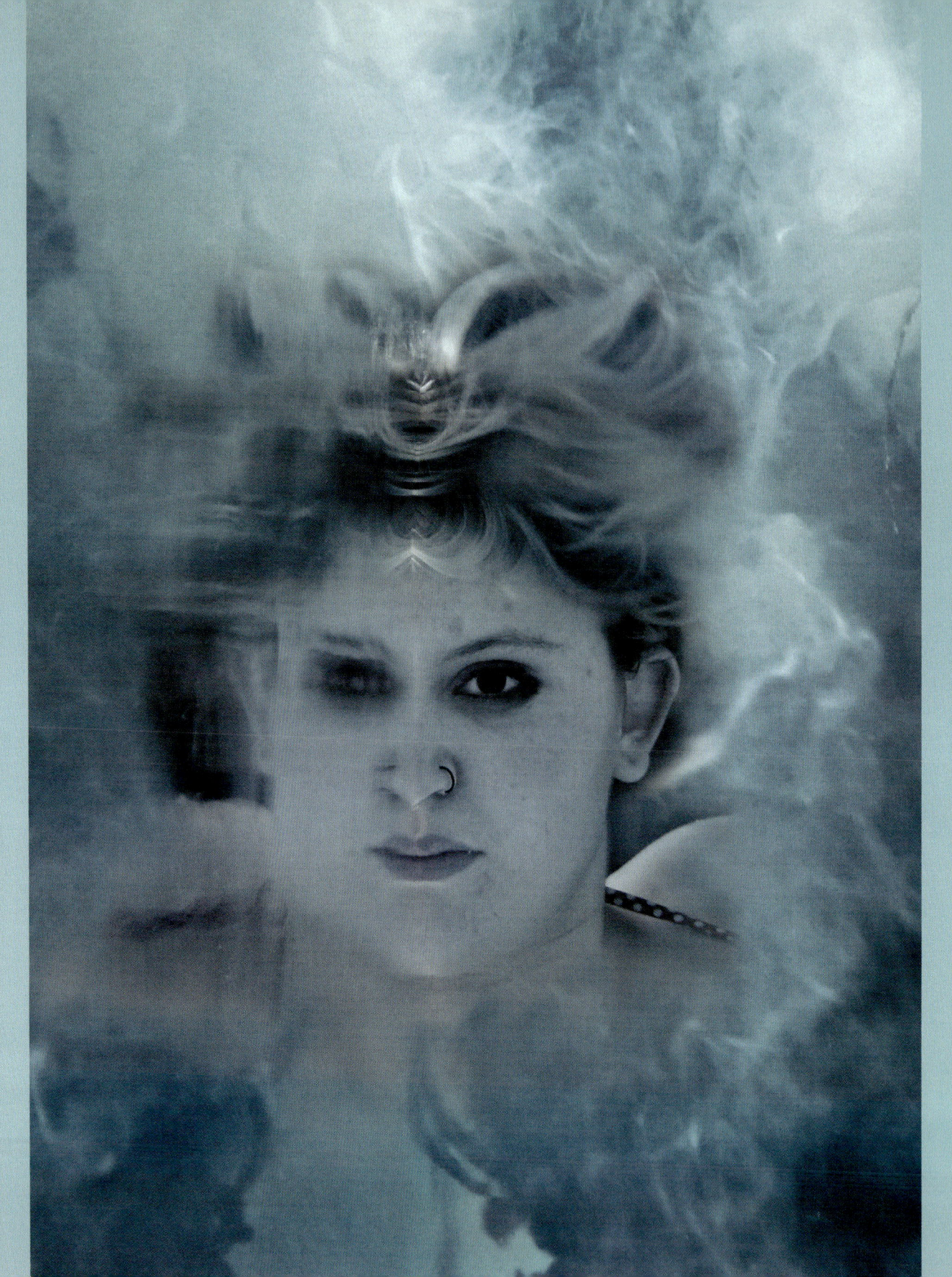

CHAPTER 11

The Other Half

Water and Air

Featuring work by Adriana Reyes-Newell

FIGURE 11.1 Untitled. © Adriana Reyes-Newell

Whereas in the previous chapter we referred to the womb as the place where intangible bonds start to appear among siblings, in this chapter we will make reference to the essentially gravity-free "amniotic fluid" that we are all suspended in before we are born. "Three-dimensional" suspension may be one of the reasons why people feel so euphoric while SCUBA diving. They are again suspended in a gravity-free, equal-pressure environment across the entire body. It stands to reason that while we may not have any conscious memory of the *in utero* experience, we may have a deeper, embedded memory of it. Touch, after all, can affect us deeply, and if we can store or release trauma physically, the process of coming into being is likely to be stored somewhere as well.

Not just the joy of this experience in and of itself, but also the overwhelming beauty of magical sea life got me started in underwater photography. Photographing through water is somewhat different from photographing through air. Light, objects, and gravity appear and act differently, and in so doing, offer unique visual opportunities. This prompted me to develop a fine art underwater photography class, which I first taught in the spring of 2008. Probably most importantly, people feel different in water than on land and become inspired by emersion into a new environment (Fig. 11.1).

What Are We Looking at?

While suspended in amniotic fluid we can't use our lungs to breathe air. Oxygen is provided via the umbilical cord. As we are born, the pressure in the birth canal pushes fluid out of our lungs and prepares them for our first breath.

This moment between a liquid and air environment is reflected (no pun intended) in Reyes-Newell's work. For her portraits she posed her models with their faces only partially submerged and photographed from a favorable angle within the water so that the other half of the face would be reflected. Had the surface of the water been perfectly still, this could have provided a near perfect symmetrical recreation of the two halves into a whole.

Since most people's faces are far from perfectly symmetrical, this could have led to a series of the two faces we potentially present under such circumstances and an exploration of what the dissimilarities reveal about how we interpret faces. This experiment was conducted and published by photographer Alex John Beck. He used a studio setting to avoid the trouble of having to shoot underwater and achieved more accurate results. BuzzFeed also lets you experiment with images of fifteen celebrities to see what they would look like if their faces were symmetrical.

How Can the Images Be Interpreted?

Instead, Reyes-Newell let the movement of the water's surface distort the other half into something less defined and more left to chance. Fashion designer Coco Chanel is quoted for having said, "Nature gives you the face you have at twenty. Life shapes the face you have at thirty. But at fifty you get the face you deserve."

This brings us back to nature versus nurture questions and, eventually, our own responsibility for our destiny. As if to underscore that point, Reyes-Newell added milk around the faces, as she set up her portraits in the pool, the first food nature intends for us to ingest. As it dissolved in the water it made the faces appear as if they were surrounded by a storm: the storm of the circumstances of our lives, the storm of our own decisions, and all of the cloudiness inbetween (Figure 11.2).

Where does this storm begin: in a previous life; way back in the primordial soup; how can we possibly know? But rather than feeling frustrated by this, we may have to accept that both circumstance and purpose drive us simultaneously. The religious and philosophical debate about the relationship of the preordained vs free will is a subtext in Reyes-Newell's images, compelling us to reflect on those fundamental questions that self-awareness insistently thrusts upon us.

Conclusion

Frustrating as the unanswerable may be, use it to fuel your imagination and enjoy the ride and where it takes you. Use the apparent echoes from the past and the future, which provide us with the illusion of stability for a moment.

These moments are powerful in these portraits of others where we may, for just a moment, find ourselves, again and again.

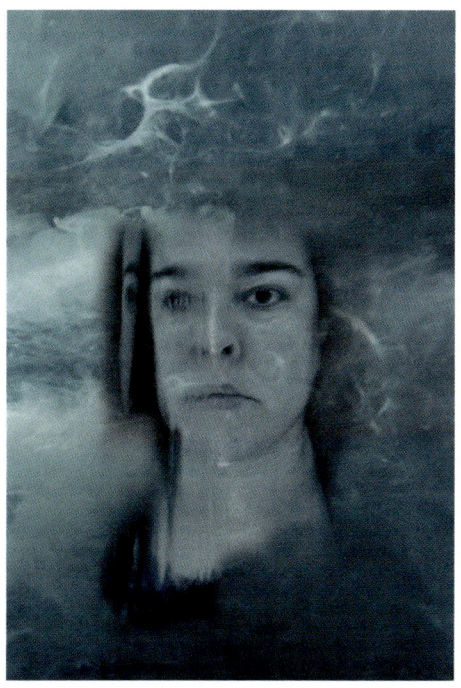

FIGURE 11.2 Untitled.
© Adriana Reyes-Newell

Assignments You May Want to Challenge Yourself With

- Underwater photography
- Facial symmetry (via water, mirrors, and other reflective surfaces)
- Portraiture
- Milk

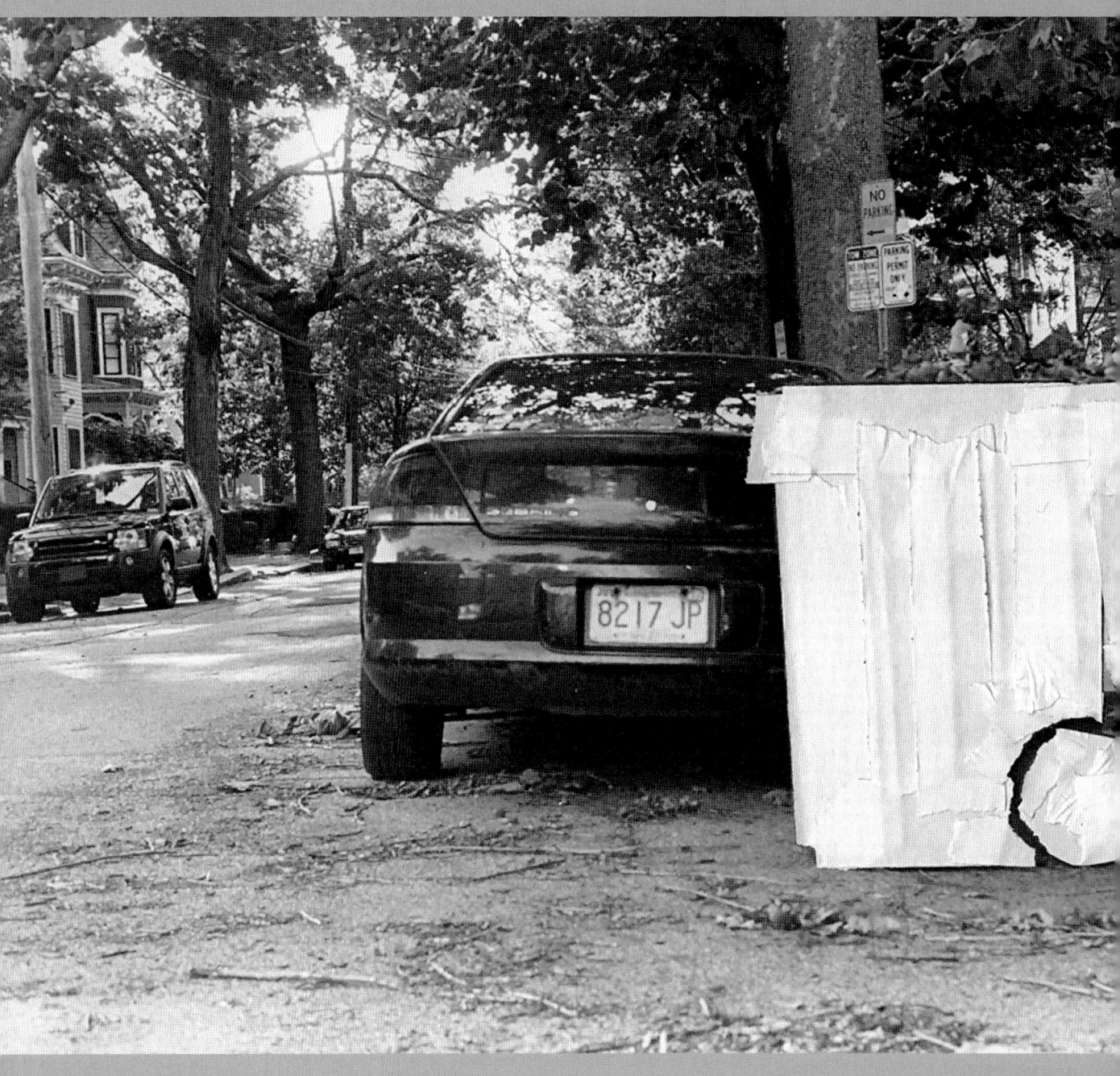

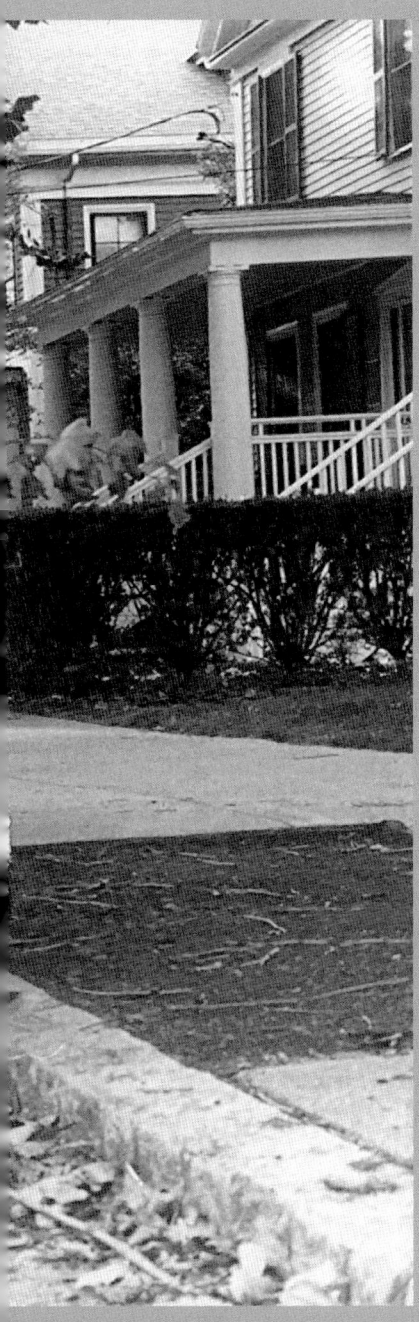

CHAPTER 12

The Original
Please Touch the Art

**Featuring work by
Jackson Reeves-Henning**

FIGURE 12.1 Trashcan. © Jackson Reeves-Henning

ONE OF THE FIRST THINGS we learn about art is that we are not to touch it; that to do so would damage the piece or might leave a fingerprint. Even though we are tactile as well as visual when exploring something, particularly as young children, the untouchability of art, as a rule, may well be the very first conscious association many people have with it.

The implications of this are potentially profound. From early on we are being taught there is something forbidden about art, almost as if touching it is innately dangerous and detrimental. Professionals, or the art makers themselves, are the only ones who know how to touch the artwork. As with a dream, we learn that holding on to it or trying to grasp it will only accelerate the process of the dream vanishing once we are fully awake. It could be argued that experiencing art is taught as a form of dreaming. We are to think of ourselves as sleepwalking pariahs in front of some deity that will vanish or die if we infect it with our physical presence. Simply put, touching art is taboo.

Glossy photographs are annoyingly susceptible to fingerprints and smudges. Even the makers will handle them with soft white cotton gloves. Large photographs can easily become damaged with half-moon creases, unless correctly handled. Even archival pigment prints are no better; the pigment can flake off depending on the paper stock. This can engender a distance between photographers and their work as much as for their audience. The deliberate maltreatment of the negative or print through staining, scratching, and otherwise distressing negatives or prints can become an act of defiance and subversion to create an aesthetic counterpoint (Figure 12.1).

During a freshman black and white film seminar critique class, the students collectively lamented their status as digital "natives" as opposed to my generation's status of digital "immigrants." We discussed this divide and, to meet where this group collectively came from, I encouraged them to embrace the materiality of the medium they were working with.

Experiment with Your Materials

Specifically, I asked them to work with their initial rolls of film. Since most of the students had not previously worked with film, most had exposures that were not entirely successful. Rather than wasting them, I suggested that they cut them up, tape them back together with other negatives, scratch them, burn the emulsion, and so on. Basically everything one is not supposed to do to film.

This led to an entirely new sense of ownership among the students in relation to their delicate negatives. This was also an introduction to integrating writing and images, as well as photographic abstraction and collage. Counterintuitive as this may seem, it also helped them understand film on a rudimentary technical basis as this assignment tangibly reinforced the effects of adding or removing density from the negative.

What Are We Looking at?

The non-archival masking tape stuck on this photograph functions in several ways.

The photograph itself becomes an original, unlikely to be reproducible with the same exactitude as a second exposure of the negative. The piece can now also be considered as being interdisciplinary. Photography is no longer the sole process responsible for its creation.

The archival quality and anticipated permanence of the piece has been altered as well. The masking tape's half-life is different from that of the photograph.

Reeves-Henning's use of masking tape to obliterate and recreate an element on his print rather than on the negative had a powerful impact. Many students felt it compelled them to "touch the art."

Work Collaboratively to Define Meaning

I asked all the students to approach the piece in turn and, with their eyes closed utter the first word that came to mind when touching the art. I wrote down the words in the order they were spoken:

Struggle
Hockey
Incoherent
Wax
Mummy
Tennis racket
Piano keys
Bandages
Clothes pins
Gymnastics beam
Boardwalk
Dead skin

By adding some verbs and prepositions, I jotted down part of a potential artist's statement:

> The waxy mummy was struggling with its tennis racket handle-like bandages that were held together with clothes pins, while it was playing the piano with a hockey stick on a gymnastics beam straddling the boardwalk feeling the heat on some of its exposed dead skin.

What Does This Do?

This had multiple implications for the student and the class. It was an example of how directing an image to speak through others can create an idea for an entirely new body of work and how the reciprocal nature of engaging the artistic process and cooperative approaches function. Taking pictures of the nouns the class associated with the tape could create an entire series of work. This reinforced the value and tradition of collaboration among artists. It also showed the students the value of attending an art school; how the collective combustion of ideas can lead to new avenues of exploration and reveal the potential of each student's work.

How Can the Image Be Interpreted?

As for the subtext, it is implicit: bandaging something is an attempt at healing, at making something better. The mass consumerism evidenced by the industrial-sized trashcans in the US certainly speaks to this need. There is also the idea of redaction collectively and individually; of eliminating evidence and compartmentalizing what we don't want to see.

How this might impact other "bandaged" images is not clear, but a few immediate thoughts seem relevant. The increasing controversy brewing over many past acquisitions of regional artifacts, such as sarcophagi and their mummies, or the Elgin Marbles come to mind, as do sports injuries of very young gymnasts who don't yet have fully formed skeletons. Another thought is of piano lessons and the tyranny of endless practice for those who weren't born virtuosos.

Conclusion

The interdisciplinary potential for photography opens, by violating a perfect surface, another door for future experimentation. The class was directed to research Patrick Nagatani's Tapist's series.

Assignments You May Want to Challenge Yourself With

- Composite negatives
- Engagement with the materiality of photographs
- Interdisciplinary elements
- Redaction
- Create collaborative artist's statements

THE ORIGINAL

As IT WAS, Reeves-Henning took off in another direction. The engagement of others with his own work led to an examination of how others, in different contexts, interact with work in museums. This became a satisfying and imaginary process that led to many great images and a portfolio in the subsequent color seminar. Reeves-Henning composed moments of others, when they didn't touch the art. In some cases, it appeared, they didn't even look at the art (Figure 12.2).

What Are We Looking at?

If someone wanted their likeness preserved before photography came along, the drawn or painted portrait was the likely option apart from the sculpted likeness. Inevitably, this leaves us for the most part with images of people of some importance and of some means. Seated, more often than not, such individuals are posed to exude the gravitas of their existence. What distinguishes this painting from many of its peers is the complexity in the subject's expression. Is it judgmental, humble, self-satisfied, or full of regret?

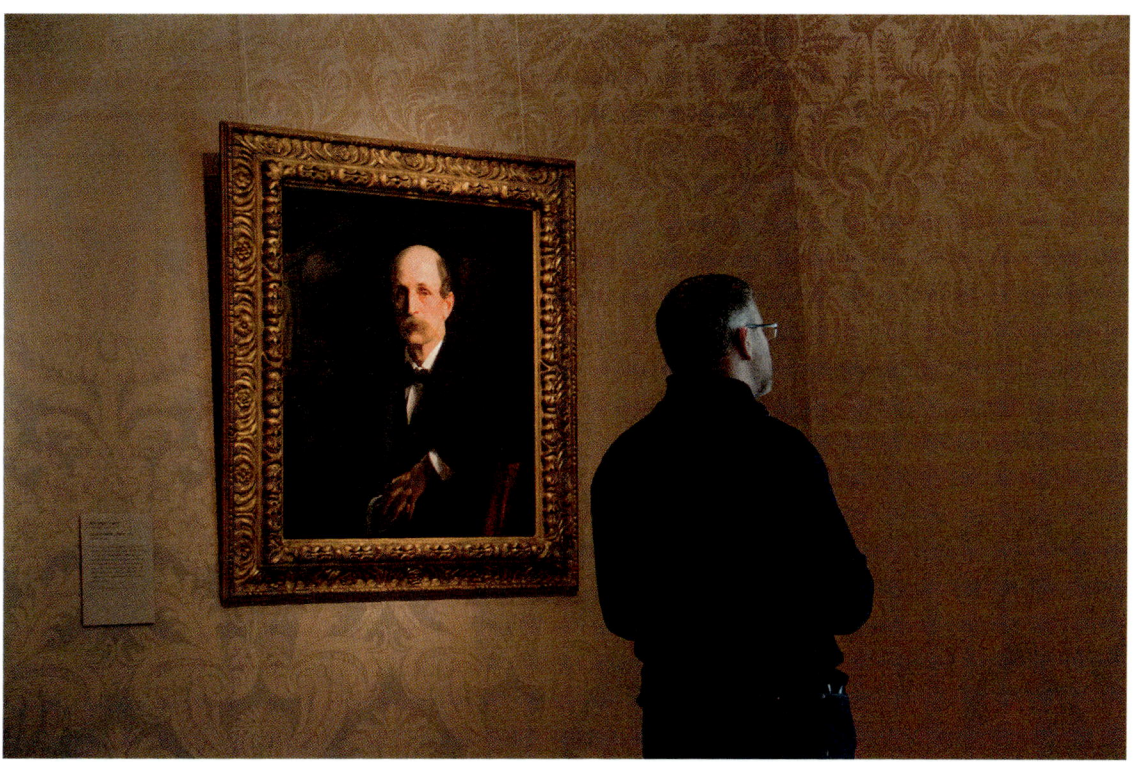

FIGURE 12.2 Untitled. © Jackson Reeves-Henning

We can assume that the painting graces a museum—because of the institutional plaque next to it although we can't read it. The professional hanging system is also mostly found in museums rather than homes. The wallpaper feels more domestic than institutional, though in the context of this piece in a comfortable way. They seem to belong together. Is that why the patron is looking at the wallpaper instead of the art? Is the patron looking at anything at all? We can't see the patron's expression, arguably the subject of the photograph. So it is the man in the painting who was old when his portrait was painted and therefore unlikely to be with us anymore. Yet, in his inscrutable awareness he makes eye contact with us. A knowing look about the other man who has turned his back on both him, the man in the painting, and us, the viewers. From the tomb of his painting the portrayed man is looking towards another man with a camera, most likely on a tripod. The easel stand he would recognize, as he would the painter's pallet—these tools of the trade have now been replaced by the digital camera, filled with logic boards and light sensors that are inventions that are now superseding film after its 150-year reign. The digital/mechanical pallet is replicating in an instant that for which he must have posed for hours back in his day when he was painted. Even though the camera is trained on him, it really is meant to capture the other man; the one seemingly just staring at the wall paper if he is even taking it in.

How Can the Image Be Interpreted?

As an audience from the future, we will only see this photograph after it has been made. Now, though, we are joined by an interloper, the man in the painting, from the past. He will not ever see this photograph but is deeply connected to it.

We couldn't touch the art in this instance, not in a museum and in any case, we are not there; not even the photograph, as it is merely replicated in this book. And still, we are being touched, in this multiply mediated exchange that has been forged by a painter a lifetime ago. Later a photographer created this new encounter; and just now you are looking at a reproduction of a reproduction in this book. This secret exchange about the man who is staring into space is hardly a secret, yet the staring man may not know of it. Is the old man pleading with us to keep it to ourselves? Is the younger man his great, great-grandson? Has he turned away to say goodbye to someone he never knew and whose legacy is with him or is he a stranger like us who merely turned away?

Conclusion

Maybe the man is a wallpaper designer. Maybe the younger man never came for the paintings in the museum at all. Maybe what we see as mere background to the spectacle unfolding in front of us represents in reality the spectacle the younger man has come to see. The damask-like wall treatment, possibly similar to the damask sheets the man in the painting used to sleep in. Maybe the art was touched after all, just not in the way we expected it to be.

Assignments You May Want to Challenge Yourself With

- Subtext, it's not what you are apparently looking at
- Waiting for the moment
- Re-contextualizing existing art

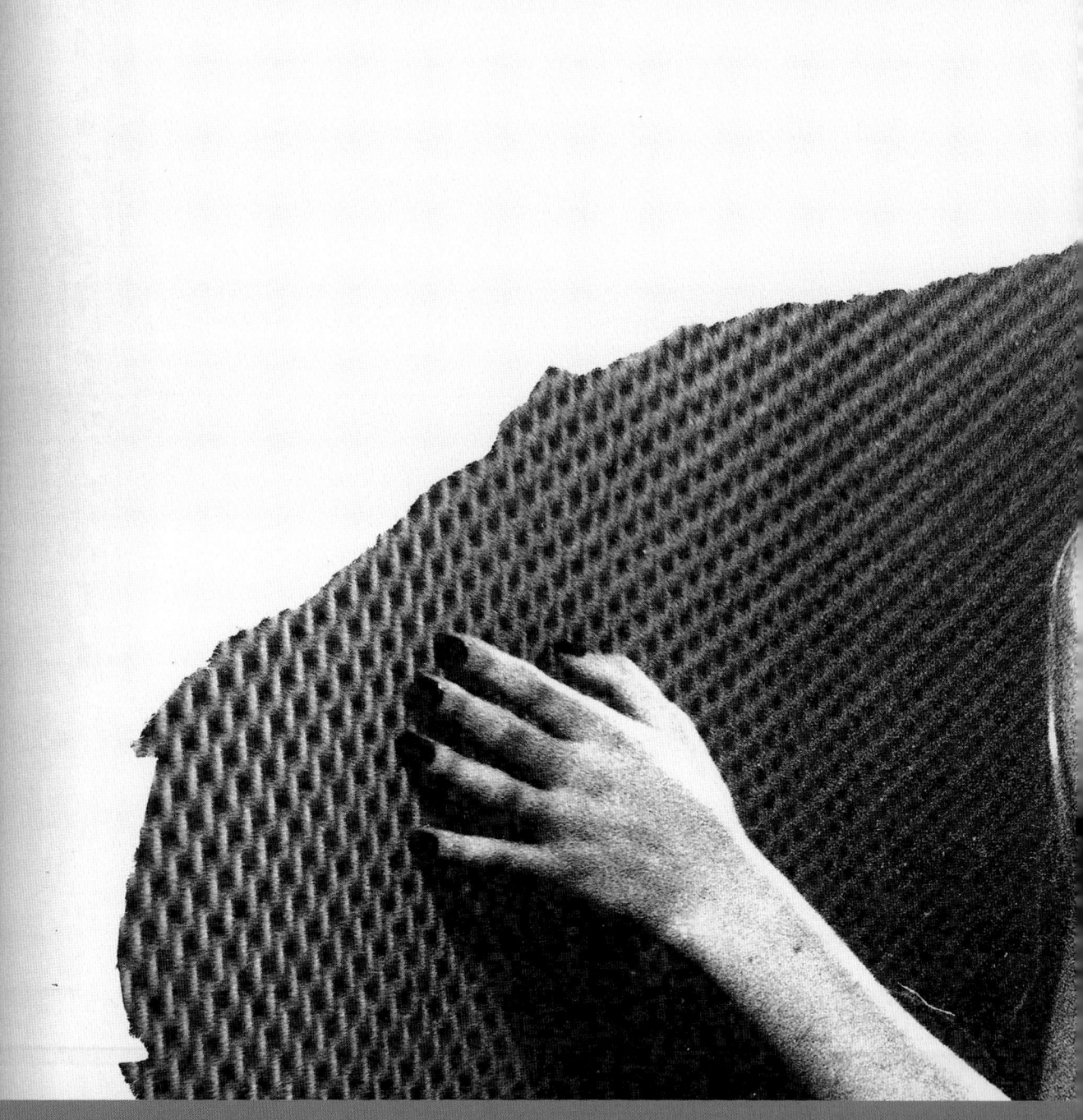

CHAPTER 13

The Tyranny of Borders
The Fractured Elements

Featuring work by Tyla Levesque

FIGURE 13.1 Kelli. © Tyla Levesque

THE EXPECTATION FOR most two-dimensional art pieces is that the frame is fully filled, whether that is based on applying paint to the last square inch of a canvas or filling the frame with photographic information. With drawings and graphic design we are more likely to accept negative space, "paper white," as part of a finished piece. This is not so much the case in photography, though I think this too is being challenged; more interdisciplinary works are being created by a combination of painting or drawing and photographic elements.

Levesque in her photographs found this absence of information, the absence of the "full" picture enticing and has used it to great effect.

What Are We Looking at?

By presenting us with a woman who is touching a high-density wire mesh fence she presents her viewers with a seemingly impenetrable barrier. She conjures associations with confinement and the futility of trying to overcome it. At the same time she plays on the experience of illusion that is now so ingrained that we often simply forget that we are in actuality looking at a piece of paper. A fragile thing that can be simply cut with household scissors, ripped to pieces, burned, or simply allowed to disintegrate if not protected behind matts, plexi, frames, and dry interior environments.

Levesque may be trying to show us that much of the information we believe is in fact an illusion; a game we play with ourselves as much as one she plays with her audience. This is an audacious reminder that what we see is not real. Since we mostly live in a constructed reality, our sense of it can be fragile and people messing around with it are not always thanked for their pointed reminders.

This becomes further complicated by the impulse to think: if the model would only move her hand into the empty space she would be free. When we realize that, in doing so, her hand would simply disappear into the void, much as the fence, we get to experience the fear of danger. We know the model's hand will simply be gone, but does she?

This is how Levesque confronts us with a choice: to stay bound by confinement or disappear. This is a conundrum and with some very practical insinuations. Visit the wrong part of town or the wrong country and while you may step out of your safety zone you may well disappear because the world can be a very dangerous place indeed. It is also a philosophical conundrum. Stay within cultural and societal conventions and you'll be safe. Challenge them too loudly and you may be seen as a heretic to whatever established order of the age and place you find yourself in.

How Can the Images Be Interpreted?

As children we are taught about boundaries early on to become appropriately socialized. The more we rail against such boundaries the harsher the consequences seem to be, for our own good of course. This is how we learn to confuse confidence with certainty and futile rebellion with genuine soul searching. The gesture of the hand in the photograph is nevertheless probing. The hand doesn't really push against the boundary nor does it break contact with it. The acknowledgment of its existence is almost tender, even pitying at that. The cut fence is not blamed for being what it is, in actuality and symbolically. Rather there seems to be a sense of wonder at its existence in the first place and the symbiotic relationship between what keeps us safe and sane; at least for as long as we are willing to believe this.

The shape of the fence resembles that of a large fish. The dense mesh is reminiscent of scales. There are countless images of people who are compelled to touch the glass in an aquarium to somehow reach the fish behind it. What the fish think, particularly if bred and brought up in that confined underwater construct about the queues of the humans who come every day and every day touch the glass and never get in, is anyone's guess (Figure 13.1).

And so it is with the man who touches his face, as if to reassure himself that he is real. The shadow resembles a masculine face but it is not his. It too has been crudely cut as if to taunt him, the viewer, and probably photography itself. By referencing the paper, the illusion of what we see forces us to acknowledge that someone's hand has taken the element of the frame, the expected confinement of the photograph itself out of the realm of our experience.

This time the composition is balanced with another dark space: some remnant of the original photograph; a dark monolith that most closely resembles the letter "I;" reminding us of the first person singular. The "I" is of course just a dark mark and we only attribute meaning to it in accordance with how we were taught to decipher such a mark. It could also be read as the number "1"—one life, one chance to find out why we are here.

Since the positive space no longer resembles anything like the fence, it is on equal footing with the negative space. Arguably we can read this image as an abstract composition with a photographic element (Figure 13.2).

What happens if we take the photograph out of this arrangement entirely and just consider the dark and light spaces and their interplay? We would be left with some Easter Island formation of a humanoid. Maybe the letter "I" or the number "1" is simply the back of the next statue in line. Both the dark and light spaces continue

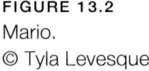

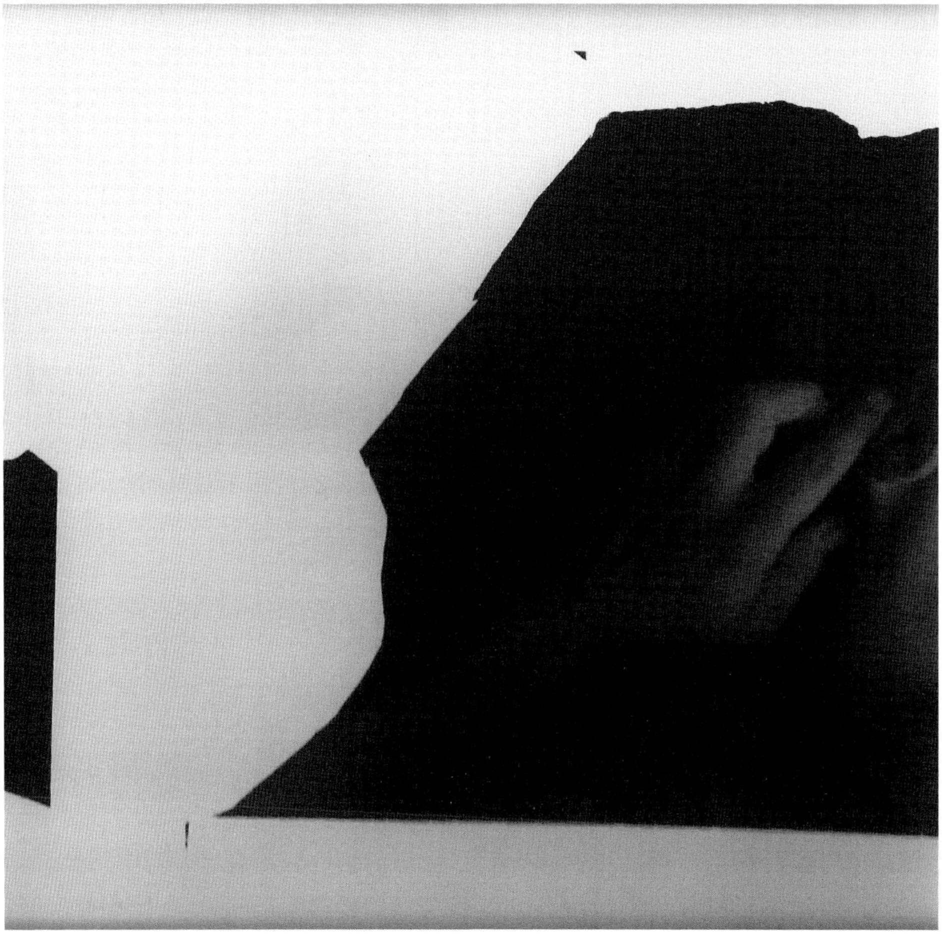

FIGURE 13.2
Mario.
© Tyla Levesque

outside of the frame. If we flip this image it is perhaps easier to see the melting snowman who seems so tired he has started to lie down (Figure 13.3).

The dark rocks against which he is resting seem to provide him with a degree of comfort. Is that where Levesque is pointing us? If everything is an illusion, who is to say with any conviction what is up and what is down? The answer is surely predicated on how we might choose to hang her image.

Is the man in the image thinking about snowmen? Are we all snowmen and snowwomen who get built up, little by little, rolled and molded into shape, decorated with individuality—just to melt away eventually and vanish?

Conclusion

It is the recognition of this transience where I connect to Levesque's work. Whether flesh or paper, snow or rocks, night or day, up or down,

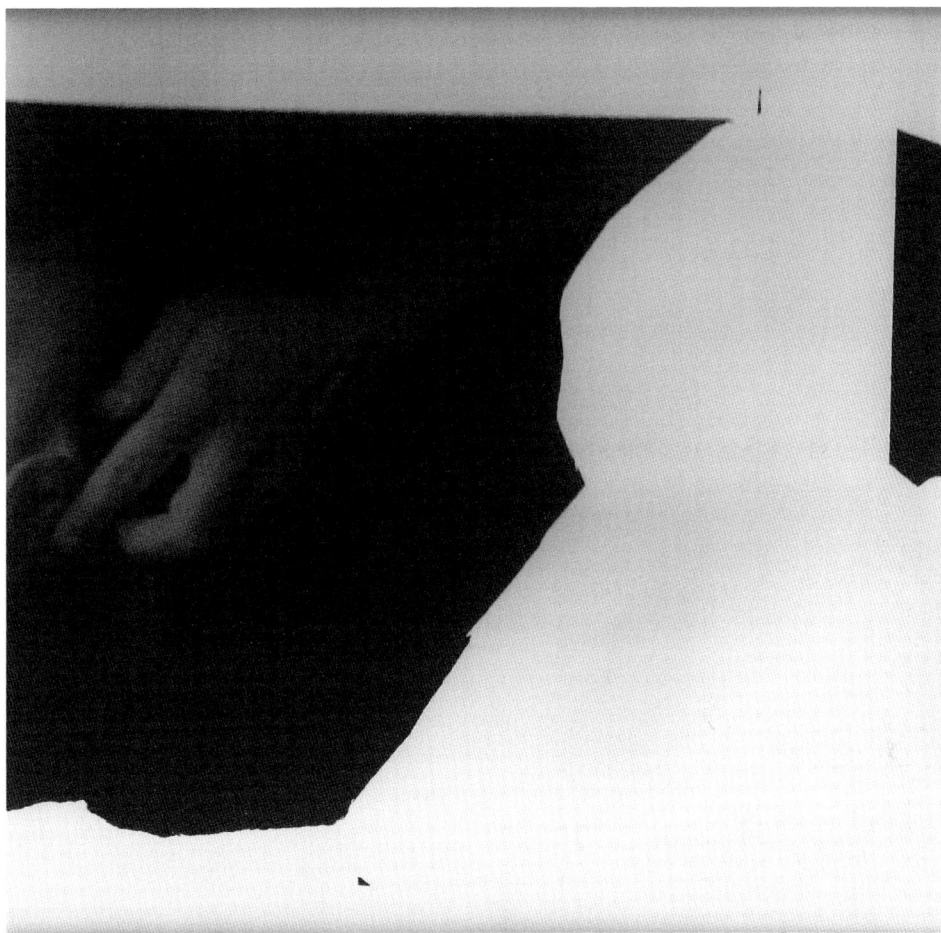

FIGURE 13.3
Mario.
© Tyla Levesque

eventually most things will disappear and if not, nevertheless change and alter their form. Maybe, if we don't insist that everything has to be perfectly formed to begin with, this inevitability can become less daunting. Maybe Levesque proposes that to leave something not entirely whole in one dimension provides opportunity for growth in other realms. Maybe she simply permits paper to hold on to its elemental nature to caution us about our own. There is always an alternative lens by which we can view something.

Assignments You May Want to Challenge Yourself With

- Mixed media
- Partial paper exposures
- Partial chemical application
- Reinterpret the idea of straight image borders

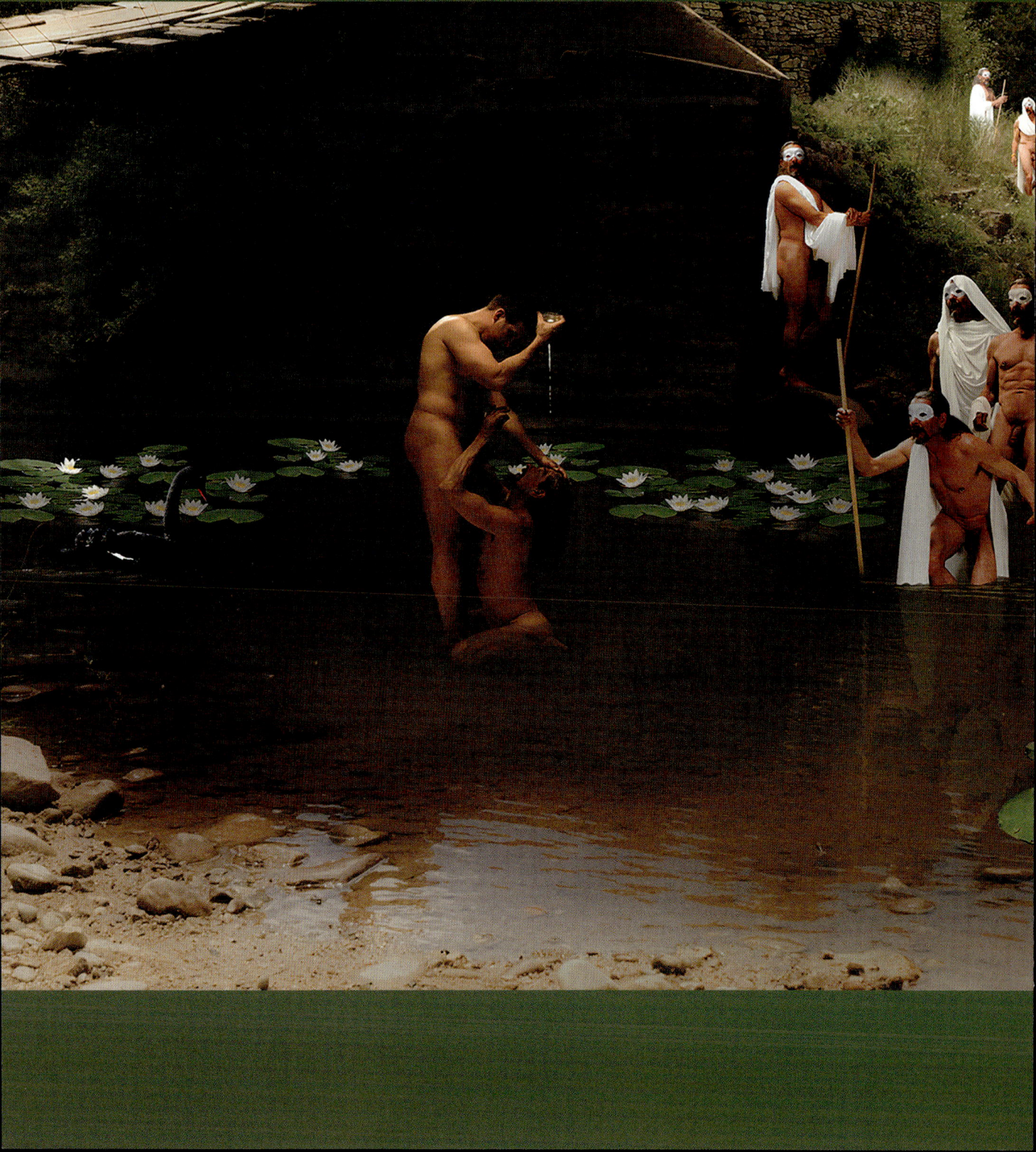

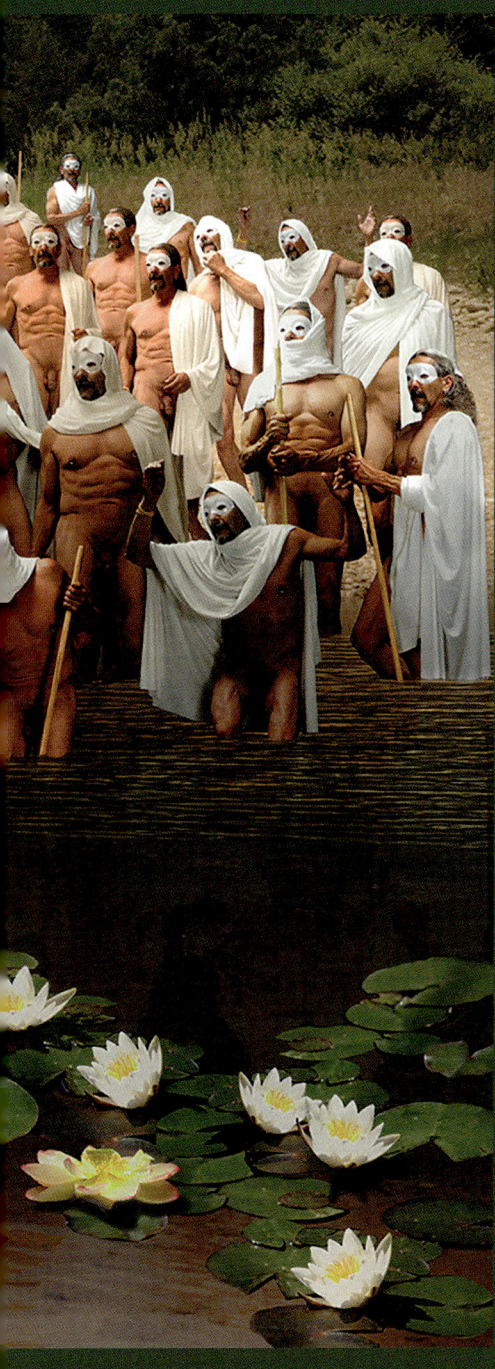

CHAPTER 14

The Holy Rosary
Belonging

Featuring work by Max Maez

FIGURE 14.1 First Luminous Mystery Baptism of Jesus by John the Baptist. © Max Maez

THE WORK BY MAX MAEZ is arguably liturgical in nature. It chronicles well-known Christian iconography that is referenced in the Holy Rosary and is found on frescos and stained glass windows. The images also likely invoke a recollection of biblical events in a most unexpected way.

Titled, by Max Maez

> Then Jesus came from Galilee to the Jordan to be baptized by John. But John tried to deter him, saying, "I need to be baptized by you, and do you come to me?"
>
> Jesus replied, "Let it be so now; it is proper for us to do this to fulfill all righteousness."
>
> Matthew 3:13–15

What Are We Looking at?

In Maez's reinterpretation of the famous baptism he presents us with an image that represents him. Whether this is as John or as Jesus is unclear since the audience is not privy to which of the two quotes in his title the image refers to. Since Maez used himself multiple times and another model only once, he alludes to a singularity and plurality at the same time. The water lily, similar to the lotus flower, appears even more ubiquitously and is associated with numerous other religions, cultures, beliefs, and virtues such as purity and truth.

Identify the Elements

Like many artists he uses himself as the model in his work. In fact, Maez appears twenty-four times, which connects him to the number of hours in each day. In twenty-three of the renditions he appears partially nude and masked, but at the point of baptism he is completely nude and unmasked. Complete nudity at the moment of baptism is loaded with potential meaning ranging from notions of purity when we are born, rejection of all material trappings, rejection of shame, and the embrace of vulnerability. Oral sex is also implied.

How Can the Image Be Interpreted?

Each twenty-fourth hour cycle occurs just before the "zero dark hour" or the witching hour, the moment of no return, when a day indisputably shifts into a new one, or into a new week, month, year, decade, century, or even a new millennium. In this context the multiple selves have achieved salvation just in the nick of time. The doomsday clock is permanently set to just before midnight. The birth of the nuclear age warns of an everlasting darkness due to nuclear annihilation and is similar to the end of times, Armageddon or the apocalyptic end of the world, which many religions and prophecies predict.

The audience must therefore ask itself whether salvation through baptism is a metaphor for all of humanity or just for one multifaceted individual. By asking this question, by pitting the individual against humanity, or vice versa, we arrive at one of the most contested, philosophical, and religious questions human kind has been grappling with since the onset of self-awareness or the perceived loss of innocence: namely in the Garden of Eden.

Therefore, does Maez tell his story or that of everyone or something in-between? Like other artists whose interpretation of their religion has caused controversy, Maez has a personal motivation for having made the images he did. As a Catholic, he was rejected for being gay and also for identifying with Indio culture. Not being seen by his religion and not seeing iconography that represented him, eventually led to the creation of work where he questions the Church by replacing religious icons with himself or with his friends. The reflection of his sexual orientation is more directly referenced in other images as the main reason for his ostracism from the Church, though the main aspect of his work does ask profound questions beyond this one particular issue.

Conclusion

What is redemption? What is baptism? What is belonging? Who is accepted and who is not? What is self-actualization in the context of society and religion? What is the artist's role in pushing boundaries? What is truth and who defines it? What is rejection? What is fear? What is courage? What is desecration? What is forgiveness?

Those are some of the questions you may potentially ask yourself when confronted with this image and ask yourself what this means to you. Some images are not intended to provide answers but rather intend to provoke questions.

Assignments You May Want to Challenge Yourself With

- Engaging ostracization
- Counternarrative
- (Re-) Interpretation of cultural iconography in all its forms (political, social, religious, etc.)
- (Self-) Empowerment

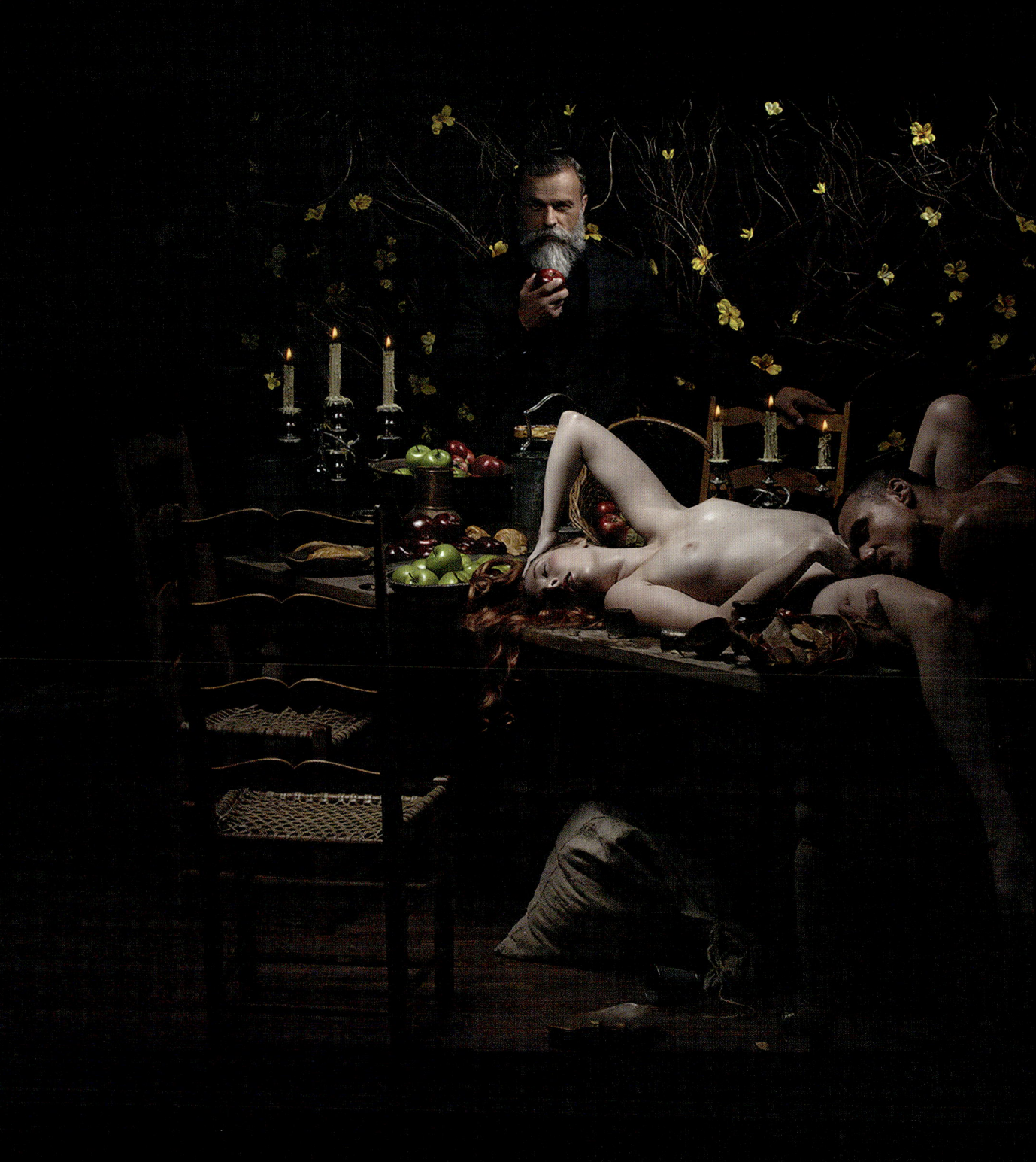

CHAPTER 15

A Conversation with God
The White Elephant in the Room

Featuring work by Johan Jansson

FIGURE 15.1 Adam and Eve. © Johan Jansson

WHETHER YOU BELIEVE in Genesis or in evolution, the story of Adam and Eve is of course familiar to everyone. Two young people live in a beautiful garden called Eden with animals that are also harmonious innocents. Apparently there is not much to do in this garden other than to enjoy it. The garden provided plenty of food. Adam and Eve are not to eat from the tree of knowledge, an apple tree, or they will become mortal and eventually die.

This raises some uncomfortable questions, the proverbial white elephant in the room, and Jansson's image makes us, as viewers, complicit if we are willing to venture there. The white elephant chemistry is based on whether we are willing to engage an image head on, despite content that addresses difficult or even taboo issues. I believe that art has a responsibility to push boundaries, to take risks, and make us question what we know or think we do. Maybe this becomes most challenging in the context of religion, as belief systems are what many draw their strength and comfort from, and most significantly, a part of their identity.

Jansson has taken this risk and we are invited to engage in his narrative.

What Are We Looking at?

As viewers we find ourselves in a situation that at the very least could be described as awkward. We appear to have entered the post Eden-phase of Adam and Eve's existence, right at a moment when they are engaged in carnal desire and abandonment. Worse still, God is also apparently there, confronting the viewer by holding an apple as if to challenge us to think about our own voyeurism in relation to forbidden fruit, and whether or not we might lead a righteous life, or even care about doing so.

How Can the Image Be Interpreted?

It would seem that this intimate engagement is either just starting or ending. Either way, the act is likely to lead to the moment of ultimate surrender: the shuddering into another realm, into nothingness, an exquisite state of collapse, of letting go completely, of being carried away into temporary separation from ourselves in exchange for a brief connection to everything else.

God's unwavering gaze is upon us here, and most of us likely have memories of personal and large-scale tragedies that are difficult to reconcile with a benevolent and forgiving entity. How can suffering be explained? We are not likely to miss that Adam and Eve are an interracial couple; a transgression that would have cost the couple dearly in most times and places.

As if all of this weren't enough to contemplate in one image, there is much more. God made Adam in His own image and made Eve to keep him company from one of Adam's ribs. None of these people seem related to one another, a situation that begs the question of what "in His own image" means. Does it mean humanity in all its ethnic and unique manifestations on earth? Also, why is God wearing a suit? Is he in fact someone else? Is the man actually the Devil, impersonating God to trick us? A wolf in sheep's clothing? Or, is this a more contemporary, corporate version of religion? Someone is balancing the books of the vast religious entities around the world so that, in turn, we are encouraged to balance the books of our own deeds; keeping a ledger of morality to account for how we have led our lives.

God is all knowing of deed and thought. Is he telling us, "I too have seen you, just like this, in the throes of lust?" Is this bearded man meant to represent the latest incarnation of Big Brother, and to be all knowing, all seeing? Is he the head of one of the surveillance and security agencies that are incrementally intruding more into all of our lives? Is the fear and guilt of fire and brimstone replaced by facial recognition software and digital fingerprints so large that anyone's life can be laid bare, even via satellites orbiting the earth like solar-celled winged angels to keep an eye on all of us?

As if knowing that the viewer will eventually need a rest from these troubling questions, Jansson offers a kind of peace in the background of the image, a glimpse of Eden at night with the temptation of some exotic and intoxicatingly perfumed flower, even if one isn't quite sure what the plant entirely looks like. For all we know this plant only grows in Eden. But to get there we have to go through God, or the artist's version of Him, after hopefully first apologizing to Adam and Eve for barging in on their earthly life at such an inopportune moment.

God has the choice of either green or red apples. The one he holds in his hand is red, red like a traffic signal on our path to Eden where we are not to set foot. This is another reference to contemporary authority and obedience and for good reason. Running a red light may well end up in death—and not just one's own. And red light districts all over the world offer the promise of physical gratification but with the risk of potentially deadly STDs. Eve too, is a redhead, reinforcing the forbidden. From the Egyptians through the Greeks, redheads were shunned and sacrificed. In this context, maybe most significantly, redheads were thought of as the product of unclean sex, fiery and hot-blooded, vampires even. Thus we must wonder about the artist's choice. Just how bloody does it get, when removing another's rib?

The twice-repeated trinity in the candelabras speaks of something unassailable on the one hand and fraught by multiplication on the other. Humans were created on the sixth day, and were meant to labor for as many, before a day of rest, and because they were created on the sixth day, the number six represents sin. Thus the six flames in the image's mid-ground become a firewall between Eden and God and then between them and the viewer.

The closest object in the photograph is the chair. As a spectral visitor, traveling across time, I don't feel I can sit there as a viewer and even be seen as this visitor from the future. Maybe only God is aware of the visit. In fact, who knows exactly what is to come. As if to underline this, there is an heirloom table and more chairs, for eventually, as punishment, Eve will give birth, albeit painfully, and then, there will be a family.

To the viewer, the white sack may appear more negotiable. Not a white elephant exactly but something seemingly bulky and heavy. What is in the burlap sack? More apples? It seems as likely as not. When God put two attractive young people into the garden, naked, and without much to do, along with a talkative snake and an apple tree the outcome seems more predictable than not. In fact, how would God's word be spread without many voices to do so? The apples are already sorted by color just as tulip bulbs once were. In the 1600s, tulip bulbs commanded exorbitant prices. While not the first example of derivative swaps, they can be thought of as a referencing the irrationality of insatiable greed, predicated of course on yet another human weakness, the yearning for beauty in all of its manifestations.

One way to look at the sack is as baggage. I suspect we come into this world with a fair amount of it and through the circumstances of our lives add to it. Maybe that is why the sack is half empty; there is plenty of room for more. Maybe this image is all about the baggage we carry right from the start, when we were told that our deepest instincts and desires were wrong, unless highly contained within a sanctified structure. Possibly, the image uses an allusion to God and Adam and Eve to distract us from the sack. Maybe we are being told that we have forgotten to look inside of ourselves, where somewhere, implausibly and inexplicably, we have an innate knowledge of good and evil, of right and wrong. Maybe the viewer is meant to pick up the sack, turn her or his back on the image, and start an individual and personal journey towards Eden. For some this will correspond with some established belief system and for others it will not.

Conclusion

Sometimes we have to take a risk. Jansson is reminding us of this, possibly that God meant us to take a risk, meant for us to see whether we can evolve and learn to balance our self-interest with the greater good in a way that is far more dynamic and unpredictable than the dogma we are made to think we are supposed to cling to.

Assignments You May Want to Challenge Yourself With

- Still life
- Contemporary interpretation of liturgical art
- Symbolism
- Photograph a white elephant

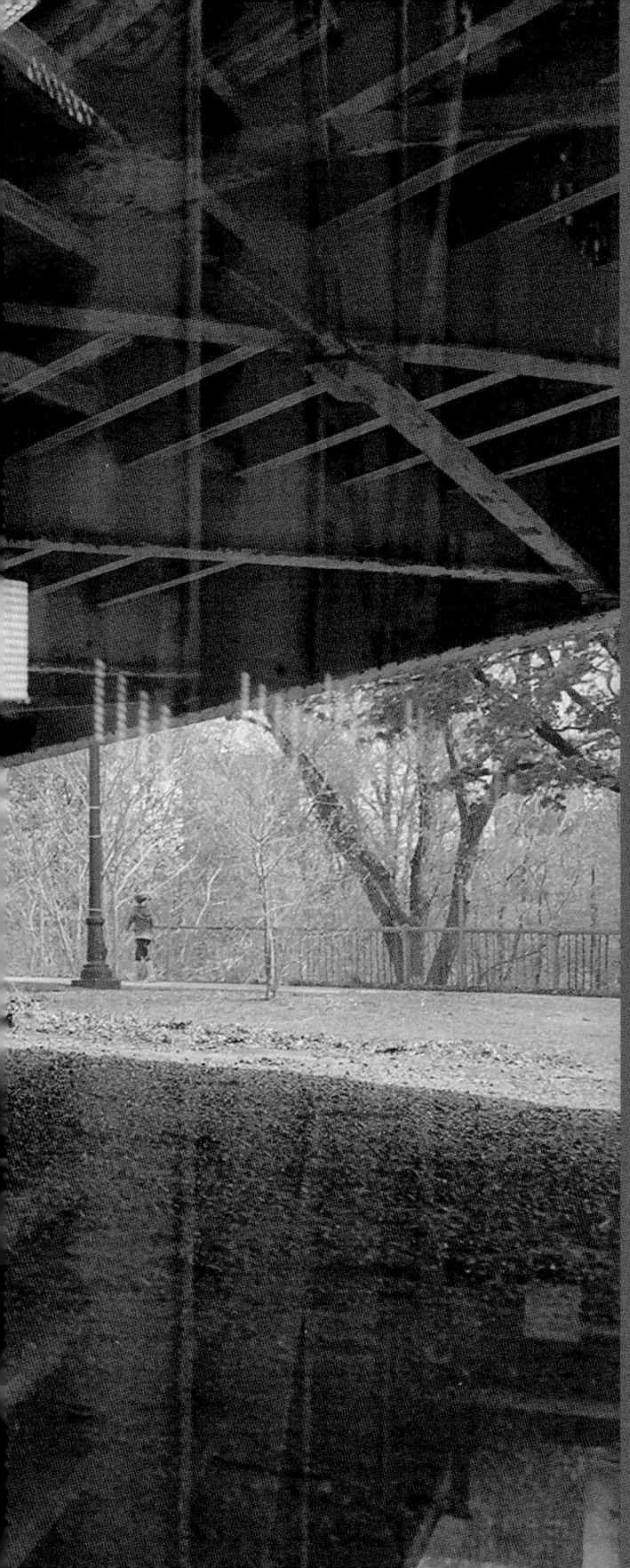

CHAPTER 16
Superstructure
Conflation

Featuring work by Steve Sikora

FIGURE 16.1 Untitled. © Steve Sikora

SIKORA'S IMAGES ARE double exposures. There are various ways of achieving this effect: expose the same frame twice in the camera, double print two negatives, or blend two images with photo processing software. Sikora partially exposes his 4 × 5" view camera negatives and then walks and searches until he finds the next complementary exposure.

What Are We Looking at?

Two disparate views and experiences become one after he has made his second exposure. The latent information on the negative is amalgamated into a new single vision, the depiction of distinct spectacles, seen in two different places and recorded at two different times.

The proverbial looking glass is the opaque focusing screen of the 4 × 5" camera and we become witnesses to the frozen collision that is time, place, scale, and light. The ensuing chaos is both engrossing and tantalizing.

Where are we? When are we? How do we feel about being there? These may be some of the questions that you may ask yourself.

The *where* may be a glimpse of a recognizable or a known place, re-contextualized with another glimpse of somewhere else that is quite different.

The *when* may become a tempting investigation into what belongs to what and what came first. Ultimately though, this seems to be a zero-sum game as the vision in which we are already caught up in is something new. The *when* may be about the "now," as we are looking, when you are seeing the image? So how do you feel about being there right now?

Does it appeal to you? Does it disorient you? Do you feel as if you are there or far from it?

There are many double- or multiple-exposure photographers who work with the technique in various ways to provide different experiences for their audience. Some are very simple and the constituent parts are easily distinguished. Some, like this image, are more complex and the experience is more disorienting. When we don't dissect the frog but instead observe it, we will become immersed in what it does rather than in the sum of its parts. Likewise, our experience of the image becomes activated when we seek to explore this conflation of time and space instead of dissecting it for its parts. Since we read the image as the Latin alphabet dictates, we read from left to right. In so doing the left also becomes the past and the right becomes the future in our observation.

How Can the Image Be Interpreted?

The vista of nature that broadens towards the image's right edge is the most intact and least convoluted part of the photograph. We see the little child seemingly lost in contemplation of nature and yielding to the authority of the fence that could easily be climbed. The lamp post becomes a stand-in for an adult and safety for its light, though that is purely symbolic since it is clearly daytime. The partially fallen leaves and child's clothing suggests fall, it is getting colder and another year's cycle is coming to a close to await winter's sleep. The lamp also dissects this scene so that if we look at it more abstractly we can imagine two coupled railway cars driving out of the picture with no indication of how many cars have already passed and how many are yet to come. This too is a subtle reinforcement of the notion of cycles, of beginnings and endings.

All through this we can see the massive superstructure of our aging and crumbling urban infrastructure. The slight piercing by the scene just described is upstaged by what looks to be construction canvas, mimicking more train cars departing the image on a higher level and intersecting the trajectory of the previous train. All this is held together by the train station from hell, with its rotting roof to its decaying foundations, which we can magically see through the earth. Down in the bottom left there seems to be another platform and a footpath crossing under the X-beam. The multilevel, multidirectional maze gains an additional dynamic by the repetitious quad columns of light that penetrate all substantive matter in the image, and travel in receding directions all their own.

Conclusion

As in dreams, gravity, solid matter, and perspective are suspended for something else. It is in this something else, where the image finds me and I find it, that I am left with the recognition and certainty of everything I don't yet know. The physiological illusion of depth, multidimensionality, and dislocation speaks not only of our age but also of bygone ages and those to come. The cycle is not just of the seasons, or of centuries, but of the time it appears to be taking for the gray matter in our brains to increase. For all the image's chaos, information, and vibrancy, like an underused processor, it seems remarkably still, one could say, almost empty.

Assignments You May Want to Challenge Yourself With

- Double exposures
- Time and space
- Trains (of thought)

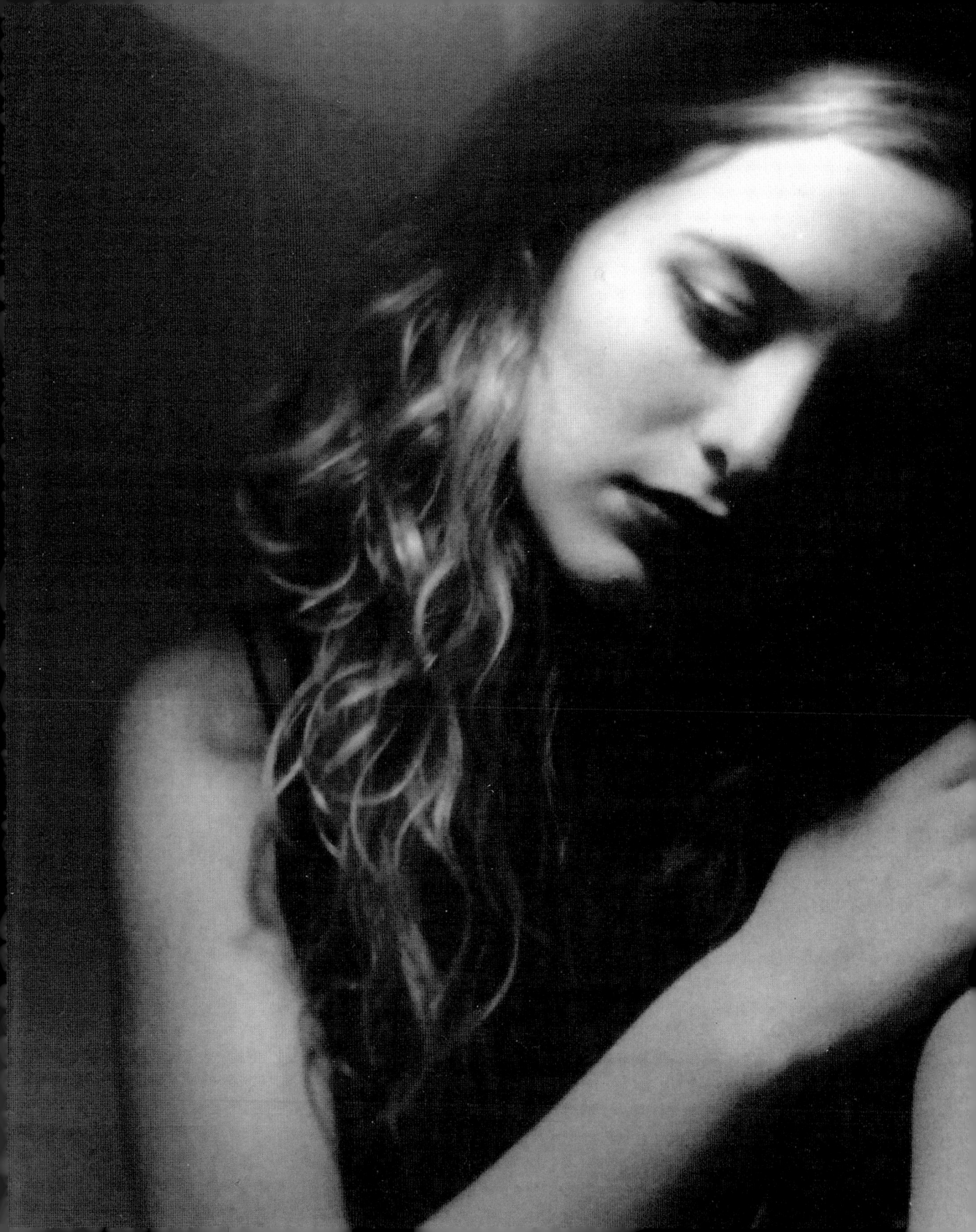

CHAPTER 17

Lady Like
Body Language

**Featuring work by
Jordan Fleckenstein**

FIGURE 17.1 Untitled. © Jordan Fleckenstein

UPON FIRST GLANCE Fleckenstein's images seem to represent a mixture of portraiture and figure studies. Though the figure is in fact dressed there is a sensual quality to the work that is often eclipsed by the nude.

What Are We Looking at?

So how is this sensuality created? The first image is charged with atmosphere and mood, both as a result of the romantic lighting and the expression of the model. Her face is lit like a half-moon; this estranged relative of the earth that sometimes shows herself entirely and often hides completely. The magnetism that the earth exerts on the moon and the moon in turn on our tides and our emotional states charges the image with its own orbiting gravity. And grave it can be for the viewer who gets caught up in it.

The moon may create an atmosphere in a metaphoric sense but has none in a scientific context. Without a protective suit, instant death and the frigid temperature of space in our solar system await. This contradiction can be attractive in and of itself, like the proverbial moth to the flame. The inviting light will inevitably burn you if you come to close. While this is cold moonlight, it still exerts that inevitable pull (Figure 17.1).

This pull is amplified by the ambiguity that emanates from the subject herself. She seems to be lost in contemplation and simultaneously on the threshold of a decision. For the viewer, this can generate a feeling of wrong-footedness, foremost because it seems unclear whether anyone is supposed to be there at all. It also seems wrong to just leave, as the moment is already too personal, trapping the viewer into having to find another clue.

How Can the Image Be Interpreted?

Reading the body language suggests that she is protective of her chest; her right arm already covers her left breast and her hair. It is this protective gesture that draws attention to what is under the dress, which otherwise might not ever have become a consideration for the viewer. Additionally, this is reinforced by the second image (Figure 17.2).

Somehow both the subject and the viewer have fallen down on the floor in what we now recognize to be a bathroom. The viewer is forced to look straight between the model's legs or at her décolleté. The sanctuary of her face is gone and the photographer is pushing the issue more forcefully now. The near symmetrical image directs our eye back to the point of graphic convergence just below the spatial horizon line. The model is sitting in a way that would not be considered to be ladylike but protects her private space with both arms.

Conclusion

Much has been written about the male gaze and increasingly about the female gaze as it asserts itself. Both the provocation and the censorship these images contain read like a testament of defiance while celebrating beauty in a way that is self-contained. The photographer and model seem to neither look for approval nor definition from anything other than themselves. Come on audience, deal with it!

I would be remiss in not stating the obvious: the first image is heavily dominated by the inverted letter **N** formed by the arms and the second image by the letter **X**. **N**o, **N**ever, **N**ow or **X** marks the spot, **X**ing you out and se**X** are some of the immediate connotations.

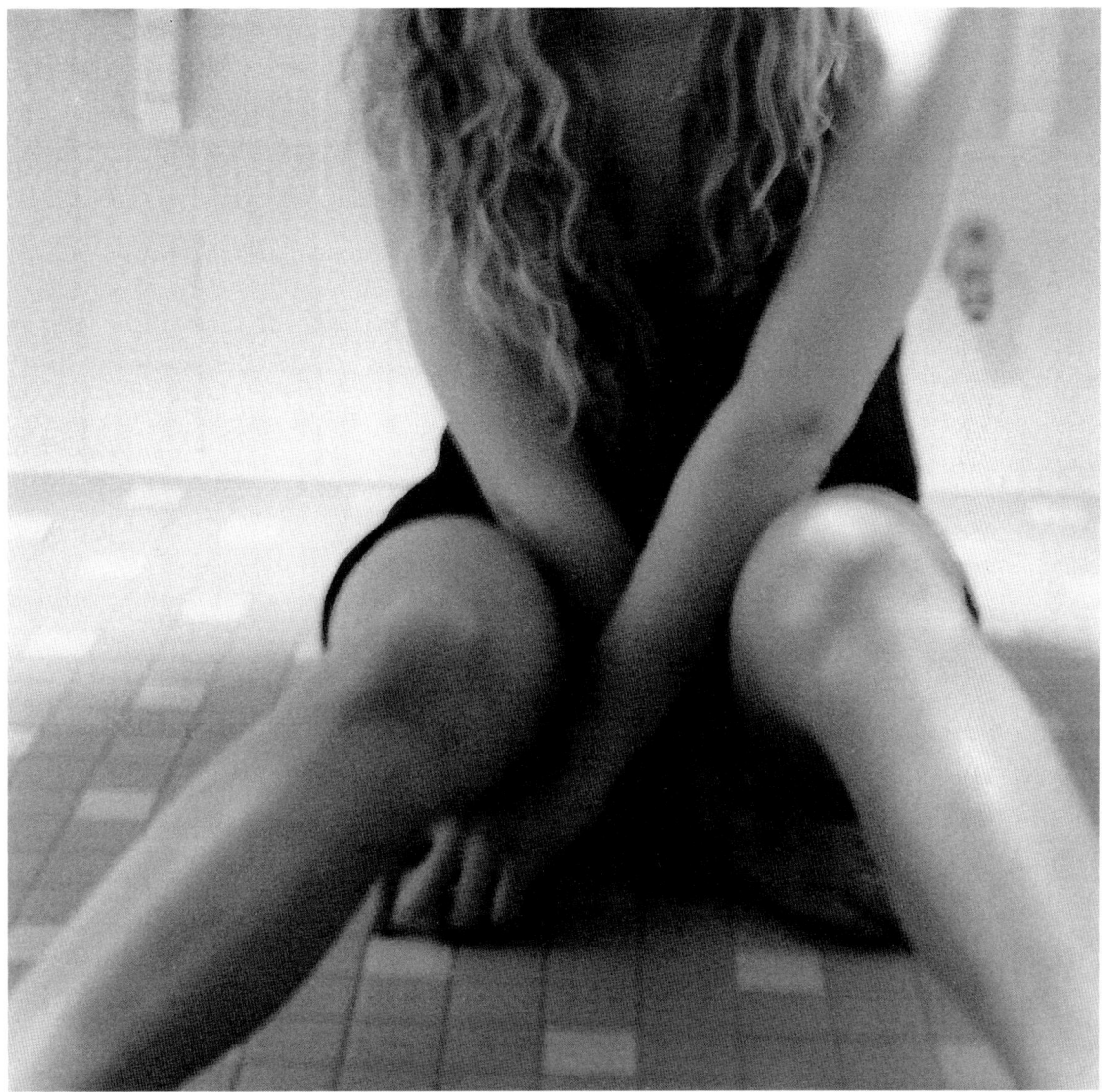

FIGURE 17.2
Untitled.
© Jordan Fleckenstein

Assignments You May Want to Challenge Yourself With

- Body language
- Gestural meaning
- Influence of light(ing)
- Alphabetic symbolism

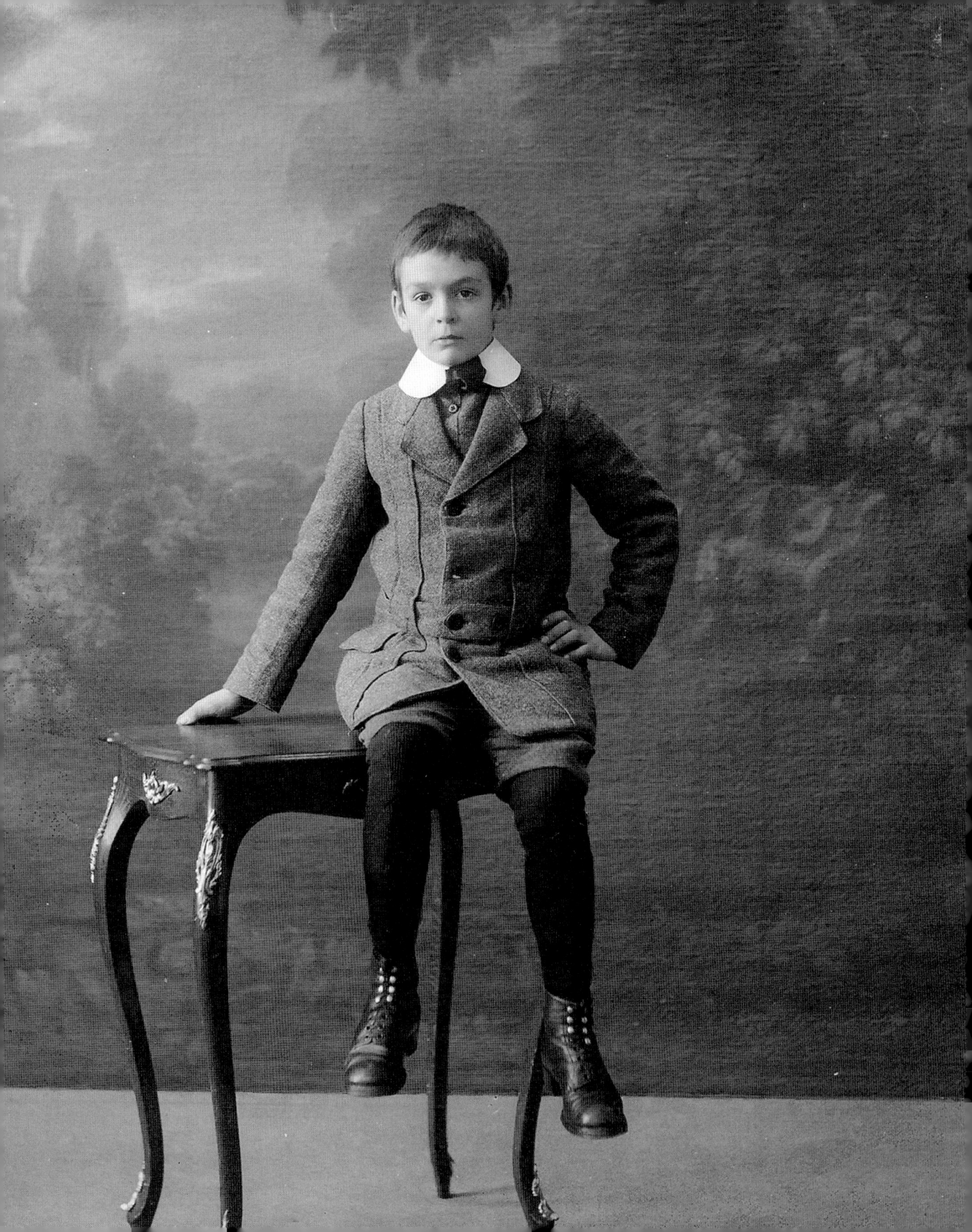

CHAPTER 18

Recycling
The Image Ecology Approach

Featuring work by Henry Aragoncillo

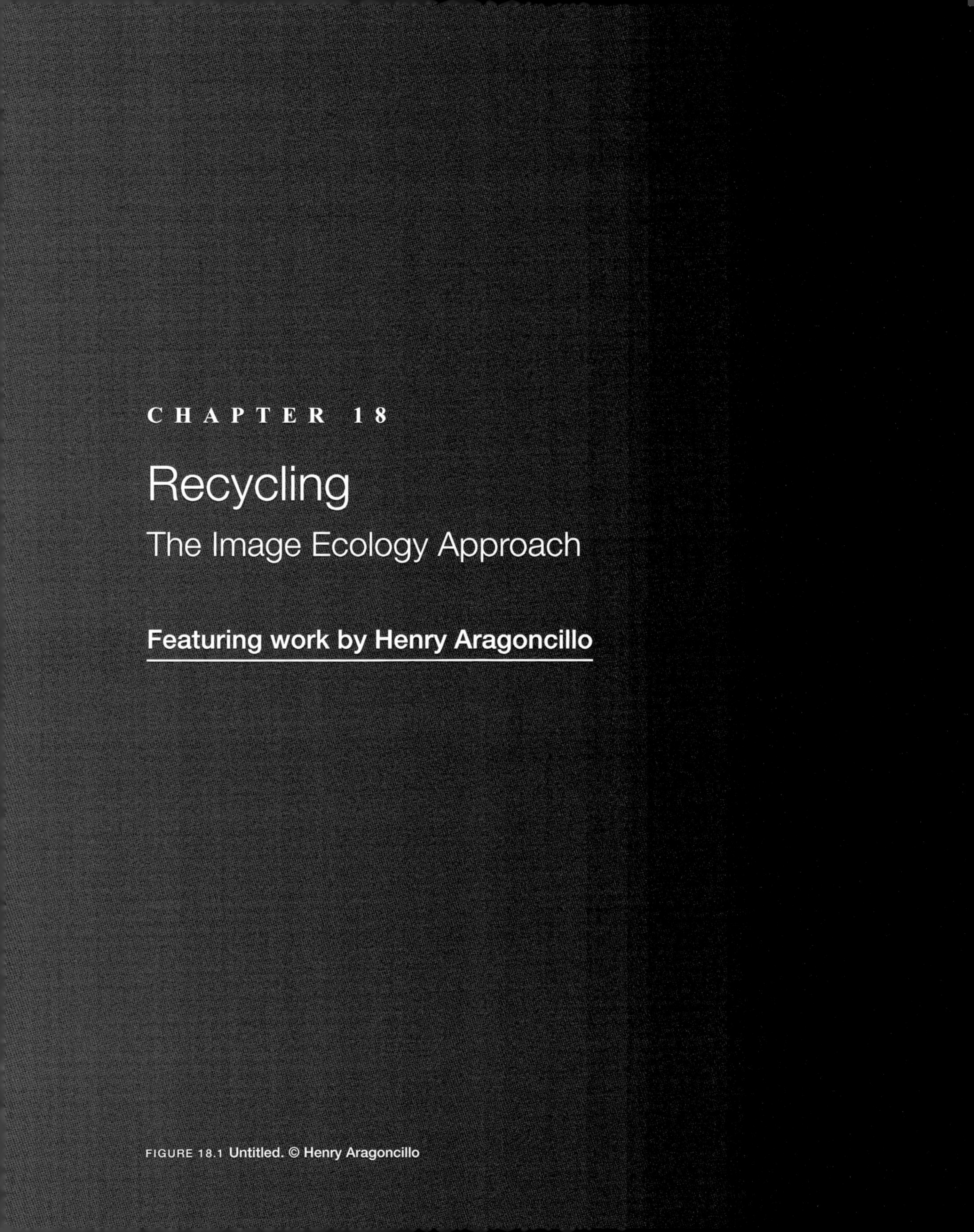

FIGURE 18.1 Untitled. © Henry Aragoncillo

THE LIBRARY OF CONGRESS website makes available a treasure trove of copyright-free historic files that image makers can download. Such works can be recycled by being transformed or combined with other work (Figure 18.1).

This form of recycling represents a specific example of visual literacy that interests me, both conceptually and in relation to our society's energy consumption. The server farms, which house our digital files, are extremely power hungry, running at a hundred percent capacity all the time, with backups and other redundant systems to protect the data. As such, the leap to data ecology or visual ecology seems an interesting, often overlooked, aspect of being visually literate and responsible.

What Are We Looking at?

The before and after example of a Library of Congress image, manipulated by Aragoncillo, explores this question in interesting ways. The idealized wallpaper or studio landscape has been swapped for an actual landscape. This landscape contains a fence and barbed wire.

The sharpness and stillness, despite the slow emulsion and accordingly long exposures prevalent at the time the original image was made, have become energized and confused by inconsistent exposures of motion. The boy's moving foot, likely to be slower than the dog's barking muzzle, is blurrier than the dog's jaw. The stability of the original four legs of the table has been replaced by a monopod that appears to vanish into the landscape, visually conflating the mid-ground and background. The nondescript immaculate floor in the foreground has given way to warped floorboards and peeling paint. Additionally, the suggested deterioration and neglect over time negates the excellent archival care of the image by the Library of Congress.

How Can the Image Be Interpreted?

The fence and barbed wire conjure associations with some of the most monumental occurrences since the image's likely inception: two World Wars, the Berlin Wall, and the Cold War. The fence posts denote decaying and soot-streaked remnants of the Industrial Revolution.

The boy's change in body language, an insinuated rebuke of a now known future, seems to elicit mild protest at being a member of an affluent class and family that may have contributed to the last deeply troubled century. The dog barking, at a potential great-grandson, appearing in a mirror facing away from the boy may therefore be a suggestion of a less affluent future generation. The audience may connect with seeing themselves as these less fortunate heirs. In the same way that animals often sense impending earthquakes long before we do, the dog's apparent aggravated barking appears not to be understood for the warning that it may represent (Figure 18.2).

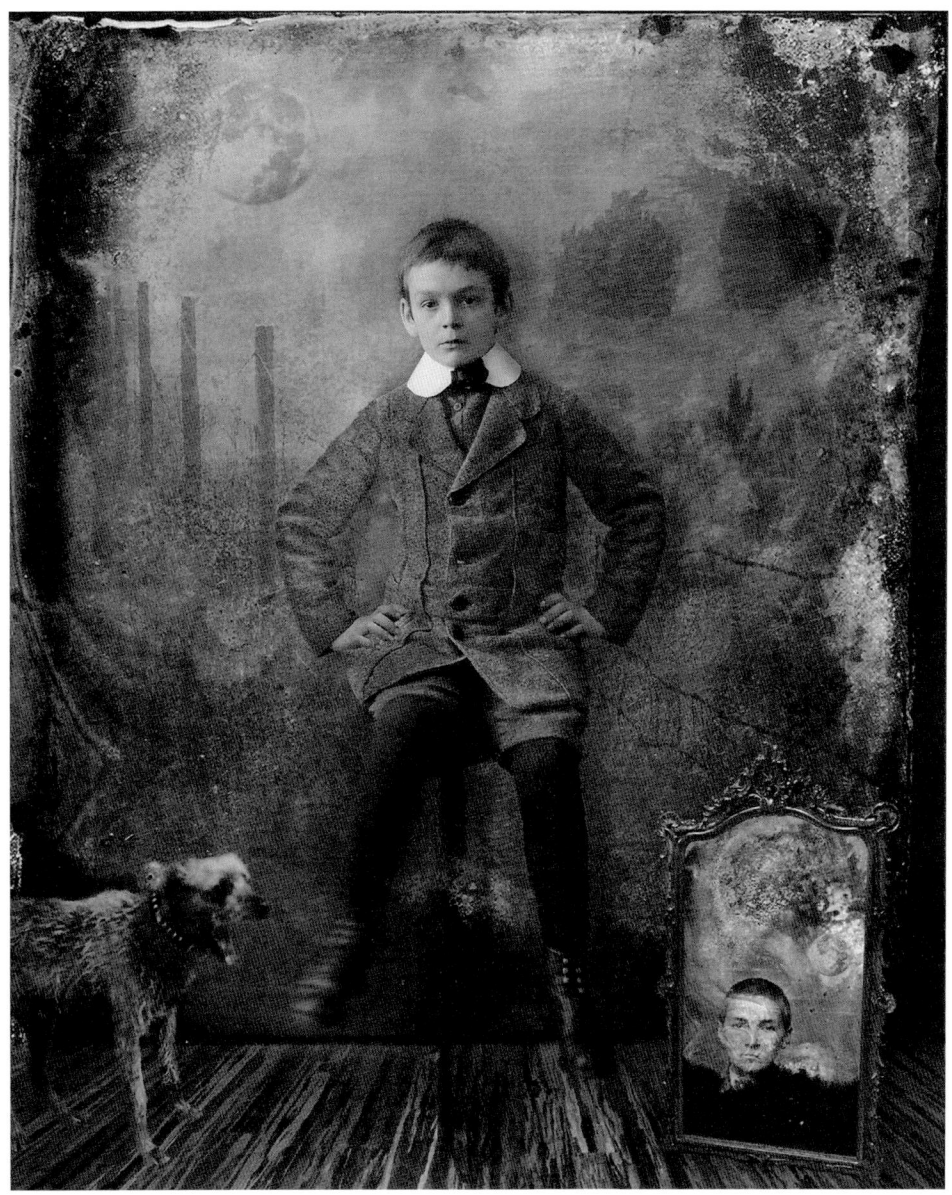

FIGURE 18.2 Untitled. © Henry Aragoncillo

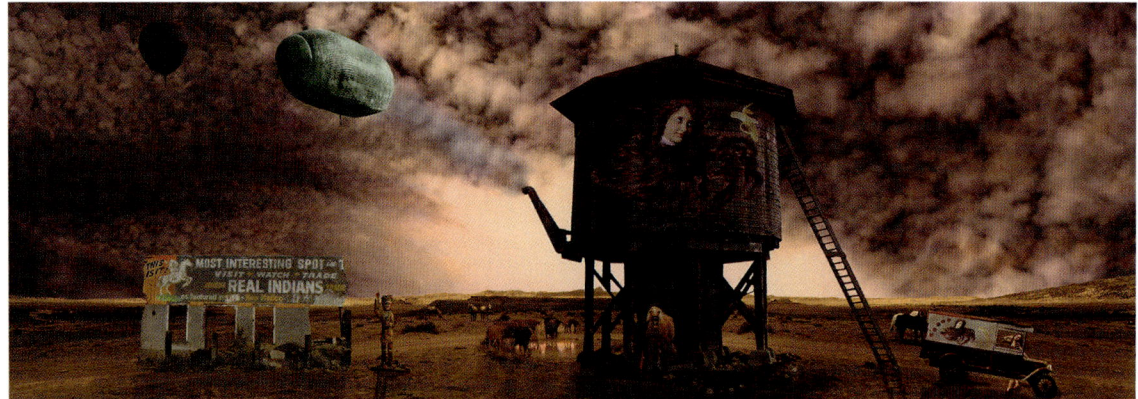

FIGURE 18.3 Untitled. © Henry Aragoncillo

Many of Aragoncillo's works are composites and set in the southwestern landscape, consisting of a multitude of elements from his own photographs and what he finds on the Library of Congress website. They are decidedly surrealist as he examines the clash of cultures and corporate and military interests. In that sense his images remain warnings via metaphor.

What Are We Looking at?

The reverence of nature by the original inhabitants of the North American continent is not represented in the reality of another version of impoverished ghettos, far from the inner cities, the Native American "Reservations." Instead, he uses the absurdity of marketing to tourists, a garish, cartoonish version of Native American cultures, as an ongoing critique in his large tableaus. The crude wooden or plastic statues of the Native Americans with head dress, the Cigar Store Indians, find their echo in those of the concrete or plastic black "boy" often holding a lantern in his hands, the lawn jockey that is still a staple on southern lawns. For me, Aragoncillo reminds us that deeply entrenched racism, packaged as stereotyping kitsch, is not any less offensive than any other expression of such sentiments. There are many supposed justifications of why these types of figures are supposedly honoring the ethnicities they represent. I think not. The time has come for those who want a garden light to hold it themselves or to invest in a thing called a lamp post. Those selling tourist souvenirs might want to consider investing in a store sign that does not continue to defraud people of their cultural dignity any more than they have already had to endure.

How Can the Image Be Interpreted?

All those who pass through the sacred, fragile southwestern lands—where Native American reservations, prairies leased to cattle ranchers, mines, closed military facilities, and enormous coal-burning plants all butt up against each other along uneasy borders—are encouraged to look with a new perspective, whether their initial interest is as tourist or as a nomad seeking to lose themselves in the desert.

In this sea of lands, once underwater, and to this day filled with fossils of sea creatures, pottery shards, arrowheads, and even the odd Confederate or Unionist uniform buttons, there are the islands of the stunning National Parks whose federal protection is constantly under threat by those lobbying to open them up for natural resource harvesting. Harvesting and exploration are of course as euphemistic as Citizens United, none of which connote what they purport to say. Like the attempts on the remaining pristine lands, our language has been disinfected and, for the unsuspecting user disaffected as well, to actually say, in plain English, what the intentions behind various acts and words are. Our words are deliberately and increasingly being obfuscated.

As you know, collateral damage means killing or injuring civilians and damaging everything else that got in the way. The Clean Air Act was well intended and indeed partially successful. However, many companies find it financially beneficial to pay the relatively benign fines, imposed by the EPA, rather than to invest in the more expensive technology and infrastructure to fully comply with the act, to protect the air, the land, and the consumers living upon it.

In Aragoncillo's work, there appears to be a deep reverence for the land and the ways in which it remains at the mercy of short-term thinking, interests, and catastrophes; he is grappling with the complexity of it all.

Front and center we have a very old-fashioned, wooden-built water tower. Aragoncillo has added a spout to make it into an enormous teapot instead. This makes us think about water in a different way, reminding us that when water gets to boiling point it starts to evaporate. The ongoing drought in the southwest of the US, the threat this poses to large areas of California, Nevada, and most of the neighboring states, once or twice removed, are well known, documented, and wash over most of the American people who just want to survive to the next payday. One only has to look at Lake Powell, and the growing width of calcium deposits upon the once submerged shoreline to know that the Hoover dam is not the canary in the coal mine but a far larger, slower dying creature in which each can see his or her reflection when looking upon it. The cost of this environmental narcissism will drown no one. Instead, in all likelihood, eventually, it will probably kill most through dehydration.

Aragoncillo's pot has reached its own boiling point: the background is taken up by the ubiquitous wildfires that have scorched millions of acres in the west to cinders. In the not so recent past a wildfire threatened the Los Alamos nuclear labs and thousands of waste barrels containing radioactive material, which were stored in unprotected ways (Figure 18.3).

Is the image of the white woman on the water tower another of Aragoncillo's allegories? What is she advertising—a product, but what kind of product? Judging by her angelic appearance, it may be that she passes judgment on the notion of product itself, including Aragoncillo's own image. Aragoncillo does not just record what he sees, nor does he pretend that it is realistic. Rather, by using the elements that he includes in his tableaus, he critiques how we might make ourselves feel better by engaging with traditional images of advocacy. He appears to lampoon that effort as much as the ingredients of his visual feasts. This visual examination of the visual stage examining the stage itself is sometimes referred to as "meta-theatre." Albuquerque, New Mexico, is famous for its annual hot air balloon fiesta. This is a visually lurid event, where mostly primary-colored balloons of all shapes and sizes spectacularly clash with each other against the azure skies of New Mexico. This festival remains one of the most photographed events on earth.

Conclusion

In contrast, one of Aragoncillo's balloons looks like a soot-covered, proverbial lead balloon, while the other looks like some variant of a green vegetable, a cucumber maybe, that would need more water than the endlessly oppressive blue skies in that part of the country now yield by way of rain.

I don't think the Cigar Store Indian is greeting us after all. More likely he too is lampooning the viewer, waving goodbye with a finality that we have not yet fully grasped. The tempest in this teapot has long since broken its bounds; in our ignorance, we merely refer to it as firefighting.

Assignments You May Want to Challenge Yourself With

- Photographic recycling
- Photographic surrealism
- Kitsch and meaning
- Constructed landscape
- Message in a bottle

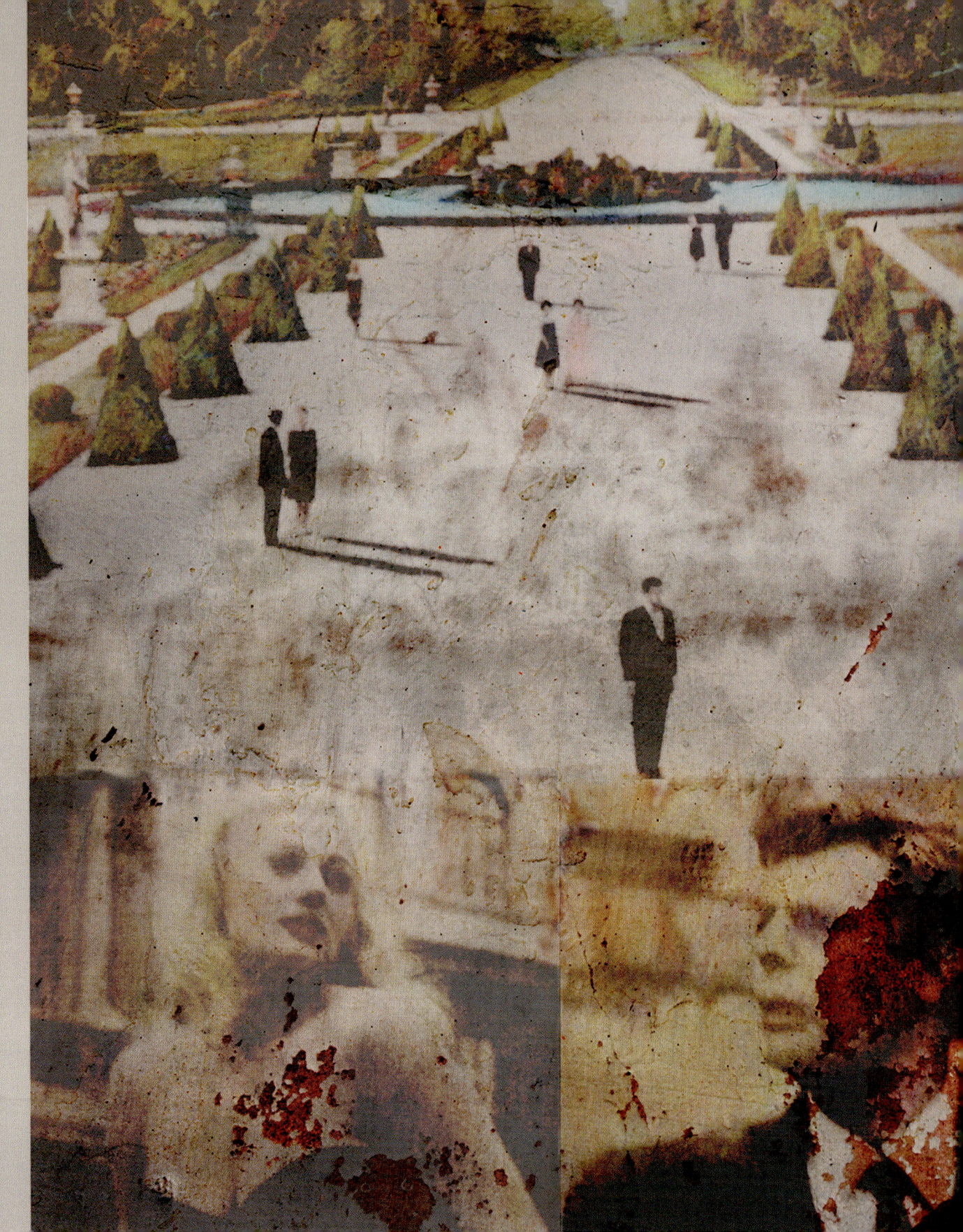

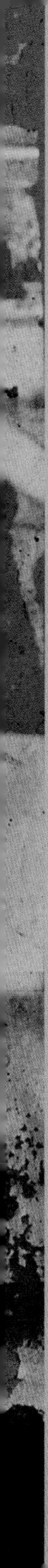

CHAPTER 19

Appropriation
Reinterpretation

Featuring work by Eleanor Rappe

FIGURE 19.1 Untitled. © Eleanor Rappe

Rappe uses part of a relatively contemporary movie poster with images of two movie stars from a generation ago to create new relationships and associations that span time. Image elements include manicured parks that in the past were built and maintained on a large scale (Figure 19.1).

What Are We Looking at?

In total, in her combined appropriations, she represents six women and five men. Three are in pairs, three are alone, and two are together and shown close-up. Let's say the three pairs are couples. Two are male and female, one is female and female, and three are single. In that case the men would outnumber women two to one, which in terms of world population would be quite wrong. Overall there are slightly more men on the planet, arguably a statistical heat. The pairs to which I assigned couple status might all be brothers and sisters and sisters.

Why should any of this matter? Quite honestly, I don't think that it does. And yet, how many couples have passed all of us by when we were alone. Their connection, whether intimate, familial, or just friends can reinforce the sense of loneliness we can all feel, even if all the singles are in a relationship and none of the couples are.

That is an intersection where cultural norms and nature are set on a collision course. That is where the safe harbor of years of reliable trust, love, and deep loyalty may be devastated by a cyclone, turning even the safest harbor into another littered beach.

There seems to be increasing consensus and scientific evidence that most creatures, including humans, are by nature polygamous and some socially monogamous, in particular when it is to the benefit of their offspring. There also seems to be broad consensus that humans don't like change. Humans prefer certainty to uncertainty, predictability over unpredictability. Why? It provides the comfort of the familiar, assuredness, and anticipatable outcomes.

What is wrong with that? Arguably, nothing. It's reassuring to know where we are from, where we are going, and where we belong. By extension it makes equal sense to be reassured to whom we belong, who belongs to us, and, above all else, that we belong. In other words, we are not alone, unknown, and inconsequential. Yet, there can be this yearning, this desire for more, for something else, for a surprise that might change the established path to the grave.

It is this contradiction in human needs and wants that Rappe appears to engage.

When we are separated from what we know and where we belong we can feel homesick. In German this feeling is expressed as *Heimweh* (home-sickness).

Unlike in English though, the German language also has a word for the opposite longing, *Fernweh* (far-sickness), the yearning to be elsewhere, the desire for something different, something new.

How Can the Image Be Interpreted?

In Rappe's image the austerity of the gardens, the formality of the closing, the utterly tamed and artificially shaped trees are set against a wilder, bigger background of mature trees and groundcover that appears to have been left in place and peace to grow at will. If people are there, we can't see them because the canopy of the trees provides both shade and privacy. This is the original home which frightens us, and for good reason. Predators and the uncontrolled fecundity of nature itself can still be threats.

Desire versus the comfort of the familiar, no matter how uncomfortable it may be; longing, even lust, versus the predictability of where we will wake up. The fear of losing ourselves, absent the framework of the expected; yearning to be unmoored and to drift on the basis of chance and spontaneity as opposed to following a set compass with a known weather forecast; openness and vulnerability against our public façade and our social identity. I am sure you can expand on the contradictions and seemingly incompatible urges that both simmer and rage in every heart that seeks more than being a four-cylinder blood pump.

So much is denied us. We deny ourselves so much. And, in return, so much is given and granted. Yet, the compromise each of us strikes when torn between impulse and security, adventure and responsibility attracts us to escape monotony, routines, and the unfathomable boredom of mediocrity.

From books to movies, music to art, we experience and (re)create that which once filled our own hearts with trepidation, tears flowing uncontrollably, because we are simply moved, and tense with the thrill of anticipation.

In the visual field, movies and TV offer a vast counterbalance to our everyday existence. Both present characters we identify with, usually larger than life and better looking than most of us.

Rappe appears to reference that as well. She shows us movie stars, Anita Ekberg and Marcello Mastroianni, the sex symbols in Fellini's *La Dolce Vita* of the 1960s: a moment in time, when established social values started to be thrown out of the window. Unprecedented experimentation and freedom, in part also due to readily available birth control pills for women, lasted until HIV/AIDS put a horrific end to the carefree promiscuity and redefinition of social norms across the social spectrum, starting with the gay male community. The illness was touted as anything from a government conspiracy to divine retribution from God. In the early days the virus was not well understood and prejudice, ignorance, and fear reigned supreme. Traditional family values were reasserted and there was condemnation of those who weren't brought to heel.

But it was too late. Too late for the many who had to die before serious investment in combating and eventually managing HIV infection occurred. Too late to push the large and increasingly out gay communities back into their assigned closets. Too late to deny women self-determination over their reproductive organs and the definition of their own sexuality. Too late to convince people that pot was more dangerous than alcohol or cigarettes. Too late to repatriate everyone back to the 1950s. Simply too late, in every conceivable way. The cat was out of the bag and while it was being chased around, a taste of The Sweet Life, *La Dolce Vita*, lingered until the inequality and recognition of double standards in terms of whom and how we love brought gay rights and women's rights to the forefront of social justice and civil rights.

When I look at Ekberg and Mastroianni as the literal cornerstones of Rappe's image, bloodied and blistering, as they appear to be, I see a reminder of this nefarious illness and the attempt to symbolically assassinate the icons of that age—to remove their likeness from a movie poster, if necessary with a blowtorch.

What Rappe is reminding us of, is that while we may be on our way, we are far from reaching a truly "equality-based" society. Opposition to gay and women's rights is only part of a far deeper and polarizing division that is blowing misogyny, xenophobia, and homophobia into the public discourse on a daily basis with an increasingly ramped-up rhetoric, promoting hate rather than love. Since this crevasse appears to fracture across the world, irrespective of borders, we might argue that climate change is upon us not just in terms of, well, climate change, but also in terms of change in the climate of how humanity will end up defining itself.

Conclusion

I interpret Rappe's austere landscape, the vast expanse of decorative rocks, as the life we might face when the dress code for everyone will be corporate or funereal again, the similarities of which are notable. The hushed conversations, the generic façades behind which we may yet again bury our diversity, plurality, and courage, may well be Rappe's warning of our collective funeral as we try to force what won't be forced, as we won't let go of all that which we must.

Rappe's image may entirely consist of appropriation but her narrative is all her own and all of ours. Let's be mindful then of how we tend our gardens in our minds, hearts, homes, and towns and of what belongs to nature itself. Sometimes stepping back can be a great step forward. This, I think, is Rappe's lament and her gift to us, her viewers.

She takes this lament a step further in her image in what I think of as an homage to elephants.

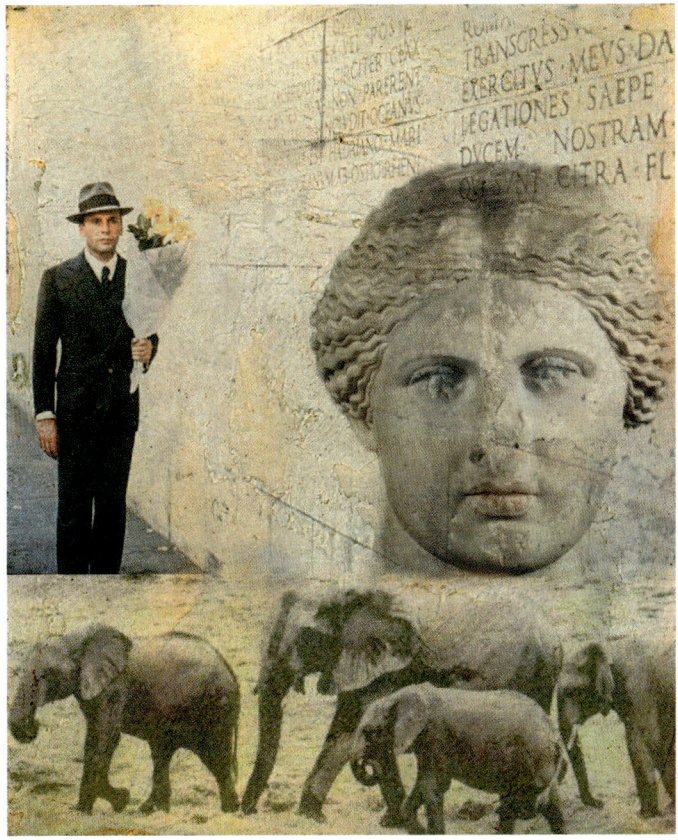

FIGURE 19.2
Untitled. © Eleanor Rappe

For various reasons, the ivory trade, the loss of habitat, the decimation of their culture, which includes sophisticated rituals and even burial grounds, this image speaks in a way that makes further elaboration unnecessary. I think of it as the funeral of all the elephants, these highly intelligent and sensitive creatures that we have driven to the brink of extinction, like so much else. As useful as it may be to analyze images, sometimes it is equally important to let an image be. To let it do its job.

This is an example of such an image for me, and grief is among the most personal experiences of all (Figure 19.2).

When did they start having enemies?

Assignments You May Want to Challenge Yourself With

- Newspaper appropriation
- Hand coloring
- Patina
- Social norms
- Too late
- Collage

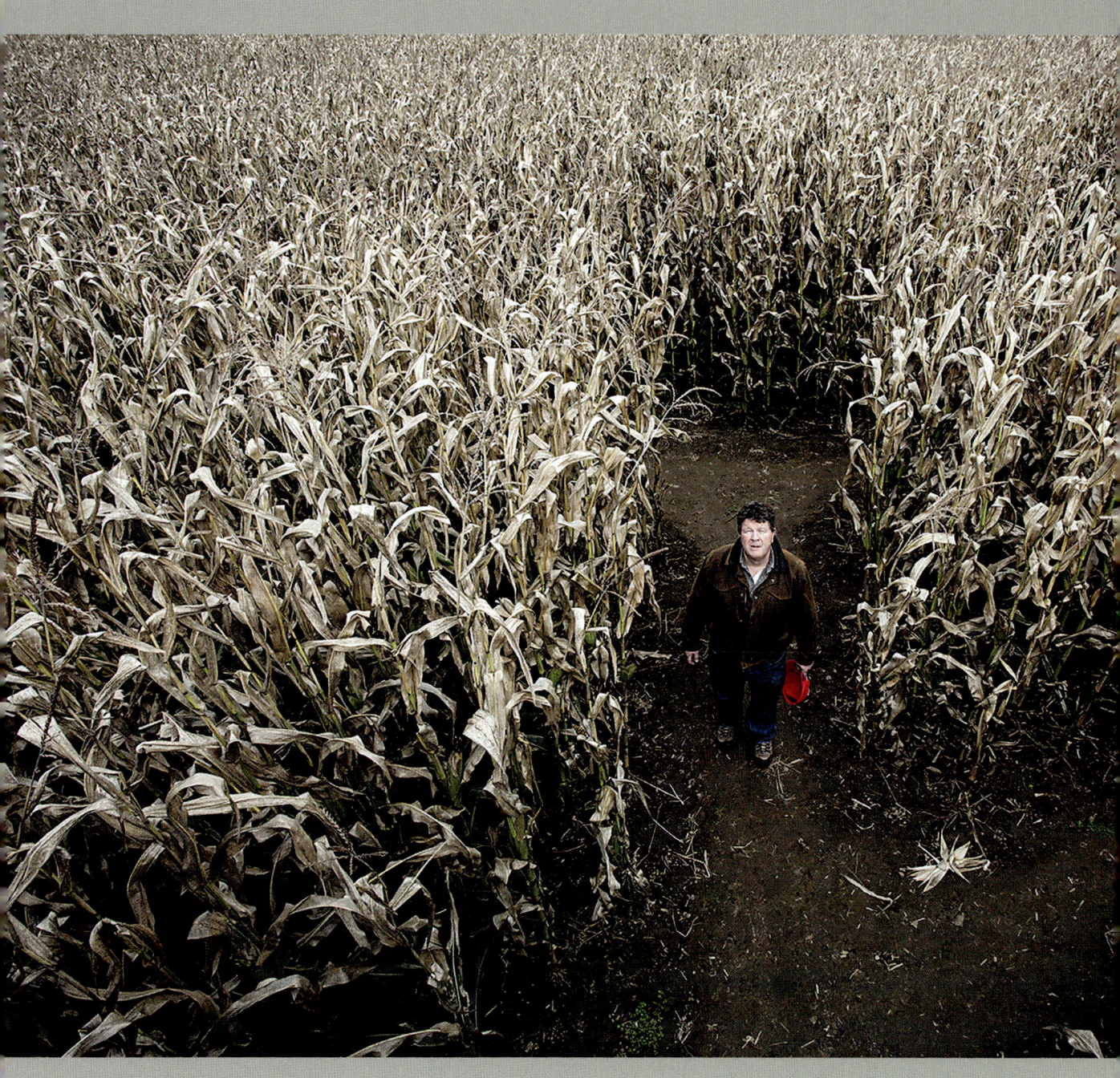

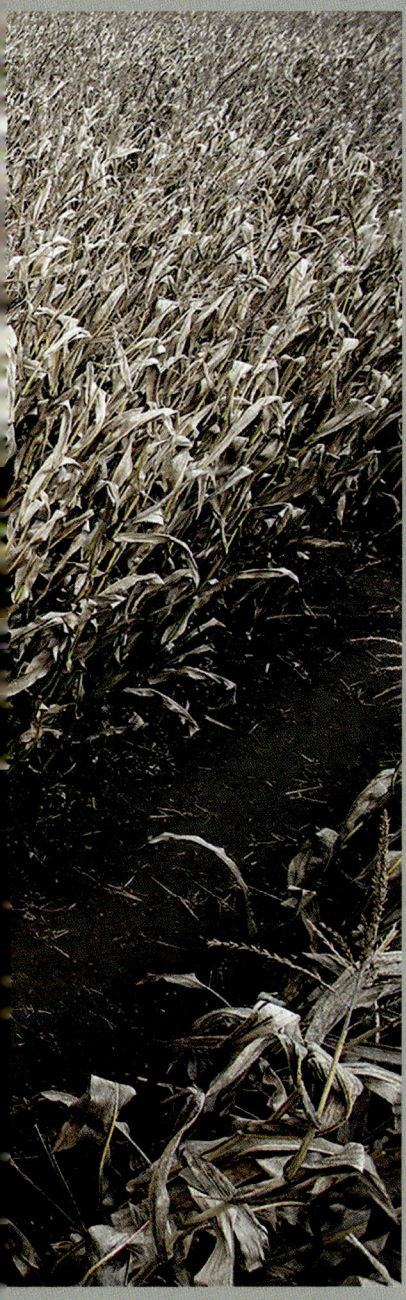

CHAPTER 20

Dad
Titled versus Untitled

Featuring work by Sara Plum

FIGURE 20.1 Dad. © Sara Plum

THE JAPANESE HAVE the expression: *jishin*, *kaminari*, *kaji*, *oyaji*: "earthquake, thunder, fire, father." All things scary!

What Are We Looking at?

This has already been strongly determined by the title of the image. Our blood relations of dad, mom, sister, brother, grandparents, uncles, aunts, cousins are the family we have been given as opposed to the one we choose and later recreate. The powerful word "dad" instantly triggers most of us either positively or negatively, and everything in between. The three letters, one repeated, so only really two letters unless we go with daddy, which still only leaves us with three letters are very important and flood the viewer with associations. My hero. My protector. My inspiration. My friend in prison. My first experience of abandonment. My first experience with physical violence or worse. However this affectionate and intimate word informs you will most likely determine your immediate entry point into this image. In whichever way this title directs you, the inevitable experience will become more nuanced. You may never have had a dad but instead a father or a sir or an anonymous sperm donor. No matter what, we all are the product of female and male genetic information that collided intentionally, unintentionally, in a Petri dish, in an act of violence or in an act of passionate, loving abandonment.

A title thus can have a massive impact even before we really get into the picture.

How Can the Titled Image Be Interpreted More Broadly?

Depending where you are coming from you may go to the cornfield, *The Children of the Corn*, Americana, back-yard barbeques or just kernels of corn stuck between your teeth. Because the corn is so densely planted it may represent a vista of individual memories or moments that collectively have grown to represent dad for you. Further still, you may see the corn as the stand-ins for all your ancestors, for all the genetic information that made him and then you. Along this vein of inquiry you may wonder about the corn itself. Is it a genetically modified organism, or traditionally grown, with a healthy dose of added pesticides, or is it organically grown? Note that although we are getting into somewhat different territory we still are informed by the title.

How Can the Untitled Image Be Interpreted More Broadly?

Easier said than done, yes? Myopia or tunnel vision has been put in motion somewhat and it is now harder to just forget about the title. As none of us experience and react in a very linear fashion, you may already have explored the following observations: as viewers we are floating above the image. We become suspended hummingbirds, just hanging, or enormous giants. The man in the corn has shrunk and is looking up to us. We as viewers are looking down on him. Is the man with the red thing in his hand about to set fire to the field and deliberately identify himself to the security camera's monitor(s) or, oh wait, it is a baseball cap and not a gas can? Check! Oh yes, the giant checkmark "✓," the most graphic element in the image. Checked off. Good. Yet, the checkmark continues outside of the frame in ways we can only imagine, as it is not contained. The "√" does it perhaps represent an equation and we didn't know because we can only see so much? How long is the maze he has to wander through to reach an end? How long do any of us have to search for where we are meant to be? And when we get there, will we recognize it, or just feel stuck?

we have the uncomfortable experience of realizing for the first time, that he too has a weakness or some vulnerability and can get lost. Maybe we hold someone on a pedestal and are curious what it would be like to experience that equation in reverse. Maybe we are Alice in Wonderland and have drunk the growing potion or maybe he drank the shrinking one.

No matter what, Plum has changed our viewpoint, literally, figuratively and instantaneously, to see dad and ourselves or others in a different way.

Conclusion

The middle-aged man is looking up at us and if we are not dying, maybe he is. As his child we may have become a caregiver too young. The sudden, disorienting, and devastating role reversal is irrevocably established. Maybe it is a less dramatic situation. Maybe we have just grown up. Maybe we realize that our hero is also just human like all the rest of us. Maybe

Assignments You May Want to Challenge Yourself With

- Familial relationships
- Role reversal
- Flying
- Compositional manipulation

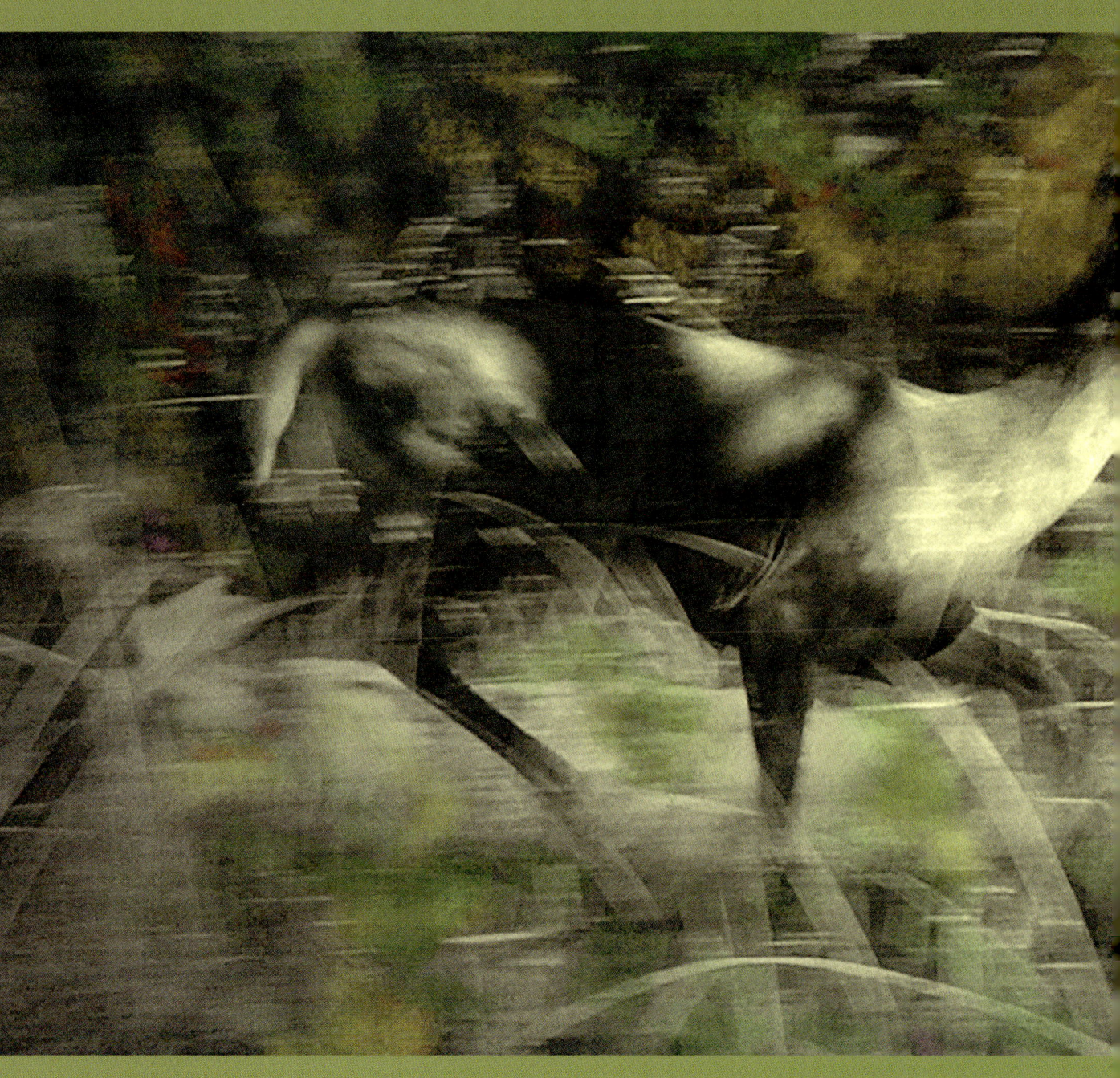

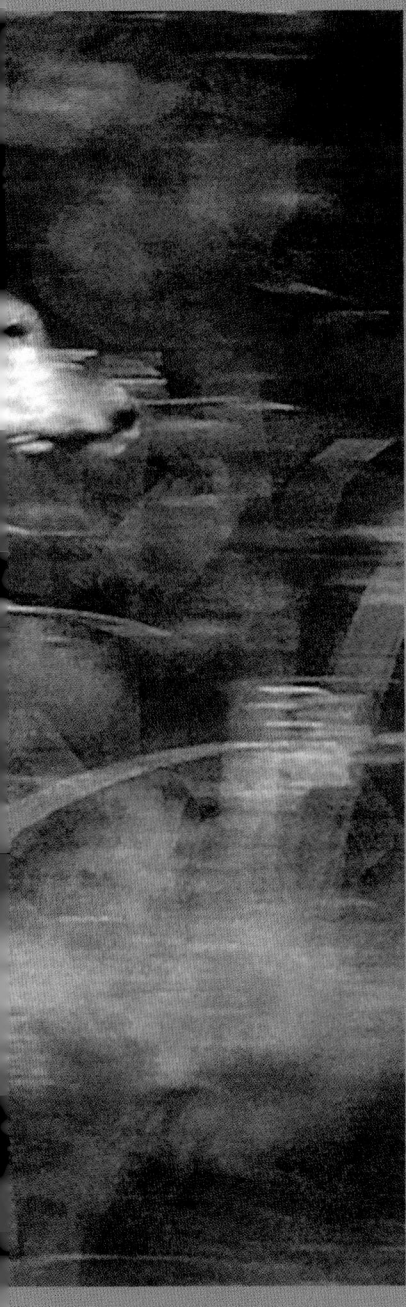

CHAPTER 21

Speed and Stoicism
The Nature of the Elements

Featuring work by Richard Saunier

FIGURE 21.1 Deer. © Richard Saunier

WHEN WE PHOTOGRAPH natural things, the landscape, fauna, and animals, we do so as we have learned from *National Geographic* and other sources that gave us the understanding of the hummingbird's frozen wings, the crocodile's gaping maw, and the monkey's stare while hanging upside down.

These striking images have the element of beauty and the scientific. They arrest the beating wings, measure the jaw's impressive diameter, and make us wonder what it would be like if our legs and feet, our atrophied tails, would work nearly as well as our arms and our hands.

For a long time these trophy shots, that require profound patience and the ability to anticipate the precise exposure that could so easily be missed, have dominated the genre of what we think of as animal photography. We call them trophy shots because photo safaris have fortunately displaced the practice of shooting wild animals for the actual trophy of their once proud heads to be mounted on a wall, while the rest of them serve as anything from rugs to umbrella stands.

Photographers like Nick Brandt and Gregory Colbert have become recognized for their animal and people, or animal only, portraits that search for the nature of the animals as opposed to just conflating them with nature. In other words their emotional being, the element that has always connected them to us as the relatives we used to recognize.

This too, is the material of Saunier's work.

What Are We Looking at?

Saunier's approach is based on showing the "element" in her element.

An anthropology with no hard-earned trust or contact. A fleeting glimpse, a momentary event that is over before we ordinarily have a chance to fully process what just dashed by.

In Saunier's image of the deer flitting through its habitat, nature itself becomes fleeting as the deer might be experiencing it, as we might, if only we could dart through the environment at such speed and with such grace (Figure 21.1).

The grasses in their curvy salutes become blurred with the animal itself as the camera pans to capture its movement. Though we can distinguish one from the other, their lines intersect and in some places become intermixed to the point where there is no discernible separation.

Beautiful as these creatures are, part of their speed ensures the survival of the healthiest and fittest among them. Without natural predators, herds can become diseased and forced to eat plants they would generally avoid. It is notable that the reintroduction of wolves in the Yellowstone National Park had a huge impact in not only controlling deer populations, but also in allowing the decimated plants and trees upon recovery to re-stabilize the riverbanks, which in a dominoes effect improved the entire ecosystem as featured on earthjustice.org.

There is a reason for the deer to have the capabilities they do, which are linked to so much more and are but a part of the far larger picture that Saunier shows us here as well.

Bison, the variety of buffalo found in the northern US, have also been reintroduced in Yellowstone National Park. Once hunted to near extinction, this icon of the American West has also made an impressive comeback and as with wolves, controversy abounds about the reintroduction of either species beyond the boundaries of national parks. Ranchers see the bison as disease carriers threatening their bovine herds' grazing lands and wolves as the killers of the same livestock.

Politics, in relation to harvesting federal lands for in-ground commodities such as coal, oil, gas, and water and on-ground commodities such as grazing lands, timber, and agricultural farming have been passionately colliding for decades. Simmering tensions that have already threatened to erupt violently in standoffs with the FBI. The fierce protection of private property and private claims to public lands contradict the reverence for

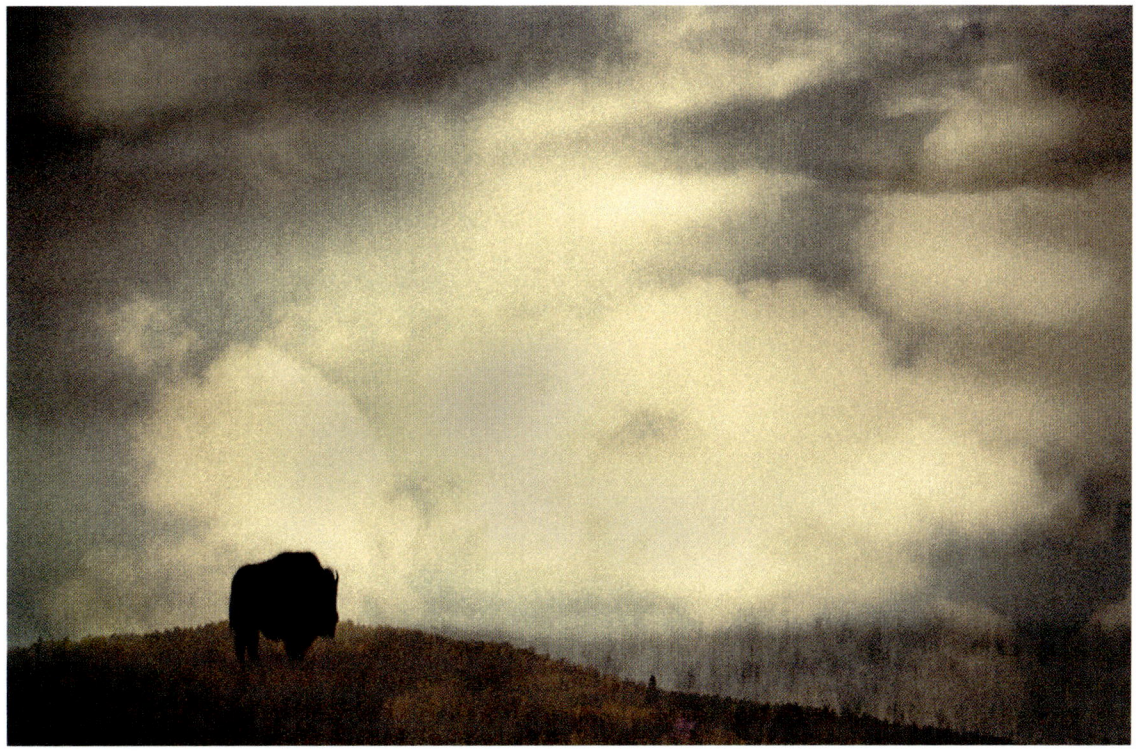

FIGURE 21.2 Bison. © Richard Saunier

the same said land that many of us harbor for different reasons. Public leasing rights can fiercely clash with federally regulated conservation efforts. What meaning do these arguments hold for the individual beast we may be lucky enough to encounter and be awed by?

How Can These Images Be Interpreted?

Just as the deer is fast, the bison is still. Unless either animal is used to people, a deer is likely to flee whereas a bison is likely not to. In that sense, they are not dissimilar from their relatives halfway around the world, the yak or water buffalo. Animals of that size are less likely to just take off, to the point where they might simply stand their ground or, if they feel challenged, may well attack. It is at this point, when the earth literally shakes under the impressive tonnage of such a large creature in targeted motion that we humans must get out of the way as fast as possible and likely nowhere near as gracefully as a deer.

Though both species are herd animals, arguably like us, we do find them on their own. It is in their individuality that Saunier has captured not so much them but our, the viewers', connection to them. Even at a distance the bison's iconic shape is unmistakable. Long before the German writer Karl May ever set foot on the North American continent, he vividly described the encounter of Native Americans and cowboys through the eternal lens of good fighting evil. His heroes, Winnetou and Old Shatterhand took on forces that eclipsed their ethnic divisions and subsumed them in favor of a higher standard of joint identity, a pure dream of America and the formation of intercultural allegiances. Meanwhile in Europe, sociopolitical stratifications and divisions were calcifying, slowly fomenting the path to WWI.

Saunier's bison were there before any of us, their eventual decimation another testament to our sense of dominion as opposed to stewardship, evidence of our sense of superiority. Trophy hunting, or the farming of bison for heart-healthy meat, is seldom a fair fight—and confuses our bloodlust with that of nature's dictates, which we are quite willing to see ourselves as part of, when it suits us, and not when it doesn't (Figure 21.2).

Conclusion

I doubt the bison is contemplating this, but Saunier forces us to. In his painterly, romanticized version of Nature we find magnificence and beauty, and our long lost relatives, which we have since compartmentalized as food, a tolerated version of nature as long as it does not interfere with immediate self-interest. We also find pets to which we surrender this connection to the point of neurosis. What is so much bigger in Saunier's photograph is the sky; it is, of course, so much older than the bison, than us, and harkens back to the beginning of our world, when the atmosphere itself was created and which is now recognized as a living thing under threat. Through its refraction and reflection of light, it is a constant mirror in which we have long stopped seeing ourselves.

Somewhere between the sculptures of Auguste Rodin and Henry Moore, between the weight of stone and metal we can sense the bison; the solidity, the massiveness, not just in terms of scale but in terms of its potential to be shaped and in turn to shape us. Saunier is shaping us with his bison, his version of *The Thinker*.

> **Assignments You May Want to Challenge Yourself With**
>
> - The nature of things
> - Prey and predator
> - Harmony

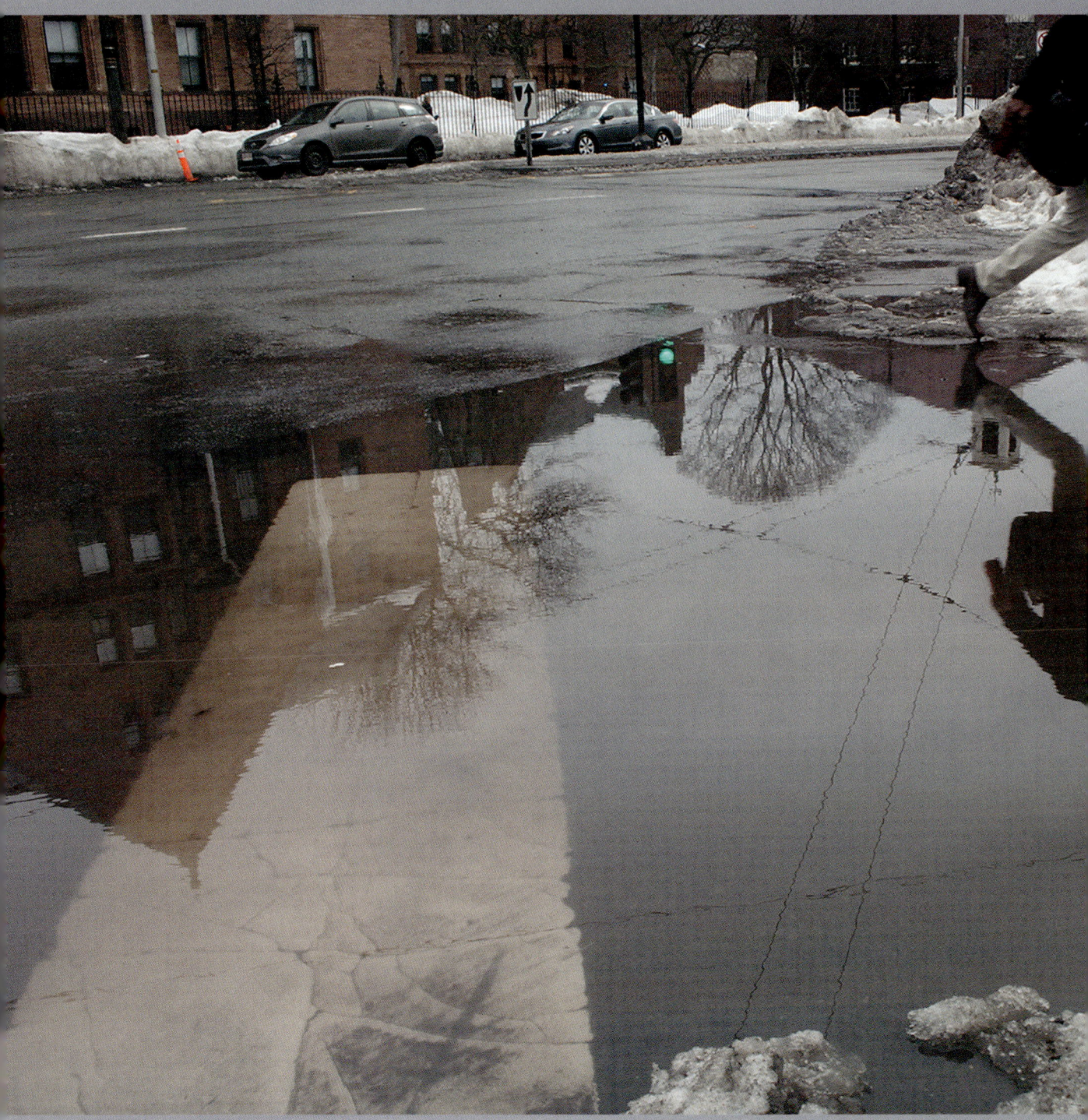

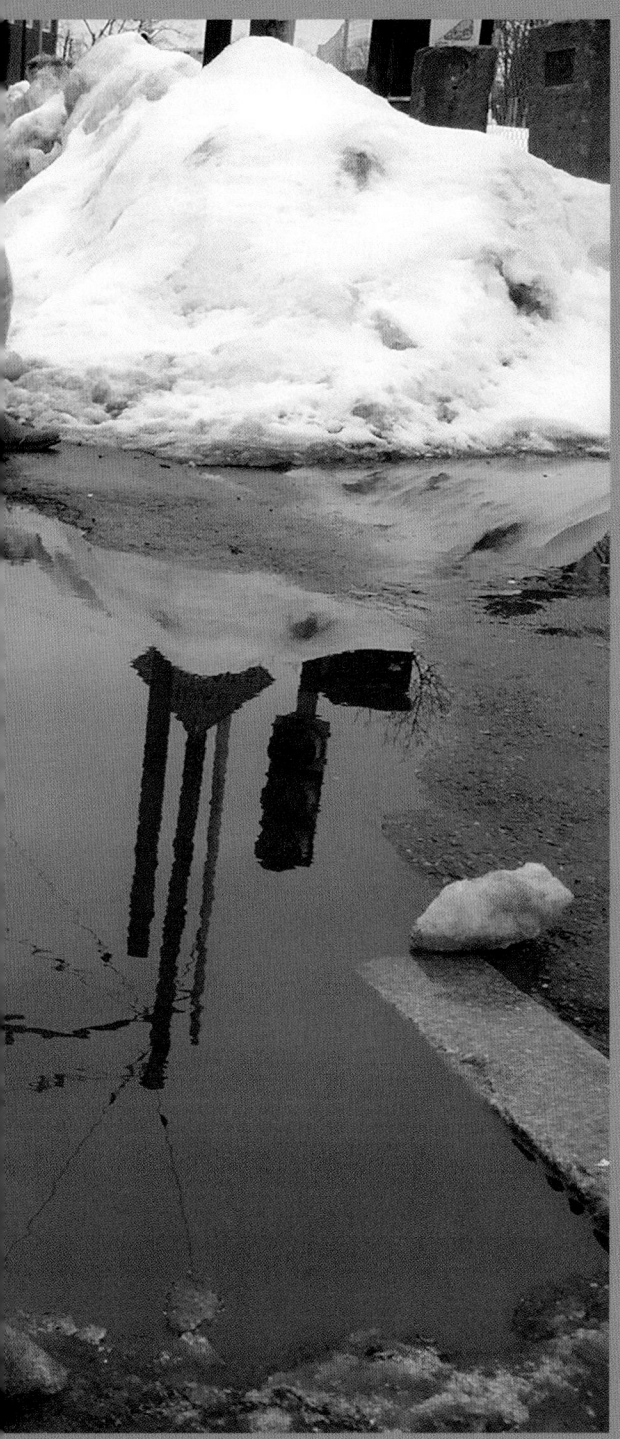

CHAPTER 22

Reflection
The Literally and the Figuratively

Featuring work by Elliott Kravits

FIGURE 22.1 Reflection. © Elliott Kravits

As WE REFLECT ON the images in this book, we are not only looking at the image elements and the subject matter, but also attempting to discern the greater meaning, the meaning that is beyond the sum of the component parts.

Kravits' image is no exception. The idea of reflection is already built in, representing the world as we are meant to see it and, in this case, a body of water rendering it upside down. Many famous images, often landscapes, have made effective use of this visual strategy (Figure 22.1).

This image functions not in the symmetrically pleasing way we have come to expect from bodies of water serenely reflecting their surroundings. Instead, it shows us a flooded urban landscape and a pedestrian negotiating the gap between the still frozen snow and the melt-water.

What Are We Looking at?

Like a white coffin's buoyancy forcing it to float to the surface, part of a crosswalk line spears the image from below, no longer functioning as intended, submerged in the murky water as it is. Its converging perspective points us in the direction of a green light, though the street seems abandoned by traffic, punctuated by a couple of parked cars. Flooding is nothing new. Cartier Bresson's image, *Behind the Gare St. Lazare*, Paris 1932, is considered to be among photographs that have pioneered frozen action images at just the right moment, the "decisive moment," with great tension and compositional complexity. While this is easier to achieve with modern cameras and has, in many respects, "already been done," this does not take away from Kravits' exploration of his city. In fact he doubles down by supplying the tension of a near impact by a foot on the water as in Bresson's image of the man skipping across the watery surface. Rather than by the heel, this protagonist is in the process of pulling his toe from the water.

How Can the Image Be Interpreted?

As we know the world is experiencing climate change. We don't budget for infrastructure, not to speak of anticipatable redundancies to accommodate future needs, but rather just maintain its bare bones functionality. Our lives, in that sense, are reactive, rather than proactive. As a society we live on borrowed time. We pay off the inflated interest on our credit cards, rather than paying off the balance. We "maintain" an inadequate bridge rather than replacing it. We treat ourselves to what we deserve rather than what we can afford. Retail therapy is endemic.

Conclusion

The other shoe is going to drop. We know it. But as long as we can keep out of the water with whatever acrobatics are necessary, the final toll matters not. To have enjoyed ourselves while it was still possible seems like a great idea, and in fact, anything else would be stupid.

REFLECTION

Therein lies the rub for me in this photograph. Anything else would be stupid and I know the feeling well. We all do. Arriving with relatively dry shoes after the fun of circumnavigating urban waterlogged swamps is, after all, a satisfying experience and an achievement in and of itself.

We have reached a point where traversing from point A to B is meaningful. If it is, this should be for reasons other than keeping our feet dry or avoiding getting splashed by a passing car. Yet, increasingly, winning such small odds provides a sense of satisfaction. To me Kravits' image dynamically alerts us to this sense of success. Crossing the road did not used to be considered a success. This image playfully, beautifully, and darkly suggests otherwise.

Assignments You May Want to Challenge Yourself With

- Climate change
- Visual anticipation
- Visual choreography

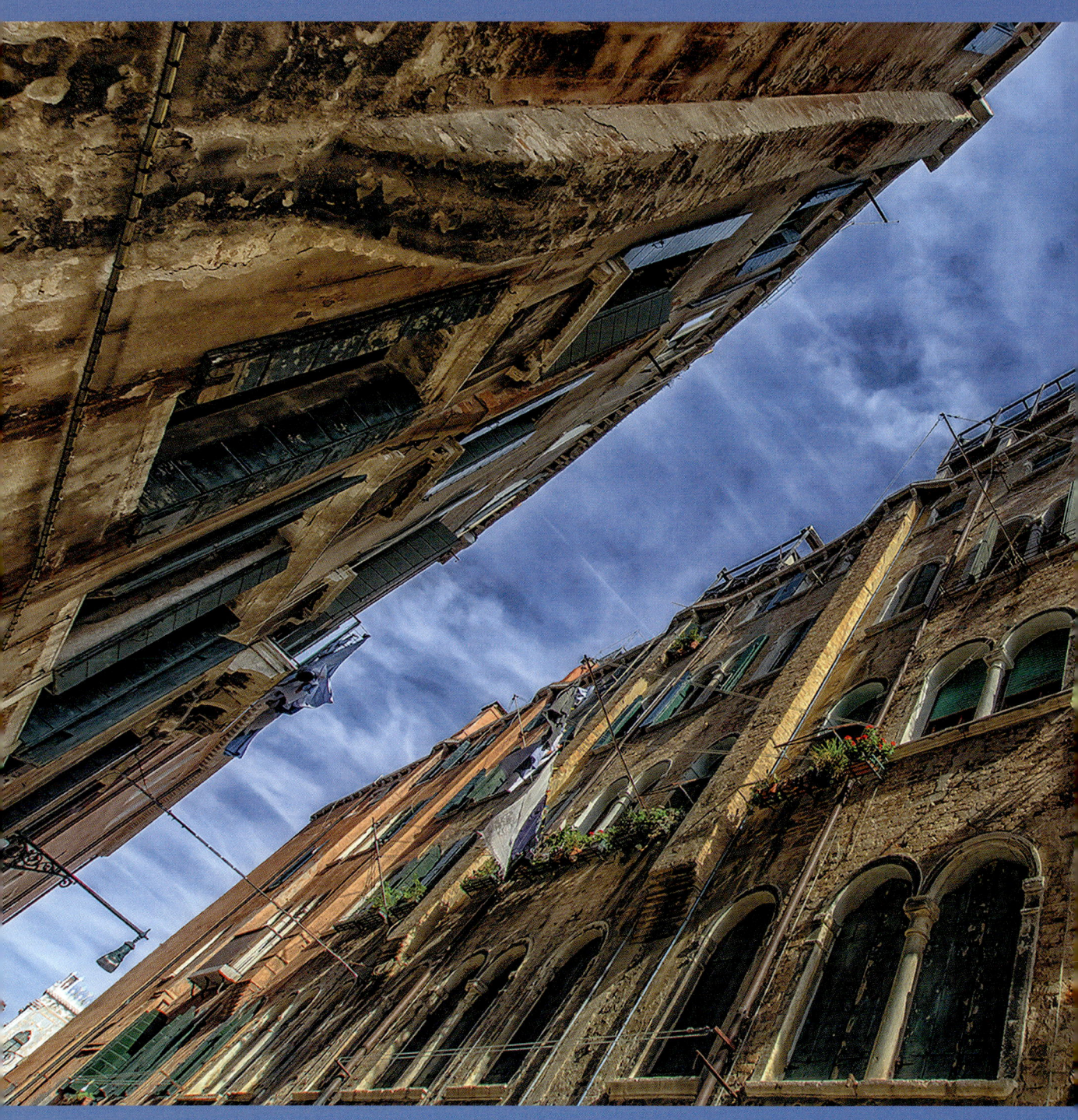

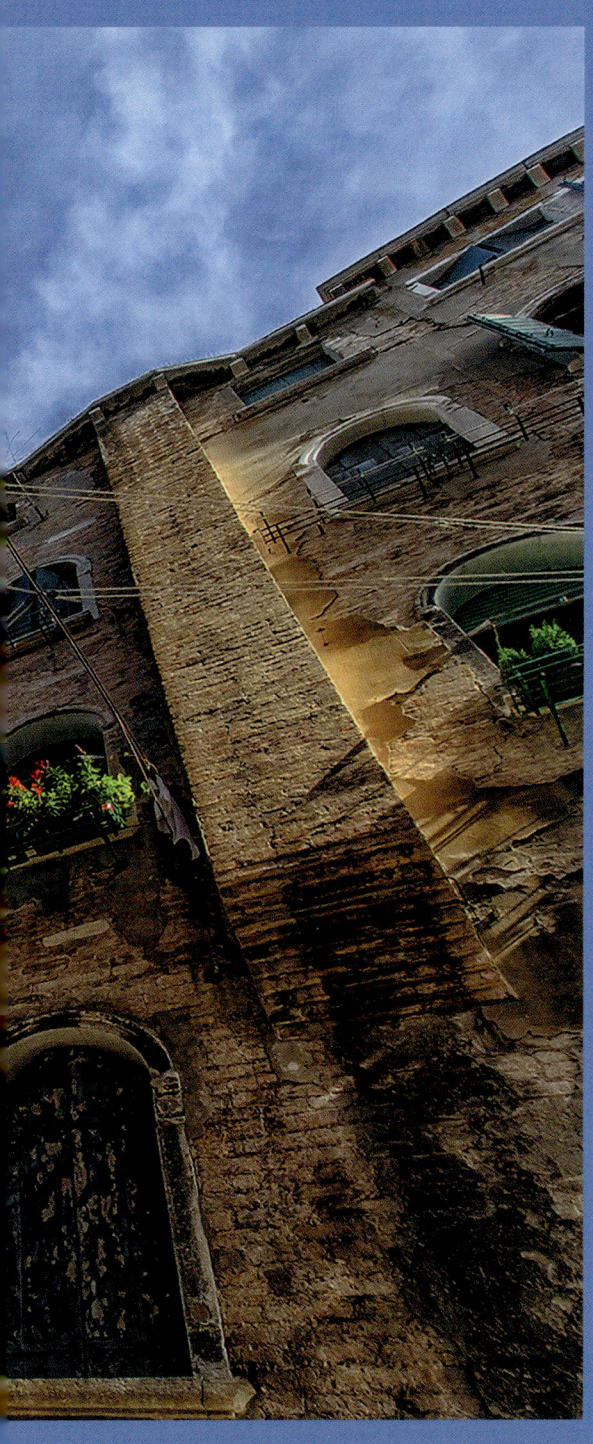

CHAPTER 23

Sky View
Upside Down

**Featuring work by
Marcos Sanchez**

FIGURE 23.1 Untitled. © Marcos Sanchez

What Are We Looking at?

SANCHEZ'S URBAN LABYRINTHS explore the experience of getting lost on well-trodden paths in a warren of ancient streets, of being hemmed in as the narrow streets of an old European town close in on the viewer. He explores these architectural canyons by seeking out the sky from the bottom of these man-made cliffs, which have over countless years been reshaped by rain and wind, winter frost and summer drought, as slowly and surely as these forces work in nature. He relieves us from claustrophobia by pointing to the sky. The intricate carvings, decorative styling, and other architectural elements of the epochs present tempting handholds and footholds, a potential temptation for any cliff climber or cat burglar (Figure 23.1).

How Can the Images Be Interpreted?

To me, we are looking at a world upside-down. A world where the sky has become a river and the water has pushed itself into the depths so far that it is unlikely to ever spill over its banks again.

In this way Sanchez is engaged in a far broader discourse than the thrill of getting lost in old Europe, not that this isn't worthy of documentation. However, by making his audience question whether they are looking up at the sky or down into a flowing river, we encounter global consciousness again. He too engages us in the discourse of climate change without hitting us over the head.

Rising water levels may be new to the world with some often-referenced exceptions such as Venice and the Maldives. For now, this reality is the subject of panicked projections across the world. Sanchez's work poetically engages this indirectly. Moving from seemingly pristine unpolluted waters, to murkier, less appealing rivers (skies) he starts to engage in a discourse about the health of the rivers themselves (Figure 23.2).

The idea of an azure river and yellow sandstone cliffs becomes less alluring, when contrasted with grimier facades and our sky rivers appearing to be polluted by inconsistent color in the water. Flecked with coloration and striation they seem less appealing. The strong linear pattern of the arched windows in the previous image has given way to more balanced facades on both sides and if we actually turn this image upside-down, the experience reads pretty much the same way.

Don't take my word for it though. Let's look at the image upside-down (Figure 23.3).

Unlike the first image this one works perfectly either way around, at least for me. In fact the iron plant hanger looks more convincingly like a tendril growing out of and attempting to cling to the wall, its curling growth looking for something to hold onto more prominently than before.

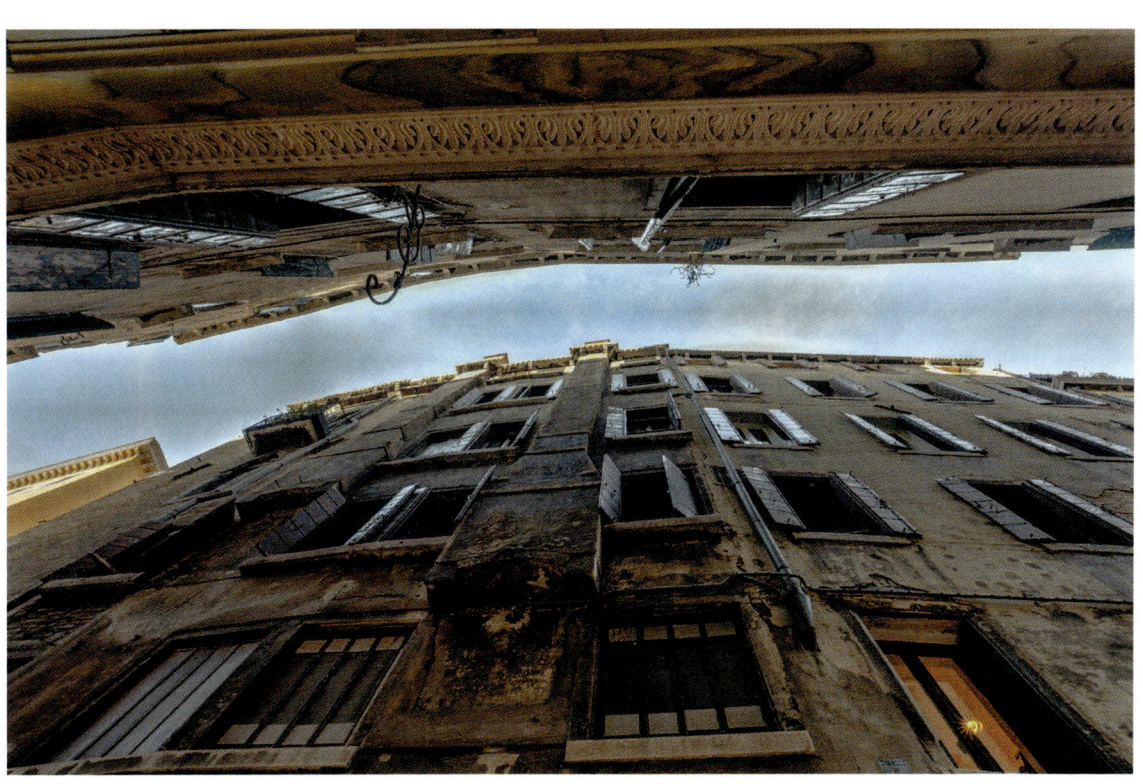

FIGURE 23.2 Untitled.
© Marcos Sanchez

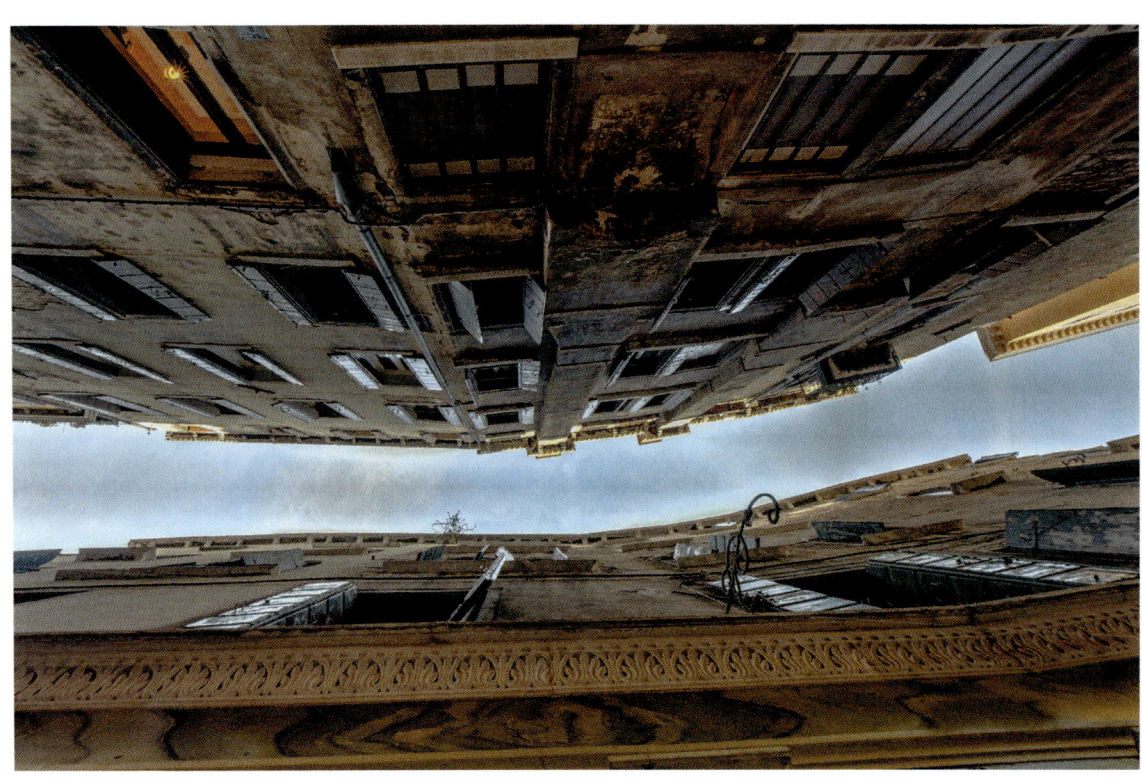

FIGURE 23.3 Untitled.
© Marcos Sanchez

Conclusion

I see a lot of potential for multiple bodies of work, exploring threatened towns around the world and alternative canyon walls that, in time, might be susceptible to being similarly flipped. Coastal skyscrapers becoming lost in the clouds and in doing so end up looking like pilings driven into a murky swirl.

Ironically Sanchez did start us off with some images taken in Venice, the town that is already partially submerged. By pointing us to the sky he didn't choose the obvious way to document the threat facing his subject matter. Instead he did it in a way that starts to speak far more broadly about problems that are likely to remain isolated for only a little longer. Therein lies his subtext and, like all good portraits, the narrative eclipses what we think we are looking at.

Assignments You May Want to Challenge Yourself With

- Global warming
- Upside-down
- Architectural interpretation

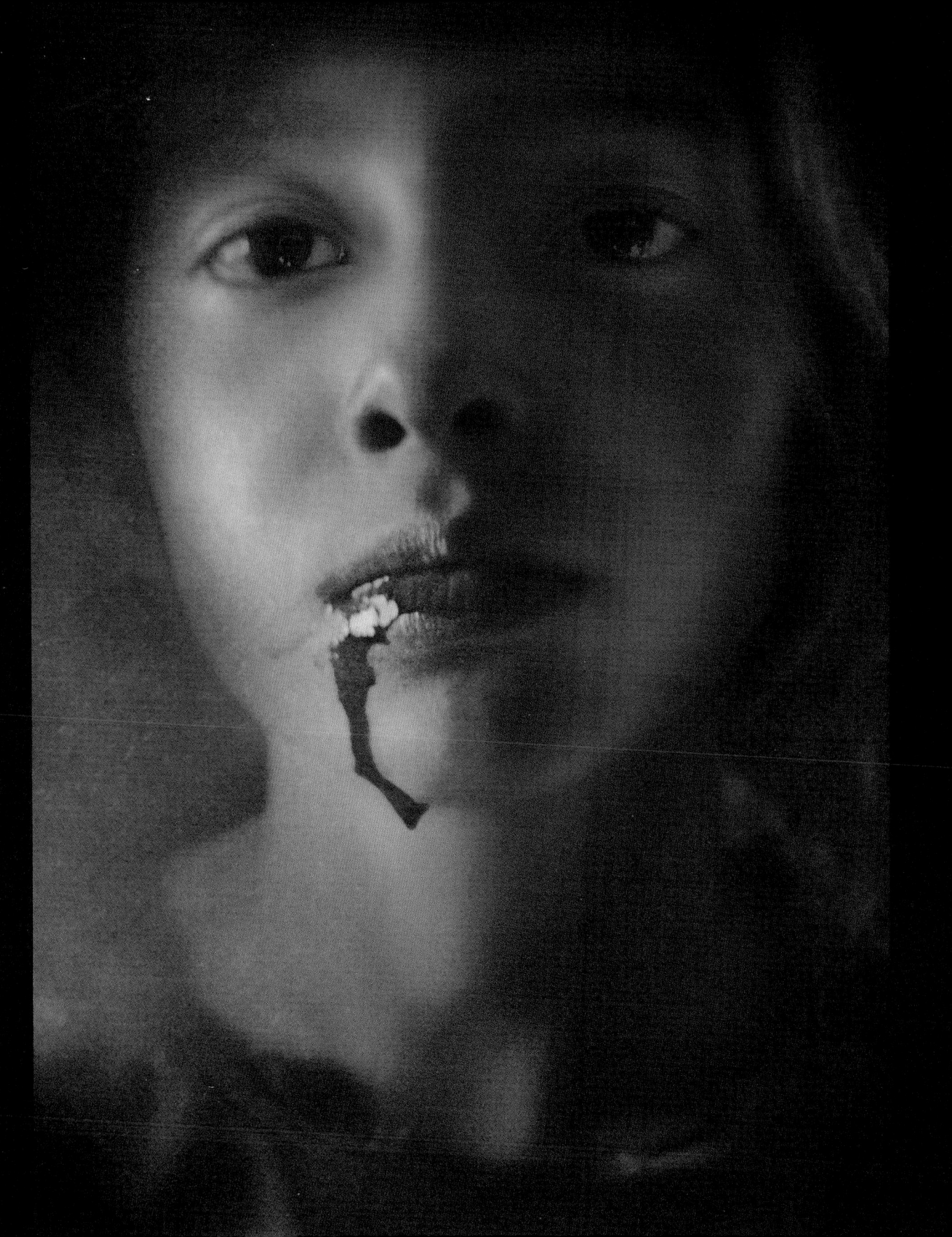

CHAPTER 24

Blood is Blood
Assumption

Featuring work by Anouk Jutta

FIGURE 24.1 Untitled. © Anouk Jutta

When encountering any image we tend to focus on what we may least expect or on its most disturbing element. Blood, the thing that flows through everyone's body, is not seen that often. It is associated with wounds, accidents, and religious exclusion as it relates to menstruation, high blood pressure, violence, and forensic imagery. The mere sight of blood can make some people feel queasy and, in some instances, can cause fainting. Thus conditioning leads to assumptions and it can be helpful to question those, in particular when we make them with a degree of certainty. But first we have to examine what the assumptions may be in this context, as in any other.

What Are We Looking at?

In the case of the young girl bleeding from her mouth, something bad is likely to have occurred. The painterly and dark quality of the photograph questions this as the evidence could have been added. Spilled blood, the loss of blood, in photographs, is mostly the milieu of war correspondents, child services, and forensic crime scene photography. When it comes to the most defenseless, children and animals, images of this type become proportionally more disturbing and even enraging. It is therefore not unreasonable to say that we have negative responses when it comes to seeing blood and that we are automatically on our guard.

Blood sacrifices in ancient rituals, leeches to cure disease, and mythologies about drinking one's enemies' blood to imbibe their strength don't do much to rehabilitate our immediate associations and in many cases continue to shock. In the end, blood reminds us of our mortality and the younger the depicted person bleeding, the sadder this becomes. Just as we have learned about the horrors of old we also know of the contemporary ones, the biological and chemical agents that cause hemorrhaging of the organs that lead to bleeding from the orifices. As much as we don't want to think about such things, a staggered wave of associations, some conscious and some more peripheral, intrude on our psyche and the assumptions continue to trend negative even further.

How Can the Image Be Interpreted?

Images where blood is worn as a badge of honor tend to be those which continue to celebrate testosterone in modern contexts, though they too have ancient roots and are ritualistic. Boxing comes to mind, the modern-day gladiator who, while bloodied, has bested his opponent and raises his hands in victory. Though there is now also female boxing, the subject in this photograph is not portrayed in a way that would suggest such a context. She looks neither victorious nor defeated. If anything, if we had to commit to naming her expression, I see a calmness, maybe defiance, but most of all the staring eyes suggest that while she is clearly looking at her audience she sees something elsewhere, something deeper, than that which is right in front of her. Then there is the tradition of the "first kill shot." No, not the one fired by the gun. The subsequent one, the one fired by the camera when the novice removes his first kill's still warm heart and often smears the animal's blood across his face, indicating a rite of passage, another successful step into manhood and into the realm of the hunter.

One may wonder what causes such behavior, such a need to eradicate the empathy for another; and while complex and even skillful in their execution, blood sports may hold at bay some fear, for a hunter is not the hunted, at least not until a bigger predator to shows up. The lineage of such impulses in our brains is lost in the distant past, where the need to assert dominance among peers and the hunting of animals may well have meant the difference between life and death.

Before we become too condemnatory about the death, say, of a deer, whose natural predators are often absent and whose numbers, therefore, need to be culled by other means to keep a herd healthy, we might acknowledge that a deer living in nature and shot cleanly has had a far better life and death than the millions of factory farmed animals who are summarily stunned, and sometimes not effectively, before being sucked into an automated animal carcass disassembly line.

Conclusion

Jutta's portrait of the melancholic look on the girl's face does indeed speak to all of that and more. It speaks to the incomprehensible fragility, delight, and despair of so many lives we will never know but to which we are never the less connected. In this regard Jutta has, at one and the same time, both profoundly reminded us and brilliantly misdirected us.

In fact the image is of her daughter. What is about to occur, as the light appears to be fading from this image, is a visit from the tooth fairy. Yes, Jutta's daughter has lost a baby tooth, another ritual of passage. Imagine if her mother had washed her face, then made her hold out the tooth on her hand as a trophy with a smile on her face. That image would have lost all its strength, that engaging subtext beyond the subject matter. It would have joined the ranks of thousands like it, and the wounds of growing up and learning about the world would not for a moment have entered the discourse of the image. For all we know, this might have been the last of the teeth her body replaced and now she knows there will be no more.

Assignments You May Want to Challenge Yourself With

- Blood
- Chiaroscuro
- Rite of passage
- Misdirection
- Uncontrived child photography

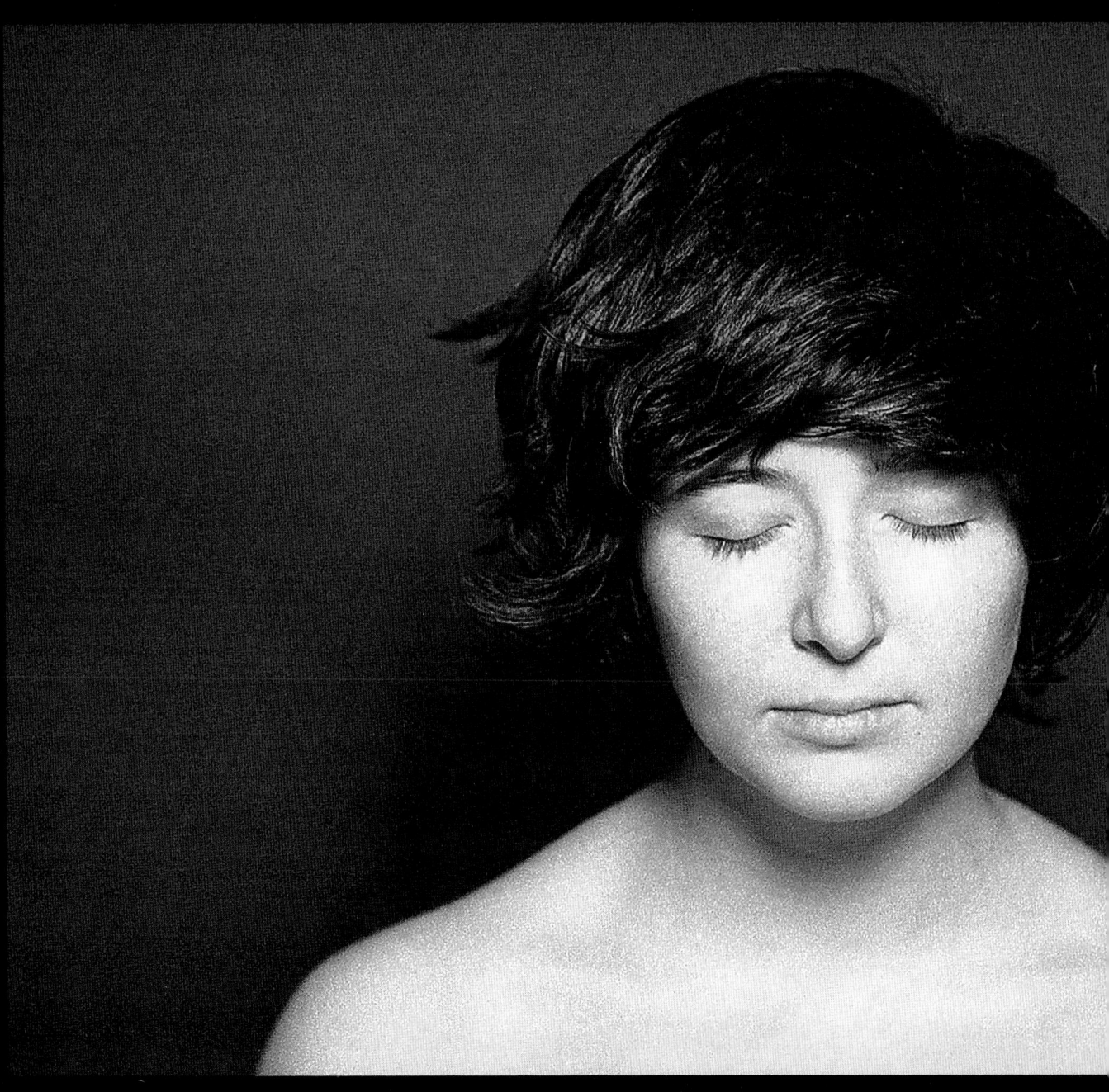

CHAPTER 25

Hypnagogia
Viewpoint

Featuring work by Chai Anstett

FIGURE 25.1 Rebecca. © Chai Anstett

LOOKING AT THE PORTRAITS of others and being photographically portrayed are among some of the earliest memories for many of us. "Say cheese" means the photo is about to be taken, that you are supposed to look happy, be clean in appearance, and otherwise ignore the majority of emotions that might be preoccupying your young self. We get used to looking up at the authority of the lens, unless the photographer bends down to our horizon line of the world.

What Are We Looking at?

Anstett's minimalist approach to her subjects seems to catch them at the mysterious moment of transitioning to sleep from wakefulness, called hypnagogia. Something is revealed about the individuality of these people even though there is no eye contact or apparent awareness of the intermediary, the photographer, who is offering this intrusive access to the viewer.

As if in a meditative trance, the subjects seem to almost be floating in ungrounded space.

How Can the Images Be Interpreted?

Viewing these images feels like an invasion of private space, a feeling reinforced by the apparent nudity of the women. There is a reminder of sitting across from strangers on an early morning commuter train when they have fallen asleep and are so relaxed that the face they wear for public consumption seems to have slipped off entirely to reveal instead a hidden defenselessness, reserved for only the very few who see them sleeping. Their startled awakening usually reveals that tired commuters who succumb to sleep do not freely give out such defenselessness. A sudden, almost confrontational, self-composing while staring at those who might have glimpsed them deprived of their public persona is a frequent reaction to waking under such circumstances. The potential

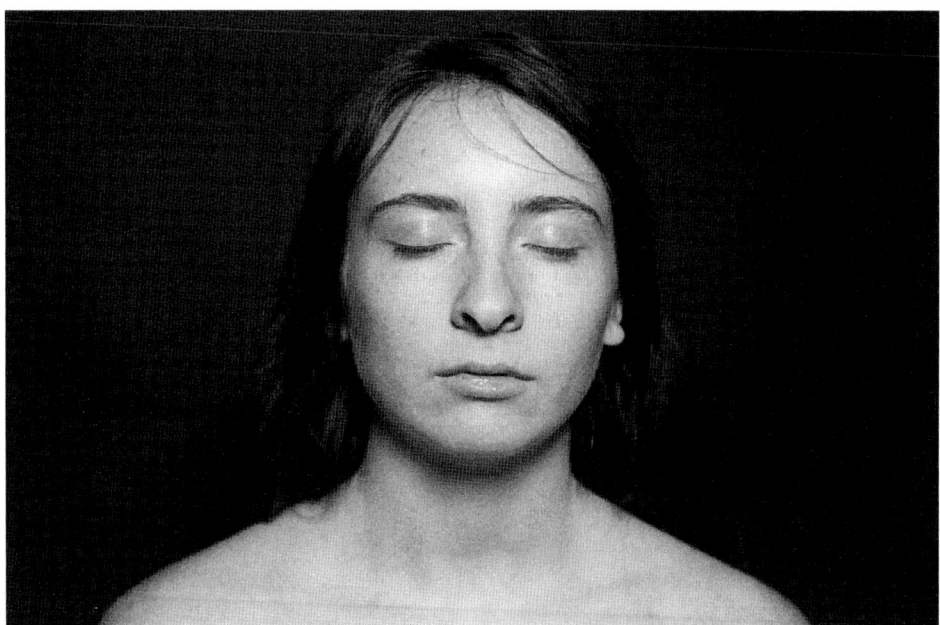

FIGURE 25.2
Emme.
© Chai Anstett

for this discomfort is an effective element in these images and asks the question what it means "to portray." How do we truly read another, in actuality or in photographs? What if they don't wake up and we just think they are pulled into initial states of sleep?

How Can the Viewpoint from the Above Approach Inform the Experience of the Images?

We already know that these subjects are not floating above us, because of the gravitational evidence of their hair. While it is not falling forward, there is an ambiguity to whether it is hanging down or lying flat, which would put us above the women. Because of the equally ambiguous figure-ground relationship, the subjects could be sitting or lying down.

If they are lying down and photographed in this clinical way, not asleep on a bed or a couch, the surface must be something else and could easily become suggestive of a mortuary table. If that were the case, choosing this viewpoint only exaggerates the discomfort for the viewer. Are we there to identify someone or are we being shown a photo for this same purpose? There is no evidence of a V-shaped incision. Is an autopsy about to be performed? And here Anstett leads her viewers to a place of compassion for these strangers. Their vulnerability is that they are young. They are at an increased risk of being victimized because of their age and because they are women. There is also the likelihood that they would be paid less for the same job as their male counterparts. The viewer is led to understand that these women could be killed or their souls destroyed, their self-worth demolished, experience-by-experience (Figure 25.1).

How Can the Element of Viewpoint Be Further Expanded upon?

We know from descriptions of near-death experiences that many patients have reported looking upon themselves, their corporeal form, from above as if floating over themselves. If we go there, then we become the women and in that moment may realize that if one is diminished we are all diminished. Think of the epidemic of rapes across so many college campuses. Our inaction and silence makes us complicit in subtle and profound ways that ultimately diminish us all and bind us even closer to these images. In this sense the viewer can be implicated in the silent protest these women strongly convey (Figure 25.2).

Anstett continued with her portraits in our subsequent color seminar class. What has been said can still inform these images, though the color changes several things. The lighting is darker and although more somber, is also less clinical. The strobes get caught on the eyelids and look like white orbs. Though still closed, they lend the eyes a weird presence; white pupils instead of black ones. Since they are slightly higher than where they should be, this makes it look like the eyes are rolling back into the skull, placing the eyeball where it should not be.

The various customs of closing the eyes of those who have died, of weighing down the eyelids with coins or stones can be traced back to the fear of the death stare, to a deep sense of respect for those who once saw and no longer do, and, I suspect, to the finality that dead eyes convey. After all we can't pretend they are asleep, and the inclination for most of us would be that they want the dead person to be at peace.

FIGURE 25.3
Mia.
© Chai Anstett

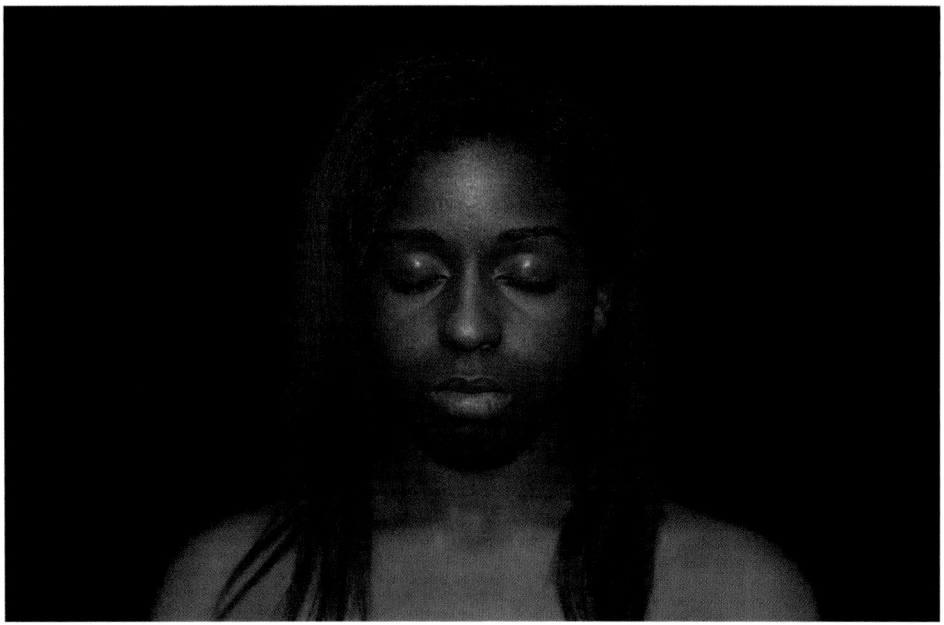

Another element is the "black darkness," in this image and in the subsequent image, which also reads as "black on black:" the dismissal of black lives whose loss is somehow more expected than say, "white on white." In fact, I don't remember that term—"white on white" ever being used. Of course no skin color is ever truly black, just as no skin color is ever truly white. This is a matter of mere gradation. Again, the idiom of "black on black" violence may be another way for Anstett to quietly insist on everyone's culpability (Figure 25.3).

IV.XX.LVII—04.20.57. A date. What is the significance? April 20th has some notoriety for being the international pot day. Fifty-seven, even 1957, has as far as I know nothing to do with that. Notably, the Mayflower II, a replica of the famed ship that ferried the first pilgrims across the sea, was launched on that date in Brixton, England to start her fifty-five day journey to Plymouth, Massachusetts. I looked that up on the Internet.

Somehow, I suspect the date has nothing to do with either event. It may represent the birthdate of someone special and it may not. We all have our stuff (Figure 25.4).

But it is a clue. In the absence of all else, we want to cling to it. This offers one way to think of the person as someone who has a date that is so important to her that she carries it with her wherever she goes. The point for the audience may simply be not to obsess over that date, but rather those that matter to each of us, visible or not. It is our own stuff that matters. When we realize that, and honor it in whatever way feels best to us, we take care of ourselves. This is the prerequisite for our being able to take care of others.

Conclusion

We might not consciously think about this when initially considering this work. Yet, as the images get

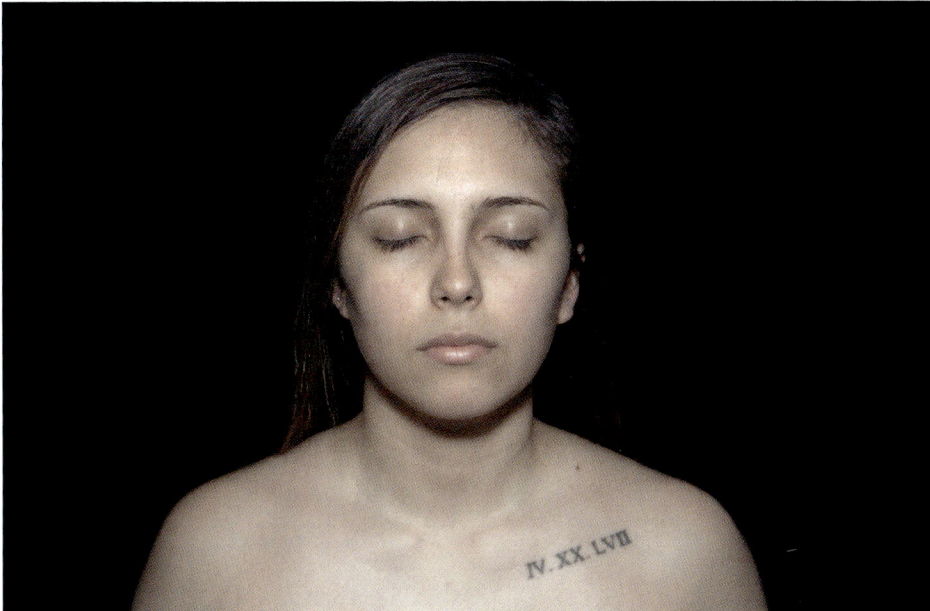

FIGURE 25.4
Rita.
© Chai Anstett

stored in our memory bank and like everything else we know and have learned, and have experienced individually and collectively, it will continue to float around the periphery of our consciousness, until we ourselves wake up and start to take collective responsibility for each other. Anstett does this with nuance and, in fact, insists quite forcefully without ever insisting at all. This then is an example of peaceful protest through her peaceful images.

Assignments You May Want to Challenge Yourself With

- Viewpoint
- Eyes closed
- Isolation
- Inequality

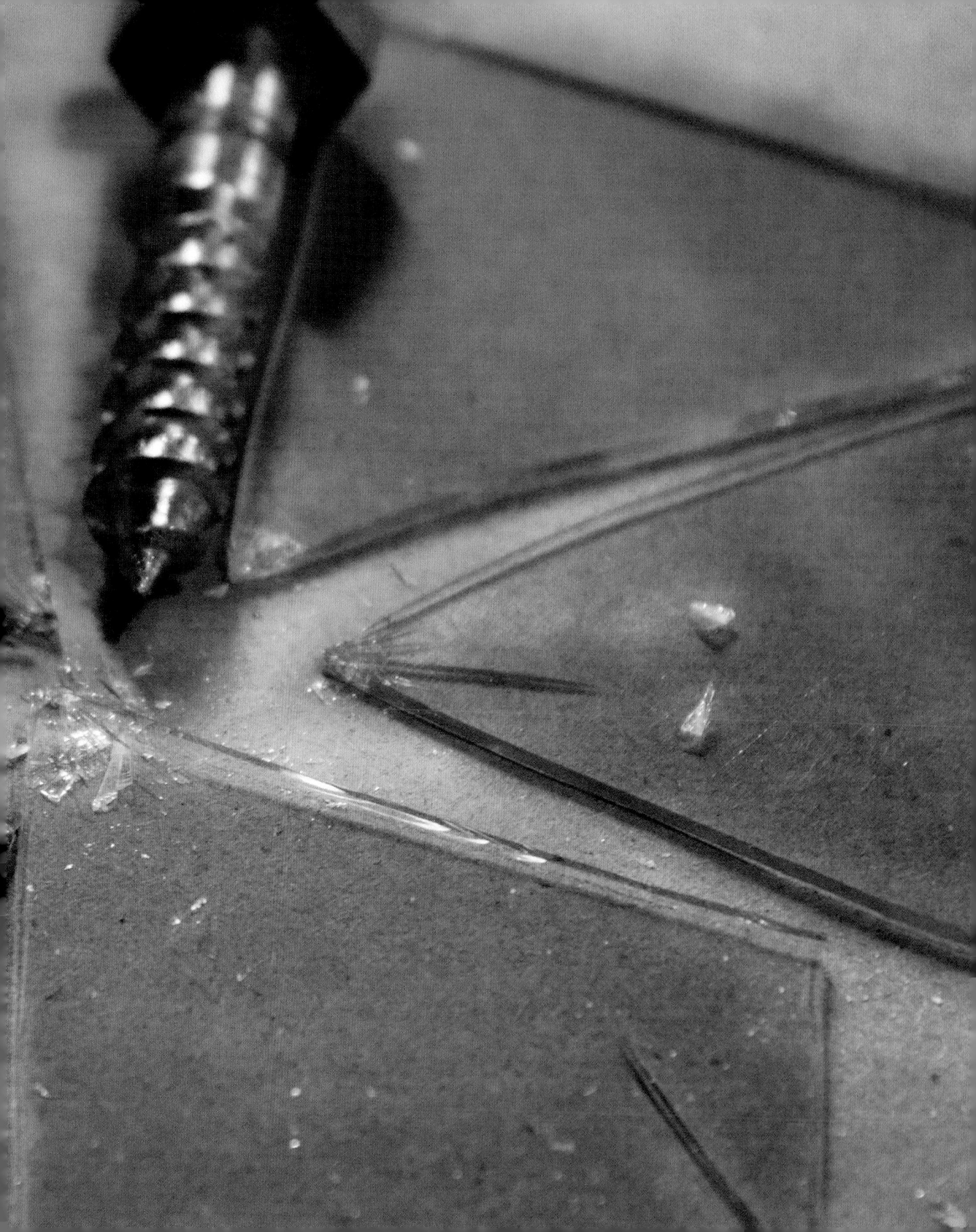

CHAPTER 26

Harmonia
Rendering the Invisible

Featuring work by Hannah Mainhart

FIGURE 26.1 Untitled. © Hannah Mainhart

THE MORNING STAR is of course no star but the second-closest orbiting planet to the sun, Venus, the closest planet to our own home, Earth. Venus is associated with femininity, just as our other neighboring planet, Mars, is associated with masculinity.

Both planets have their own place in Greco-Roman mythology, much of the foundation for our contemporary civilization. The forbidden love affair between the god (of war) Mars/Ares and the goddess (of love) Venus/Aphrodite resulted in the birth of their beautiful daughter Harmonia. Of course, Harmonia eventually gets killed and the associations exerted on our cultures by the symbolism of our neighboring planets have caused anything but harmony.

Images of people suffering fill the annals of art history. During the Renaissance the focus seemed to be on saints. Think of Christ, the Pieta, and St. Sebastian pierced by arrows to mention but a few. Many are rendered to look exsanguinated, to visually emphasize blood loss and approaching death.

The worship of sufferers, the reminder of their sacrifice, to benefit a greater good, and in the case of Christ to suffer for all so they may be forgiven for their failings, is rich material, referenced not only in the era when the Church was the main patron of the arts but also photo-journalistically later on. Think of Robert Capa's image of a falling soldier during the Spanish civil war, published in *Life* magazine; Nick Ut's image of a naked Vietnamese girl running from napalm bombs, which won the Pulitzer Prize; Ladislav Bielik's image of a man facing down a Soviet tank in 1968; and, only twenty-one years later, Jeff Widener's photo of a Chinese dissident standing resolutely in front of a column of Chinese tanks in Tiananmen Square. There are of course many more, and far more gruesome images of suffering during war and human cruelty. However, these are among the iconic images that have resonated in ways that have redefined perceptions of what was occurring in the face of overwhelming odds. To quote Gene Roddenberry's *Star Trek* character Spock: "The needs of the many outweigh the needs of the few," and in a later iteration ". . . the needs of the one." Self-sacrifice has therefore held sway in hero imagery and frequently not in images of personal suffering, often dismissed as self-indulgent or self-destructive.

Larry Clark's black and white images of heroin users and later Nan Golden's color exploration of dysfunction and personal isolation are examples of efforts to address suffering in private, apparently not linked to the needs of the many but to the needs or even the desperation of the individual. Everlast's *What's It Like* or Amy Winehouse's *Rehab* are musical examples of addressing individual suffering and in so doing challenge societal edicts you may have come across. Glamourizing self-destruction or self-indulgence are the primary objections to such works. Yet, personal pain exists, and needs to be chronicled, possibly all the more so for its apparent irrelevance in the face of exponentially increasing tensions around the globe in nearly every context imaginable.

It is against this background, and the weight of ongoing stigmatization and dismissal that Mainhart has chosen to engage the world of mostly unseen pain, linguistically characterized as "self-harm." She too was criticized for visually engaging, even glamourizing and potentially triggering urges to commit self-harm.

This lengthy introduction is due in part to establish a context for her work and in part to suggest that you, the reader, may want to skip the rest of this chapter, just as students were allowed to leave the class who felt triggered when her work was under consideration.

It is not for me to either censor or impose the work on anyone. My decision to include Mainhart's work in this text is no different than the reasons for the other images we have looked at. The work has a viewpoint and demonstrates a sustained inquiry and is rich with subtext. Mainhart takes on the renaissance strategy of some of the aforementioned images directly, by rendering her subject's skin as "exsanguinating."

She applies this not only to people but also to situations.

What Are We Looking at?

Broken things relate not only to people but also to environments. Think of the rustbelt, failing infrastructure, inner city areas that are no-go zones, upper-class ghettos where everything matters but the kids who live there. We already know that those whose odds are in their favor don't necessarily succeed, just as those whose odds are against them sometimes do. Generally this may not be the rule as the absence of values and unquestioned privileges aren't a cure-all, although they do open doors. Nurture versus nature is a complex issue; does our genetic inheritance work or clash with our environment and all the unforeseeable events that occur when people start families?

The stuff of abandoned buildings can become the instruments of self-harm such as the broken glass and sharp metal objects depicted above (Figure 26.1).

How Can the Image Be Interpreted?

In Roman times the suicide of Lucretia, who could only think of saving her honor by taking her life after being raped, appears to be referenced here, although the Renaissance paintings and etchings of her seem to be more sexualized by the more frequent depiction of a dagger held between her bare breasts. We are unlikely to know the true number of raped women and, to a lesser extent men, around the world. Statistics

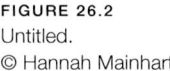

FIGURE 26.2
Untitled.
© Hannah Mainhart

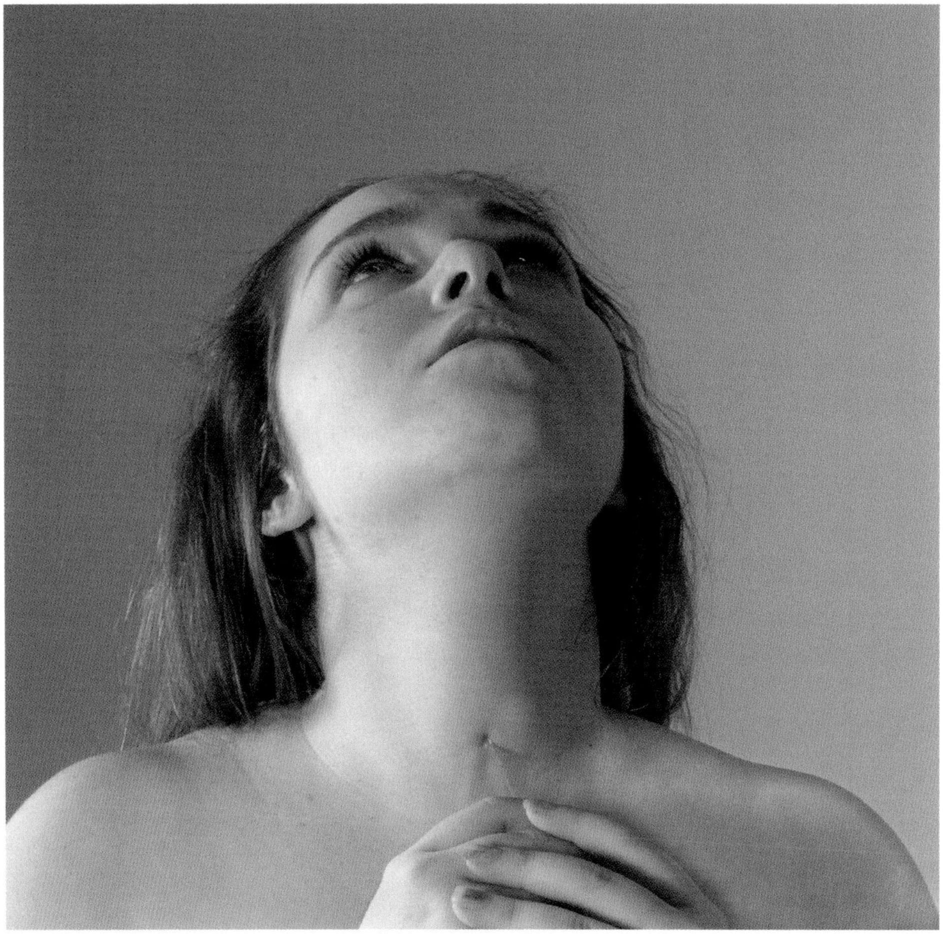

reflect an alarmingly high percentage, though it is impossible to know how many because, by definition, unreported rapes can't be tracked and therefore can't be known. The devastating effects of such crimes on the victims are not quantifiable and survivors cope in many different ways.

It is not uncommon for victims to blame themselves and to turn their pain on themselves. Self-hate or lack of self-worth often have convoluted roots and may not easily be uncovered. Even if they are fully known and understood rationally, the emotional devastation often remains. Insidiously invisible as such injuries are, the mind often turns on the body as punishment or, to make visible what can't be seen (Figure 26.2).

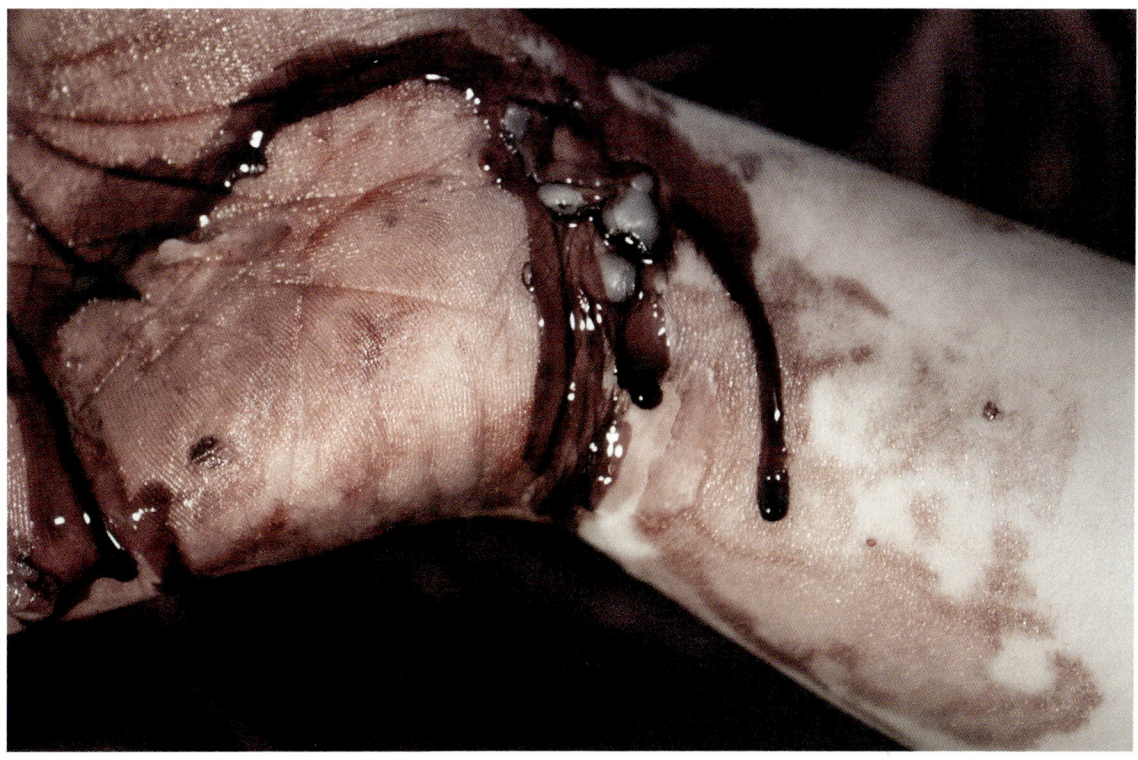

FIGURE 26.3
Untitled.
© Hannah Mainhart

Conclusion

The visceral recreations of Mainhart's insistence to show what becomes physically manifest upset some viewers (Figure 26.3). Yes, the images are difficult and convincingly staged. What, however, does it say about us that we can consume far more horrendous depictions of death, torture, and injuries in the forms of mostly entertainment but also the news that makes these, comparatively benign images of an exploring photographer, so challenging. For me it is her sincerity and courage to start conversations about difficult, strongly "stigmatized" subject matter. Think of the root of this word—"stigmata." The tattoos or brands left on a criminal in Greco-Roman culture. More contemporarily, the wounds left on Christ's body through crucifixion.

Assignments You May Want to Challenge Yourself With

- Self-harm
- Saints
- (Silent) suffering
- Renaissance art
- Advocacy

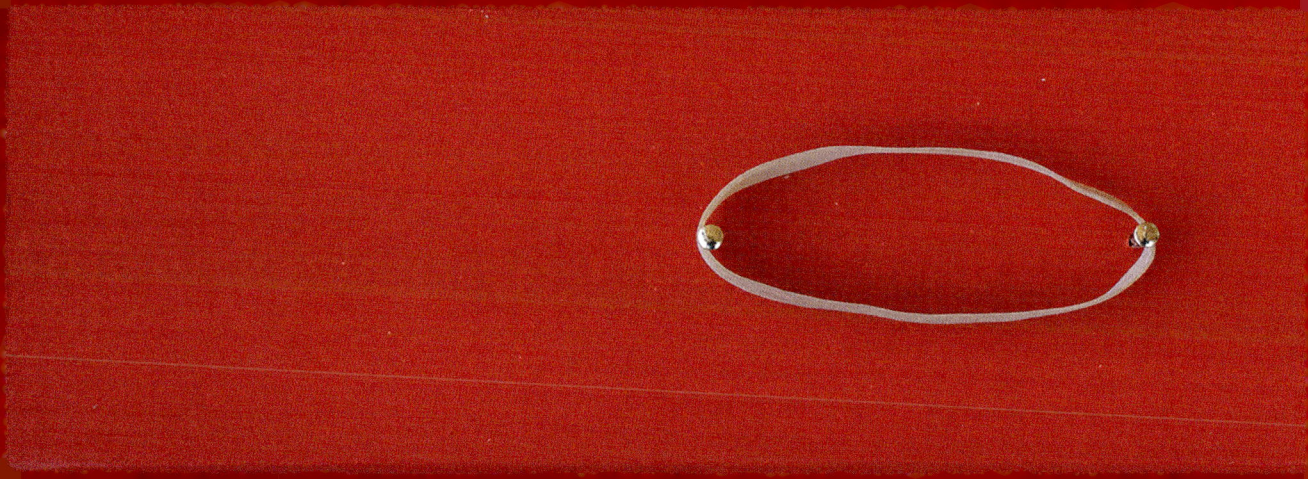

CHAPTER 27

Snap
Breaking Point

Featuring work by Elaine Carson

FIGURE 27.1 Relaxed. © Elaine Carson

The UBIQUITOUS RUBBER BAND has many uses and Carson uses them in her constructed metaphors. Rubber bands have an intrinsic attraction for people. They can temporarily solve the most outlandish problems and they are fun. They can be used as a self-propelled sling with the thumb to serve as a launch pad. Which kid in class has not studied the accuracy of such projectiles with more dedication than the subject matter they were supposed to be paying attention to? During adolescence this often represents the first clumsy attempts to get the attention of someone we fancy. When this gets met with eye rolling and a slight smile, this awkward transition into flirting holds the promise of encouraging more articulate attempts in the future. If, as is mostly the case, the eye rolling is followed up with an exasperated shaking of the head, then, most definitely, more sophisticated methods will have to be found.

That we entrust the rubber band to send these first messages of interest in another is possibly linked to more than inexperienced overtures. There is always the security of plausible deniability—"Sorry, this was actually meant for someone else, bad aim and all that." More significantly, the rubber band has instructed us in chemistry and physics before we knew what those terms meant. Rubber bands have chemical properties that allow them to be stretched, to a point, before they break. This relates to the thickness, length, and durability of the band itself for they eventually become brittle and lose their flexibility, at which point they simply snap. Similarly, the physics part teaches us about storing energy in the tension on the band, which relates to momentum, distance, and trajectory.

This nifty device, therefore has associations with playfulness, discovery, education, and, yes, romance.

As adults, it will do to get our hair into a ponytail, attach cling film that doesn't cling to a bowl, secure rolled up images and so much more. We gradually forget about the magic of the thing and eventually think of it as nothing more than a temporary solution to a practical need that is often not at hand when needed most. A bag of rubber bands, thoughtfully stored in a supposedly easy-to-remember spot in some drawer, suddenly becomes utterly elusive when attempting to recall exactly in which drawer that bag actually ended up. As a result many of us are grateful that the mail, when there's more than one item, comes held together by such bands, often the only useful part of a pile of junk mail.

It is in these early lessons and associations that Carson seems to have rediscovered the wisdom contained in a rubber band (Figs 27.1 and 27.2).

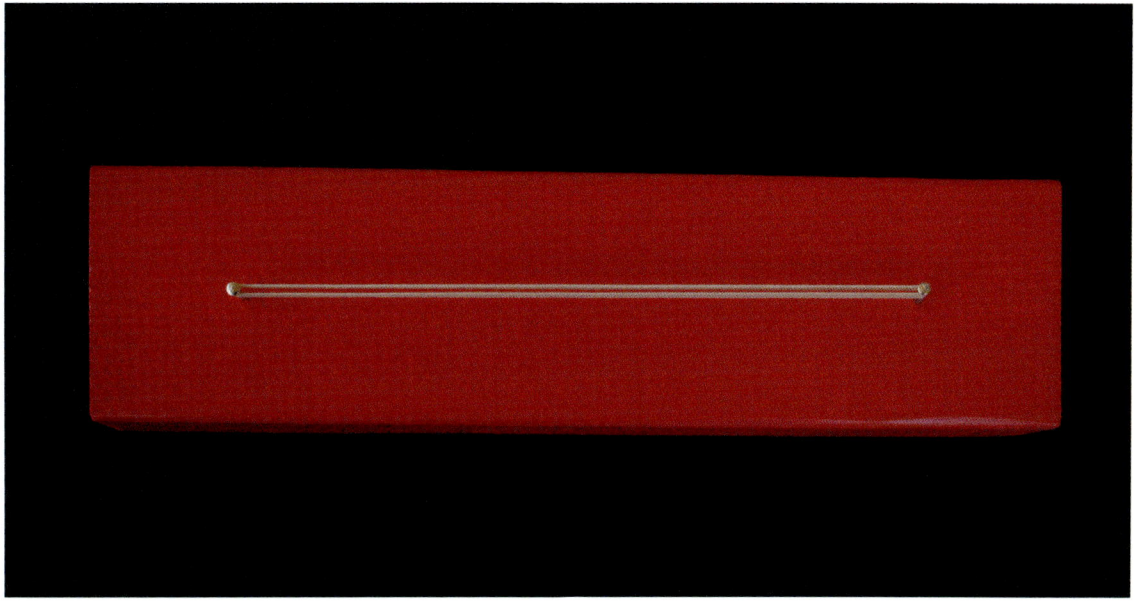

FIGURE 27.2 Stressed. © Elaine Carson

What Are We Looking at?

Carson's seemingly simplistic images may appear to state the obvious, the difference between relaxation and stress. If that is so obvious, why is everyone constantly stressed and rarely relaxed, if ever at all? The images are visually appealing. The elements in the photograph are sparse just like what they claim to represent. The red platform, floating in space, adorned only with its golden nails and a generic rubber band.

The only difference between the two images is the placement of the nails. That is it. Everything follows from that one simple choice. In one image the nails do not exceed the length of the rubber band and it is in its natural state. In the second image the distance exceeds the length of the rubber band and it is severely stretched. Image number one exerts no pressure on the nails, image two does. Not only that, image number one looks like an imperfect oval. Image number two like a parallel track. We can't really refer to it as a long rectangle because the rubber band assumes the curvature of the nail at the two points of attachment.

Now we have words like oval, parallel track, point of attachment, all of which remain predicated on how the nails are positioned in the first place or, to use a more familiar cliché, how we move the goalposts.

How Can the Images Be Interpreted?

This begs the question of who places the nails, the symbols of both crucifixion and the preferred method to not only hang a crucifix on a wall but the majority of two-dimensional art. Nails, it seems, are simply too practical not to be used to hang a religious icon, even by the very method it mourns.

Another way to think about Carson's work is as the misshapen circle and its subsequent stretch into the parallel lines. Neither serves a purpose as such but both intrinsically describe the difference between tension and no tension. When looked at in sequence, this becomes compounded when repeated. Breathe out—breathe in, asleep—awake, at peace—in pain, undercapacity—overcapacity, healthy—ill, or getting ill. We all know stress is a killer. Yet, this is more admired than a state of idleness. We are constantly expected to be active. To be inactive is frowned upon though we already know that a rubber band that is not stretched lasts longer than one that is. The latter state will eventually lead to the breaking point. The weakest molecule of a constantly stressed rubber band will become the weakest link in the chain that can no longer hold the tension. And then it snaps. We actually do better when we both relax and challenge our minds and bodies. Exercise of either makes us stronger but that necessitates relaxation. Not the kind where you go on holiday to do something but the kind when you go on holiday to do nothing. Since this is arguably a waste of a good holiday, Carson may encourage us to do that at home every so often, which is to do nothing. Nothing at all. Try it, this is one of the hardest things to learn and one of the most recuperative and energizing activities, since to be truly inactive would require death. This doing nothing at all requires commitment, discipline, patience, and utter determination by the practitioner, commonly referred to as meditation. If you believe that there is absolutely no way to fit an extra twenty minutes into your life, try to get at least a reasonable amount of sleep.

Conclusion

The proverbial burning of the candle at both ends temporarily provides more lumens but for a much shorter time because the candle has to burn horizontally rather than vertically and thus drips the wax that fuels the wick much faster.

This is the wisdom that Carson is showing us with her rubber bands. She reminds us that a thing that once, long ago, taught you good lessons, may yet have more to teach you, if you are willing to stretch yourself a little.

Assignments You May Want to Challenge Yourself With

- Constructed imagery
- Everyday household items
- Metaphor
- Significance in the insignificant

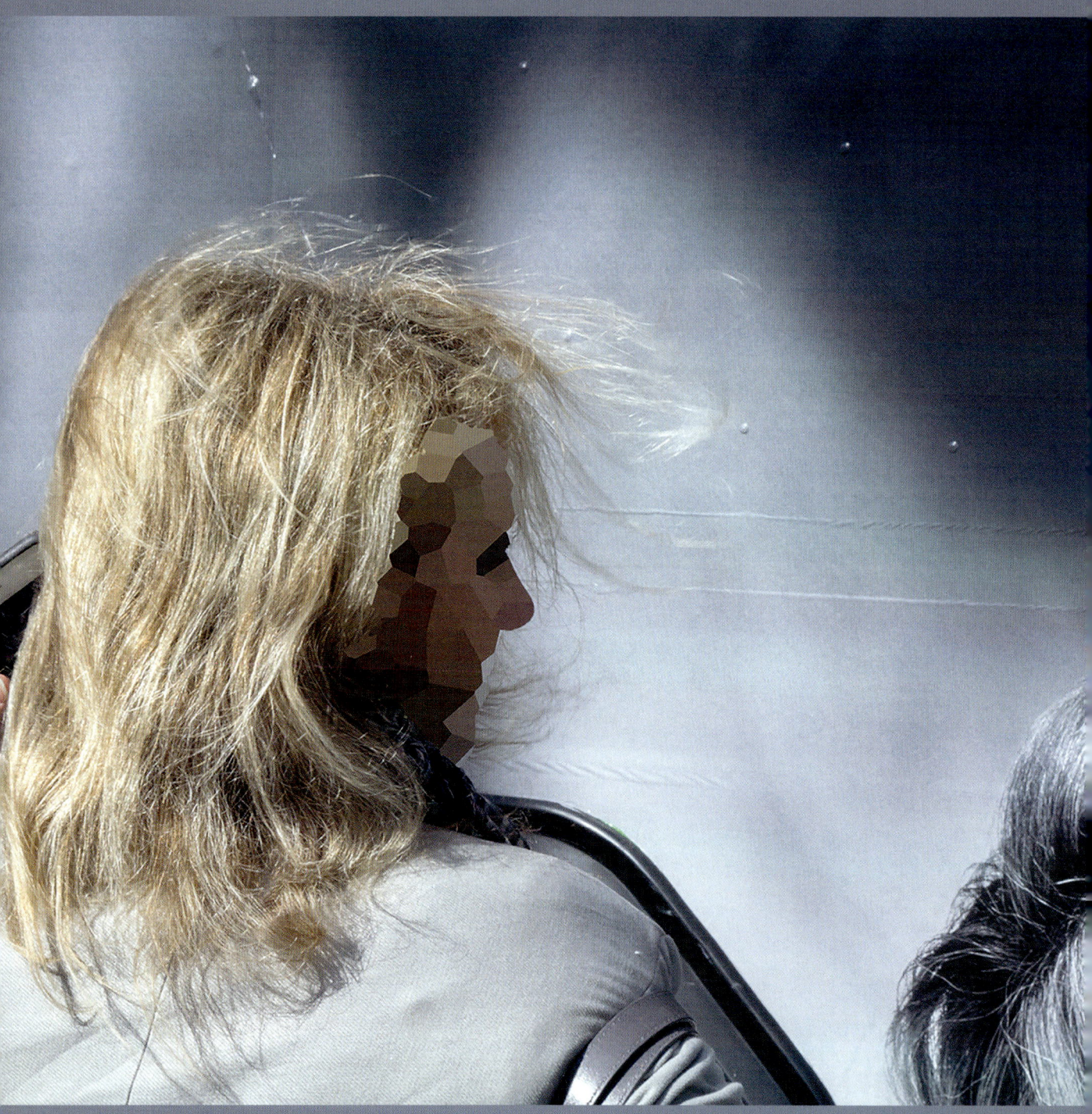

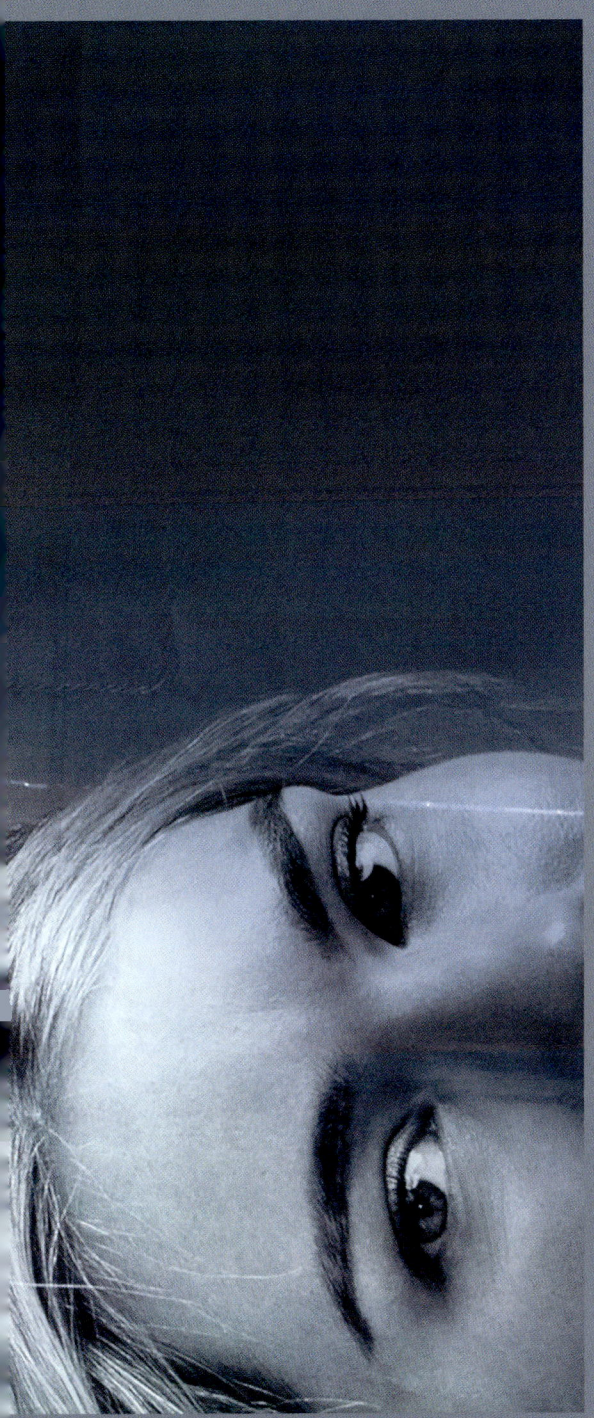

CHAPTER 28

Recognition
The Need for Invisibility

**Featuring work by
Thap Saengsouriyheth**

FIGURE 28.1 Untitled. © Thap Saengsouriyheth

MUCH HAS BEEN REPORTED about the increasing surveillance of people via a myriad of tracking devices. Whether your location can be triangulated by your cellphone, or pinpointed by your credit card use, an automated toll road payment device, this is but nothing compared to the ceaseless videotaping of your person.

Whether you are withdrawing cash from an ATM, waiting for a train, driving a car, boarding a plane, walking down a sidewalk, moving through a public building, or shopping at almost any business you are likely to be filmed, your image captured, and possibly your voice recorded in these environments. This is not to speak of tracking your social media and phone conversations or your website visits, online purchases, physical address, and so much more. What identifies you more than bureaucratic and biometric data is your own image. All that is required to link it to you is a computer program with an algorithm that matches any reasonably sharp frame grab, captured anywhere, to an image that is in a database such as your driver's license, passport photo, and presto, facial recognition software can identify and track you almost anywhere.

Reasons for this are mainly twofold, security and commercial profiling. Trading such information for both reasons is nothing new but it has expanded exponentially with the promise of greater security and consumer targeting. Laws vary greatly around the world and are substantially different in how much an individual's data is protected. Ironically, the EU holds itself to much higher standards than the US. I say ironically, because so many Europeans emigrated to the United States for the individual freedom it promised. Some Asian countries are fairly strict in how personal data can be used and much of the world has no laws at all. This is interesting because no matter how protective the laws of any given country may be, security agencies and large corporations operate on an international stage, and what must be legally safeguarded in one place may not be regulated at all elsewhere. Such loopholes are like black holes, which make it unlikely for the ordinary citizen to be able to look over the event horizon.

So what is an individual to do?

What Are We Looking at?

Saengsouriyheth's work is rooted in obscuring faces to emphasize the prism of all our mixed gene pools, our self-effacement under the tyranny of unachievable, idealized advertising, and broader concerns with self-image, identity, and profiling (Figure 28.1).

He does this effectively and with elegantly choreographed aesthetic anticipation as he makes his candid images. When contemplating them I was struck by another thought. In a reversal of how freedom is interpreted between the US and almost anywhere else, Americans have the right to protect themselves with arms and other devices, in some states with negligible restrictions. One of these other devices is the radar detector. The police use radar to catch speeders and in turn American drivers, if they so choose, can install radar detectors in their cars to be forewarned of such speed monitoring. This cat and mouse game is advertised as helping the accidentally inattentive drivers to keep their insurance rates down, which would almost invariably increase were they to be caught speeding.

How Can the Image Be Interpreted?

Saengsouriyheth's images led me down another path though. In contemplating his work, it suddenly struck me that the "Incognito Face" or "Incognito Pendant" or however such a jamming device might be named, is not yet hanging around everyone's neck. This is not so much a personal radar detector but a jammer to obscure the appearance of someone when filmed or photographed. This would be a device that either distorts the three-dimensional heat signature or throws off a camera's focus to the point of rendering an image useless. On a recent trip to an impoverished island nation, I also visited a resort with a harbor full of luxury yachts. These multi-decamillion vessels were gracefully basking in their bays. As obvious targets for piracy, sophisticated security systems must have been a given for all of them. Some were ostentatious, not just in their appearance but in their warnings on the side of the hull. A huge skull and bone insignia, comparable to the international warning sign for poison was prominently painted on the hull of one of them. While I interpreted this symbol as a warning to stay away, it too might have had a subtext, maybe someone thought it funny to make reference to corporate piracy practices that might have paid for the vessel in the first place. What drew my attention was the most elegant and understated yacht of them all. Not the biggest and not painted in white but coated in something that looked like Teflon. I turned my lens on it to photograph it for its beautiful design and sleek futuristic appearance. Unlike with the skull and bone ship, the autofocus would not lock on. It whirled frantically between useless points of focus despite areas of contrast like the windows and the hull. The only remedy was to photograph my subject by manually pulling focus.
My attempts to research the technology the yacht may have been equipped with turned up nothing useful. It is highly likely that whatever technology was in use was designed to prevent lock-ons from more nefarious devices than cameras.

Still, it took that one experience with the yacht and Saengsouriyheth's images for me to make the leap between the two. Whether the technology is cheap enough, small enough, and readily available, or restricted for use under limited circumstances, are all relevant questions. It seems unlikely that such a device will be making its debut imminently nor will it be on the latest must-have gadgetry stage.

Under the watchful eye of "Transit Watch" insignia, Saengsouriyheth captures a man in makeup and costume, likely an advertisement for a theatre production or

FIGURE 28.2
Untitled.
© Thap Saengsouriyheth

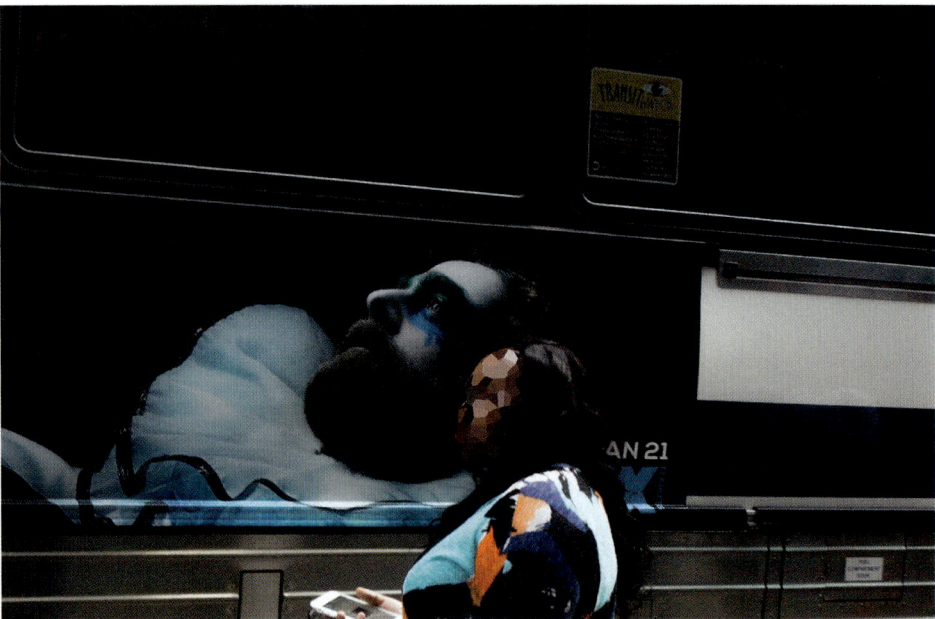

opera. The woman beside him is again obscured with her cellphone in hand as in the previous image. So what are we looking at? The photograph of a photograph sets the emotional stage for us. The unreadable face of the woman gives us arguably less to go on. The man looks sad, defeated, his costume ruff more similar to a bib and his makeup reminiscent of a black eye. Is he incapacitated to symbolize a victim of domestic violence in this iteration of the photograph? Is the virtual communication between viewers, stranger, and ad a silent vigil to our collective disconnects, an exponentially manufactured experience of emotion reported in this manufactured image (Figure 28.2)?

As a viewer I am grateful for how these images lead me astray. For I recognize that loneliness. I recognize it as I wait for a train and commune with images plastered on the other side of the third rail. By contrast, the actual faces around me avoid eye contact and sound, defended by earplugs with their eyes glued to a screen, just as my own are. This is code to avoid offense of any kind in large urban settings and a longing to escape the perceived boredom of transit that has transformed our lives. The personal invisibility devices are indeed already with us.

You may counter that commuters used to hide behind newspapers, books, and eventually Walkmans before the digital translation of all of that emerged. True, though the printing press and magnetic tape are technology too, as is photography. I don't think that most of us are interested in the technology per se but

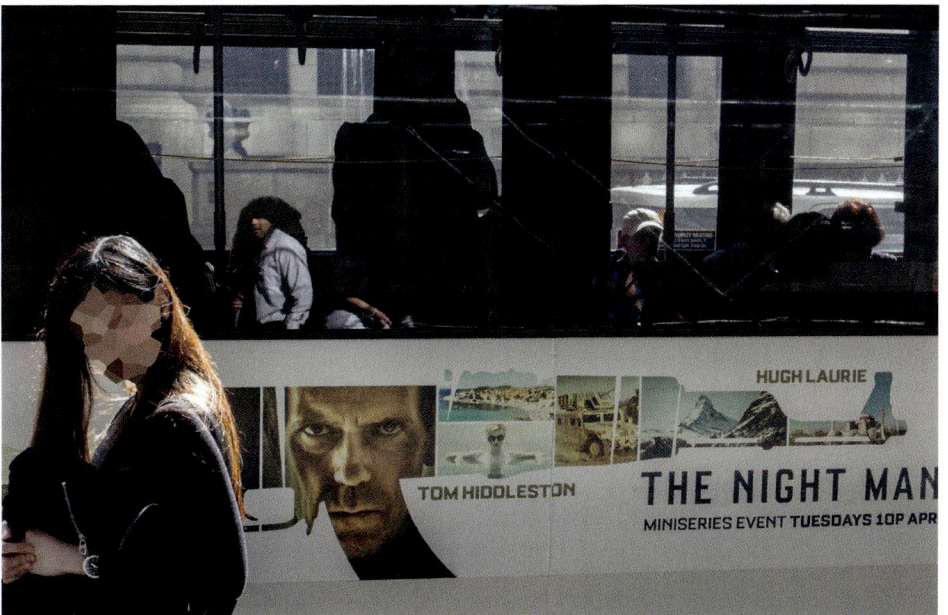

FIGURE 28.3
Untitled.
© Thap
Saengsouriyheth

what it can do for us. As consumers, it transports us away, to fill the increasing void with melody and prose, fantasy and dreams. One aspect of this consumerism, especially on mobile devices, has ushered in a new era of shopping via apps and click-bait. In so doing we remove ourselves a step further from other fundamental relationships of interaction, such as the trader and customer. As social animals, this still begs the question for how long will we be able to sustain this virtual diet and how it will impact our ability to actively rather than passively connect, engage, and experience.

Conclusion

Saengsouriyheth's work is therefore not just asking where we come from but also where we are going. Is our need for oblivion and to isolate ourselves self-perpetuating? What will it take to escape the centrifugal forces of such seductive self-reinforcement? When will the binary bread for the masses go stale?

For now let me leave you with the "Night Manager" as we continue to pull the wool over our eyes (Figure 28.3). Night, night.

Assignments You May Want to Challenge Yourself With

- Technology
- Integration of advertising
- Integration of words

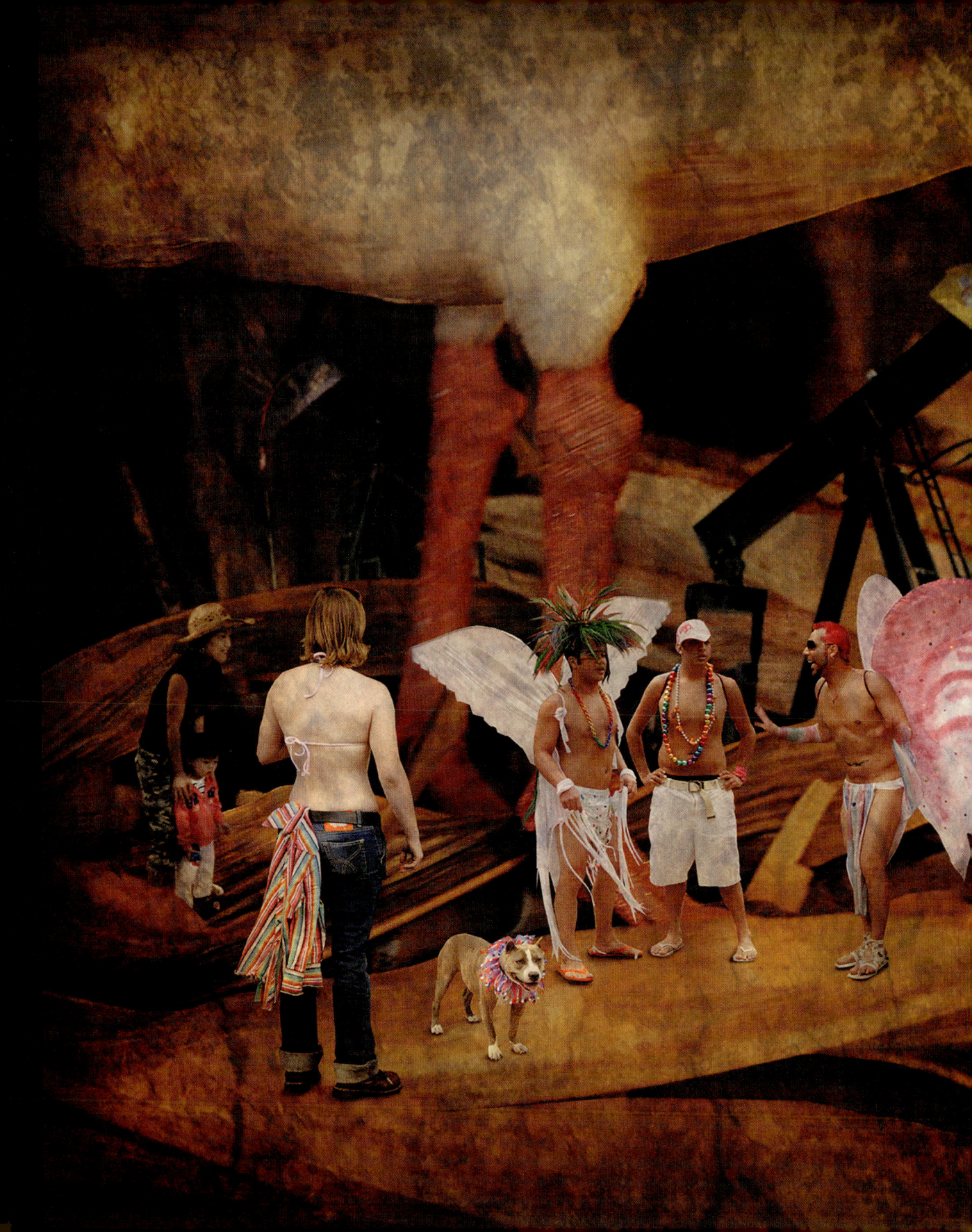

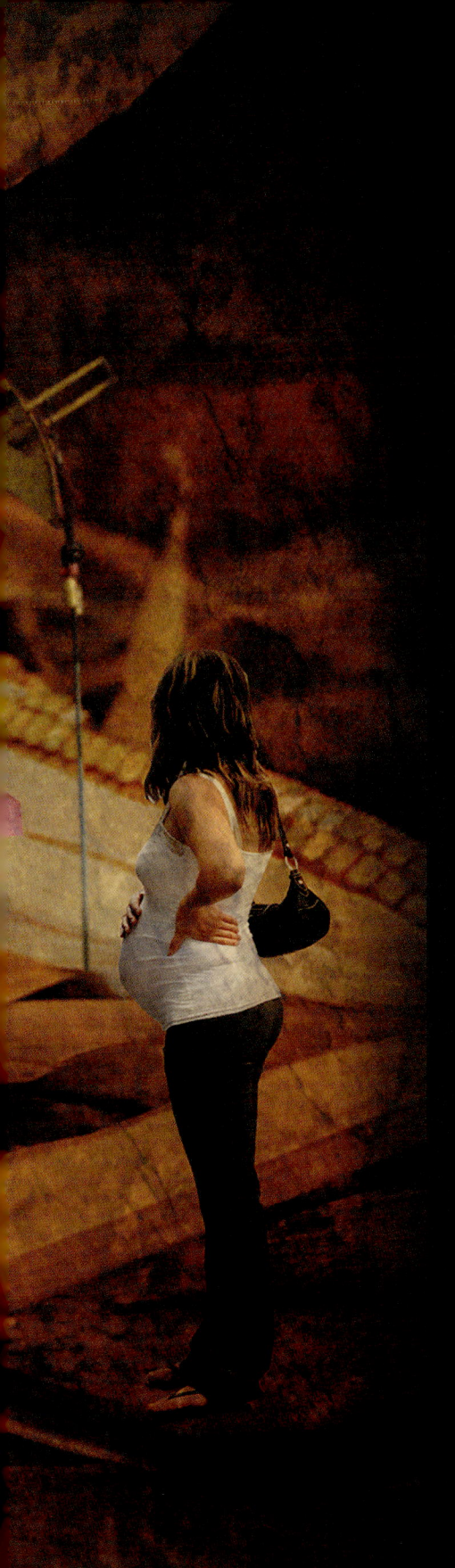

CHAPTER 29

Big and Small

How We Give Thanks

Featuring work by Paul Lewis

FIGURE 29.1 Untitled. © Paul Lewis

LEWIS' IMAGE IS BOTH big and small. Indeed, that is obvious. The plucked turkey is bigger than the oil pump. So what? We could leave it there because that is obvious, right?

What Are We Looking at?

He uses things we understand in America, Thanksgiving and oil. In the case of somewhere unfamiliar with the concept of Thanksgiving, it would be a duck or chicken and oil. So we get in trouble already, a big chicken . . . a coward. You a chicken? "Cluck, cluck, cluck," we recognize that taunt in quite a broad context through the global dominance of US media.

To irritate us a little more, it could be speculated, Lewis is indeed transposing us there. Oil prices, leases, and futures are suddenly conflated with the idolized and idealized holiday when the Pilgrims and Native Americans were breaking bread and, supposedly turkeys. That story has differing versions, too. In any case, the turkey's visual dominance anchors the image somewhere in that collision. A mighty cloud with talons for lightning that seems more of a threat to itself, as in a Hindenburg disaster in the making.

Let's see what else is going on as you may be expecting at this point some lecture about sustainability, planetary resources, food inequality or, even more aggravatingly, animal rights, presidential pardons, and the need for safe energy. In some of the images we have discussed, we have already touched on this collective consciousness/awareness discourse and therefore we might consider this territory already covered.

Territory, covered—let's go all out. The continental colonization is old news, the pregnant woman redundant, the gay parade overkill, and the hippy parent in camo pants with the intercultural adopted child par for the course. So what are we looking at, really?

How Can the Image Be Interpreted?

We know a turkey is smaller than an oil well. We know that genetically modified corn, organic corn, or any corn is smaller than people and oil wells, and that people will eat what they can afford and use the energy that will transport them to the job that will put that food on their table for which they will often give thanks. Not to speak of a rare holiday, albeit one that enjoys some notoriety about being more prominently dysfunctional than other ones.

This image apparently insists on addressing the enormity of the insignificant and the treasure to be found in kindness. It conveys the power of humanity's melody against the seduction of the pain of demagoguery.

It equally pits political correctness and political greed against the need to put food on the table. It also covers the pragmatic, even painful choices against idealism and dogma. It reminds us that our own children, family, and friends will trump everything when push comes to shove. What an impossible choice to make. What may be rational, even right and just, usually goes straight out of the window when pitted against loved ones, family, or just, love.

Love is the only currency with no stock market fluctuation. Love is vaunted as the most powerful force in the universe. Love is the experience that puts people voluntarily in their graves and dooms empires. Love is the thing that slips faster through your hands than water if you try to possess it. Love will visit ugliness and pain in measures that are incomprehensible when it is denied. Love is only pure when it is selfless.

This gets confused with loving to discover a new well. This confuses falling in love with someone, only to suppress and control what caused the fall. It confuses love that is jealous, love of possessions, power, and wealth.

I suspect that Lewis did not set out to make an image about love when he set his disproportionate and contradictory components in his collages on a collision course. Yet, this dispassionate exploration of the elements brews a most passionate concoction of the elements. This hopeless recognition that we are not yet ready to figure out how we can exist without pain for others and in so doing make our own future less likely every day. In that way, to me, he speaks about love and how, more often than not, in the end, it will tear us apart. We have not yet learned how to truly live and Lewis observes this phenomenon with about as much passion as a metronome.

Conclusion

Sometimes the greatest emotions can be found in the simple accounting of facts. This leaves plenty of space to contemplate them. The solution will be different for each, as always, and when we recognize that we belong and are interdependent on each other and everything else, we may gain an understanding of how food belongs to everyone and love for a commodity-based economy can't have a real future.

Lewis' secret seems to lie in that he protests too little as opposed to too much. He mires us in sociopolitical mud until we find no terra firma to anchor one of our boots. Unlike his namesake of a hundred years ago, we are firmly left on our own to find our way back out of this rabbit hole.

Assignments You May Want to Challenge Yourself With

- (Dysfunctional) holidays
- Scale
- Love
- Animal rights

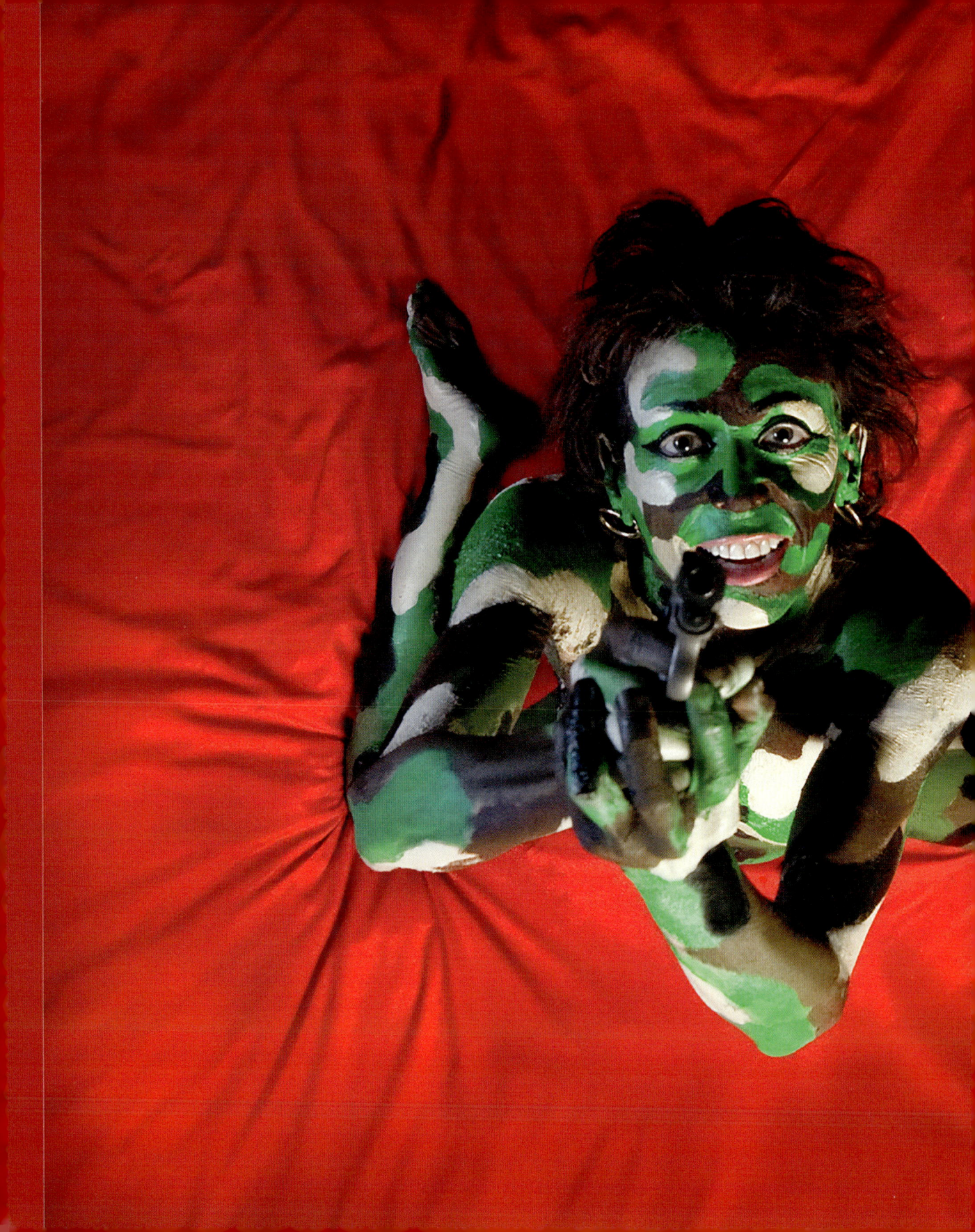

CHAPTER 30

Ammo and a Happy Meal
Be Theatrical

Featuring work by Sherry Selavy

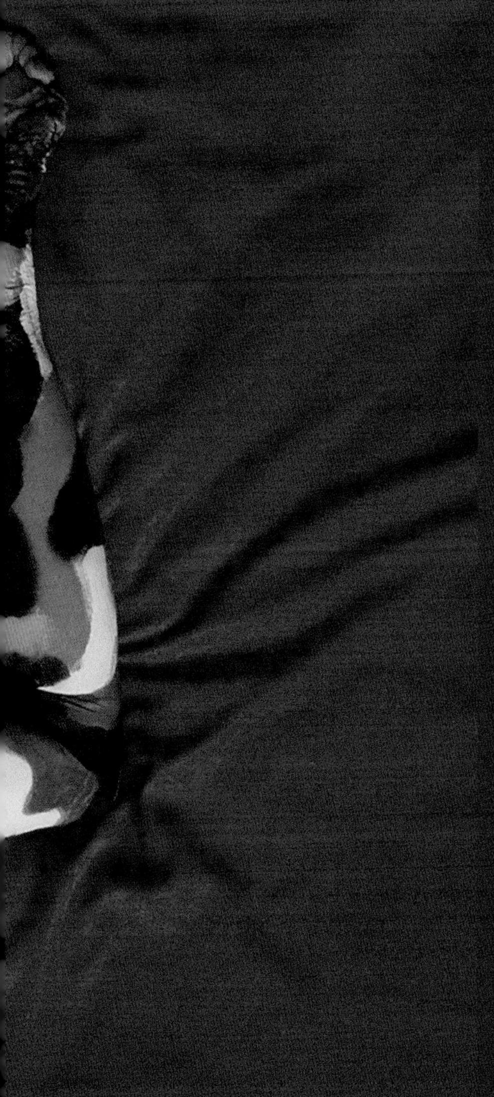

FIGURE 30.1 Untitled. © Sherry Selavy

LIKE MANY ARTISTS Selavy often uses herself as the model for her images. You may be familiar with Cindy Sherman's work that parodied stereotyping and fame, which in turn made her quite famous herself.

The legacy of self-reflection—figuratively and, when used in photography, literally—has enjoyed a long history more often than not categorized as a self-portrait. Often the inquiry is deeply personal and sometimes the self is the most convenient stand-in for pursuing matters seemingly outside of the self. Since I believe that art is personal by definition, this has certainly not stood in the way of artists taking on any theme; and, as in all cases, the most effective works become transcendent, with the additional element of gravitational pull generating its own power.

In Selavy's first image under consideration here, this venerated gravity in art is quite literally employed and possibly ridiculed by suspending the audience above the subject in a way that might not feel entirely agreeable (Figure 30.1).

What Are We Looking at?

The "Say cheese" grin directed at the lens feels as contrived as that of a frog's—when contemplating a juicy fly. While, ordinarily, this might lead to a discussion about a deficit in an image because of the over-evident awareness between the subject and the photographer, this becomes overwhelmingly predatory in this case. No small feat, since the audience is looking down on a naked woman on a gaudy red spread. How would this image read if it consisted of just those elements and visual structure? This matters maybe most in so far as this humiliating visualization is turned on its head. The body is de-sexualized with makeup; makeup not for beautification, but makeup for war. Then there is the matter of a gun being pointed at the audience. Selavy turns the tables between victim and predator. With any luck, most of us will never have a gun pointed at us. We know that this is not an experience we would likely forget and would mostly go to considerable lengths to avoid.

Yet here we are. Even though it's just a photograph, this still elicits a form of consternation, a feeling of being threatened. We did not choose to find ourselves in this one-sided dialogue and yet the totality of everything that is being suggested is likely linked to opinions we feel quite passionate about. For example, portrayals of women in the adult entertainment industry are suggested, as are those of women in army combat units. There is also the impudence of threatening to blow our heads off with a semiautomatic with no way for the audience to know whether the slide has been racked and a round chambered. If this situation were real, the likely fight or flight response would have to be recognized as futile in equal measure.

How Can the Image Be Interpreted?

As an audience, we are as good as checkmated. Selavy gives us all the time in the world to contemplate this; and while we may simply turn our backs on the image she has already made her point. What about those who can't? What about those who can't walk away? What about the ones for whom the circular abyss of darkness becomes the last? What about them? The victims of murder, every day, everywhere, all the time.

If you connect the outermost points of Selavy's outline and connect those with lines you can end up with the Star of David. Israel is among the few Westernized democracies that conscripts women as well as men. So we are looking at a cultural phenomenon that is increasingly a reality around the globe where women are deployed in active combat roles. This may represent one of the greatest changes occurring in breaking down gender roles around the world at the beginning of this millennium.

Selavy also looks like a frog about to pounce. So what happens if we kiss her? Will she turn into a princess?

Indeed she does (Figure 30.2).

What Are We Looking at?

Now she conflates our addiction to fast food with body type and body image. The convenience, comparable affordability, and nutritional deficits associated with regular consumption of fast food and accompanying soft drinks flood the media as do the equally unhealthy, often-unrealistically slim body images that at times come close to depicting someone suffering from the illness of consumption. Again it's already too late by the time we turn our backs on this image. The association game she plays with us here makes us think of bodies that either consume too much or consume themselves. From B.E.D., binge eating disorder to anorexia, Selavy places her Happy Meal between her thighs, unabashedly doubling down on stereotypical sexual desirability and how this consummation contradicts the consumption. She makes the point that people who predominantly eat fast food or people who starve themselves, or subsequently make themselves throw up put their health at great risk.

How Can the Image Be Interpreted?

By borrowing from what looks like a variety of exotic accoutrements associated with Far Eastern dancers, deities, and myth, this princess holds no allegiance to a sole culture and thus references many, if not all traditional diets that now compete with Happy Meals.

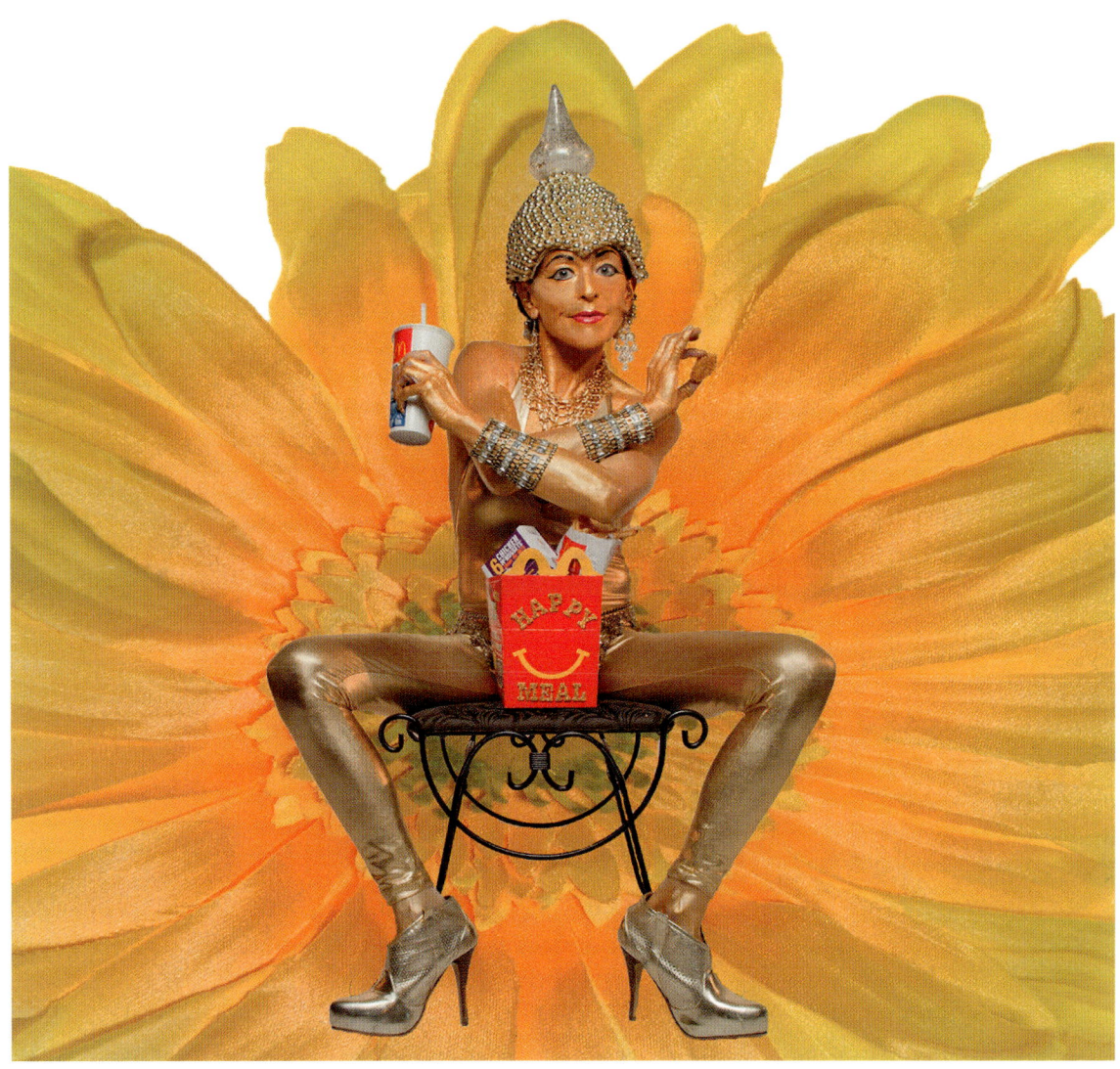

FIGURE 30.2 Untitled. © Sherry Selavy

The military camouflage has now been replaced by the gold standard of money. Whether Selavy is referencing the Golden Arches, which are of course actually yellow, or Asian deities covered in gold, seems less important than the reference to money whether out of reverence or the expanding food industrial complexes. The gold nugget in her right hand is in fact a chicken nugget, the thoroughly abused goose in this fairytale that nevertheless keeps laying the golden egg each time it's slaughtered and replaced by the next.

Obesity can kill, anorexia can kill, and the unsanitary conditions when chickens are killed to become nuggets can sometimes lead to fatal Salmonella infections.

We are again reminded of those who can't walk away. It could be argued that Selavy seamlessly asks us just when we've eaten a happy meal? A meal prepared with love for that which we consume and love for ourselves. We often seek in love what we think has been denied us most: equality, respect, safety, fun, trust, acceptance for who we are, and the recognition of all the multifaceted aspects of our being. If we learn to treat ourselves well, we may in turn expand our empathy to encompass others and, like Selavy, may even have fun making work about it.

Conclusion

In combination then, which is the more violent picture? What kills more people? Diet or bullets?

What undermines more cultures? Money or war? Not simple binary issues, I know. This is intertwined, convoluted, and complex. What is not difficult to predict is that more people with less food is not likely to lead to a good outcome.

Assignments You May Want to Challenge Yourself With

- Personal theatre
- Women in combat roles
- Fast food
- Body image
- Insinuation

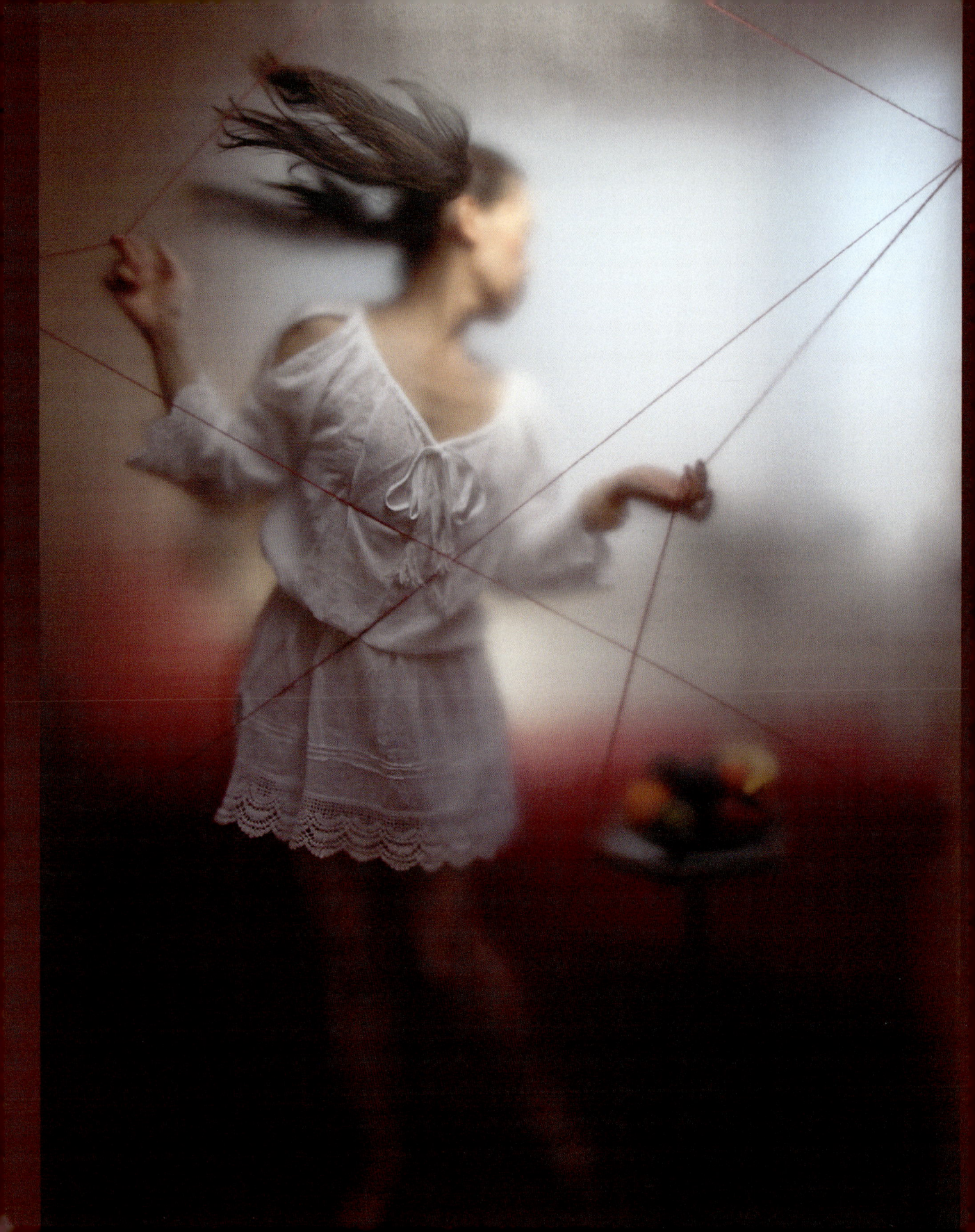

CHAPTER 31

The Spider and the Net
Catch and Caught

Featuring work by Trang Vu

FIGURE 31.1 Nom du Théâtre—Tara. © Trang Vu

A SPIDER'S NET is a pretty clear proposition. You either spin the web or you get caught in it (Figure 31.1).

For Vu, it has a different meaning, but we didn't know what that was when embarking on the reverse critique. Whether we get there by an artist's statement, researching the meaning of red string in cultural contexts, or just following our response remains the very issue this book hopes to address. If you only connect via mediation, information, explanation, do you really connect?

If not history, then mythology is kicking us straight back in the head or what we can remember of it. The Egyptian goddess Isis with strong links to female empowerment; Nike/Victoria with more links to female empowerment; and if we include male manifestations, sleep, Hypnos/Somnus; the Greek father of dreams, Morpheus; and also Hermes/Mercury, traders who in their practices may have come to the attention of the IRS, a couple of millennia later.

With or without remembering the classics, there is always Asterix with his winged helmet, who along with his friend Obelix beat up innumerable Romans as part of the parody that took most European countries, and some beyond, to task in the popular French cartoon series from the 1960s and 1970s.

What Are We Looking at?

Okay, without remembering anything at all we are still faced with a female figure whose flying hair is reminiscent of wings. Both of her hands are touching a string or wire and, if it carries a charge, electrostatic hair may be one of the immediate explanations. On closer examination though, the hair has not turned to frizz nor is it smoking, so electrical shock is ruled out. The body language is wrong too. Physically, it looks like a strong wind is blowing her hair, yet it leaves her white dress and posture unaffected. The string appears to have tension on it. It crisscrosses in and out of the frame. Where it goes beyond or how far, we will have to guess. Despite the tension that keeps the string in a straight line from the points where it is anchored there appears to be a degree of flexibility, possibly elasticity in it.

Where it is gently pulled and held, the straight trajectory is broken, not really altering its course but via another anchor point that breaks one straight line into two. A dance that teaches us geometry then? An aesthetic element that dissects the body into uneven parts? Frames within the frame, including the fruit on the table from apparently the four corners of the world. A dream, maybe? Despite the extensive and delicately embroidered dress it looks loose, as if designed for comfortable sleep rather than street clothing.

If we were able to step back, zoom out, would the construct reveal more? Might we see a web? Is she caught in it or building it? All that seems wrong. To me she appears to be listening to it. It does not appear to cause physical distress when the circuit is closed but it is like an insight that is being conveyed, roiling her head but not her body. What would happen if she closed the circuit elsewhere? Would her body act as an efficient conductor of the string to shut off part of the grid, the net. Is this the construct that we are looking at?

Is this about choice versus the preordained? Is it about Karma that we cannot change, only merely adjust?

How Can the Image Be Interpreted?

Investigating an image can be a bit like detective work. Even though we aren't looking at a crime scene, unless faced with law enforcement imagery, surveillance, forensic, or archived evidence, we may want to eliminate what we can easily understand and focus on that which we don't yet know. This keeps us trapped in the image until the whole thing makes sense. As we know, this investigation is different for everyone. For many the joy of the image may lie exactly in the fact that it does not answer back easily and the unresolved questions become the very essence of enjoyment for them. For others it may be the invisible wind taking the subject on an inner journey. The apparent haze through which we encounter what we see may be the entry point that resonates; for others, it will be the fruit, or the dress, or the dance, or plenty of other elements we have left unaddressed.

For me it is the red string.

We know it has some flex in it. Enough tensile strength to be stretched into a straight line and that it is red. A red line, we've already said this but maybe we missed what it might mean the first time around: the red line. Most subway systems have them. So does everything with a heart. The heart, our central station, pumps blood along our arteries and the veins. However, no train track or blood vessel travels in a straight line for long. Even abstracted subway maps have curves in them. So what line is red and connects in straight increments? Yes, that most intimate of things, our history, genetically and culturally; our bloodline.

Now the haze and hair make perfect sense too. So much is murky for most in relation to their ancestry. Even if genealogical records span centuries, eventually the dust of time will cover the line and make the trail go cold.

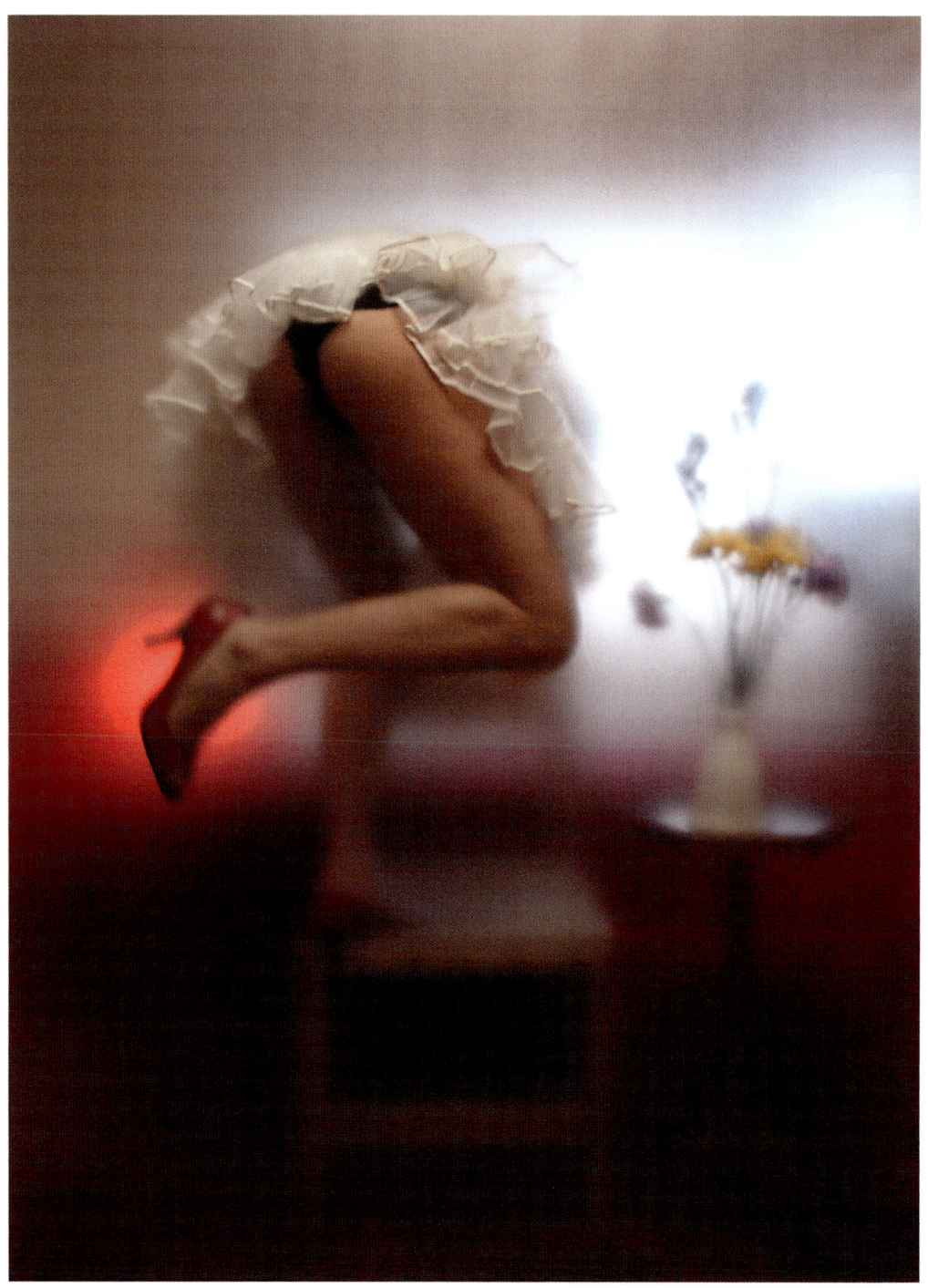

FIGURE 31.2 Nom du Théâtre—Lucy. © Trang Vu

My bloodline, your bloodline. It might have been separate for millennia, but somewhere under that pile of dust, even time can't deny that it will eventually cross, along with that of the rest of humanity—and going much further back, everything that emerged from earth's elements in the primordial sea.

Vu, among other things, is reminding us that our family dynamics and identities play out over generations. This is possibly not entirely understandable from the perspective of one lifetime alone, that the single link our lives represent connect to other links and, eventually, to everything in the end. Maybe some of Vu's ancestors were Boat People. Maybe she is touching the string where the choppy sea blows wind into that chapter of her red string. I suppose we all have a red string. We are born with it.

Whatever image one might expect to follow in the series, it probably wouldn't be this one. Nevertheless, there are visually consistent threads; the red string has been replaced with red stilettos; the white nightdress with a white tutu, albeit one that doesn't leave much to the imagination, at least from this vantage point. So what we are looking at now and why?

What Are We Looking at?

The haze remains, the fruit is replaced with flowers. The subject is dissolving into white space. What is front and center is arguably the reproductive area of her body with the red shoes. This grown-up version of Dorothy is most definitely not in Kansas anymore. Nor does it look like she clicked her heels to disappear in a vortex of wind as before but instead the white light. An experience frequently described during near-death experiences. In that regard the image does tie in with its predecessor. We are reminded of where life starts and what we possibly see when it ends. While the previous image was dominated with linearity this one deals with circularity. We see images like this of women's bodies in the context of beaches and even in beach volleyball. So why would this image be seen as sexualized objectification as some students thought of it?

After all, it looks like the woman is escaping. She uses a chair to do so, but in this image it reads like a ladder. How many women still experience sexual harassment in the workplace? How many women who have succeeded in climbing ladders have their accomplishments dismissed as having slept their way to the top? And even if that were true, why would that be an indictment of the women instead of the man or men? It would be the men abusing their power.

How Can the Image Be Interpreted?

As in the previous chapter these images could be loosely categorized as self-portraits or performance art. The artist has total control over her body and how it is portrayed. Who is anyone to say how women or anyone should portray her or himself? These images are carefully constructed and conceived, leaving little doubt that the maker was fully aware of the likely criticism that might be leveled at her.

So why did she do it? We can't be sure but we can speculate. The most obvious answer may not be found in images but in words. Racial slurs have been adopted by those at whom they have been directed for centuries. Why? To redefine ownership and whom such words empower. Is it really a surprise then that women may do the same? That they take of their bodies the very thing that has either been objectified and for which they have simultaneously been shamed for millennia. And here I am made to eat my own words again. Sometimes context is highly relevant. We live in a time when something can be said and shown that literally assumes opposite meaning, entirely defined by context.

Regardless of how close we can get on our own and how much we can be helped along by the artist, hopefully this will lead to an evolution in linguistic and visual perception where meaning gets recontextualized in such a way that eventually, even if the roots are not forgotten, we can't take anything for granted and have to listen and look in more nuanced ways. And right there all of us may grow up a little more and have an opportunity to escape what we claim as culturally unassailable or hardwired by nature.

Conclusion

We have done it many times in our evolution. We must be careful then that we don't prevent the exploited or displaced from redefining themselves on their own terms in order to avoid our own sense of guilt or discomfort. For as long as we believe in freedom of speech and, therefore, even make the sacrifice of tolerating hate speech, we must be very mindful that we keep perspective, that outrage remains proportional to what we see or hear. If not, we run the risk, with the best of intentions, to turn political and cultural correctness not into a tool for genuinely changing verbal and visual rhetoric into something more aware and respectful, but rather into just another tool for shaming, condemning, and dismissing. In that way Vu may simply warn us about what it is exactly that we pass on in our bloodlines, that which is so much more than DNA.

Assignments You May Want to Challenge Yourself With

- Genealogy
- Cultural clashes
- Female gaze

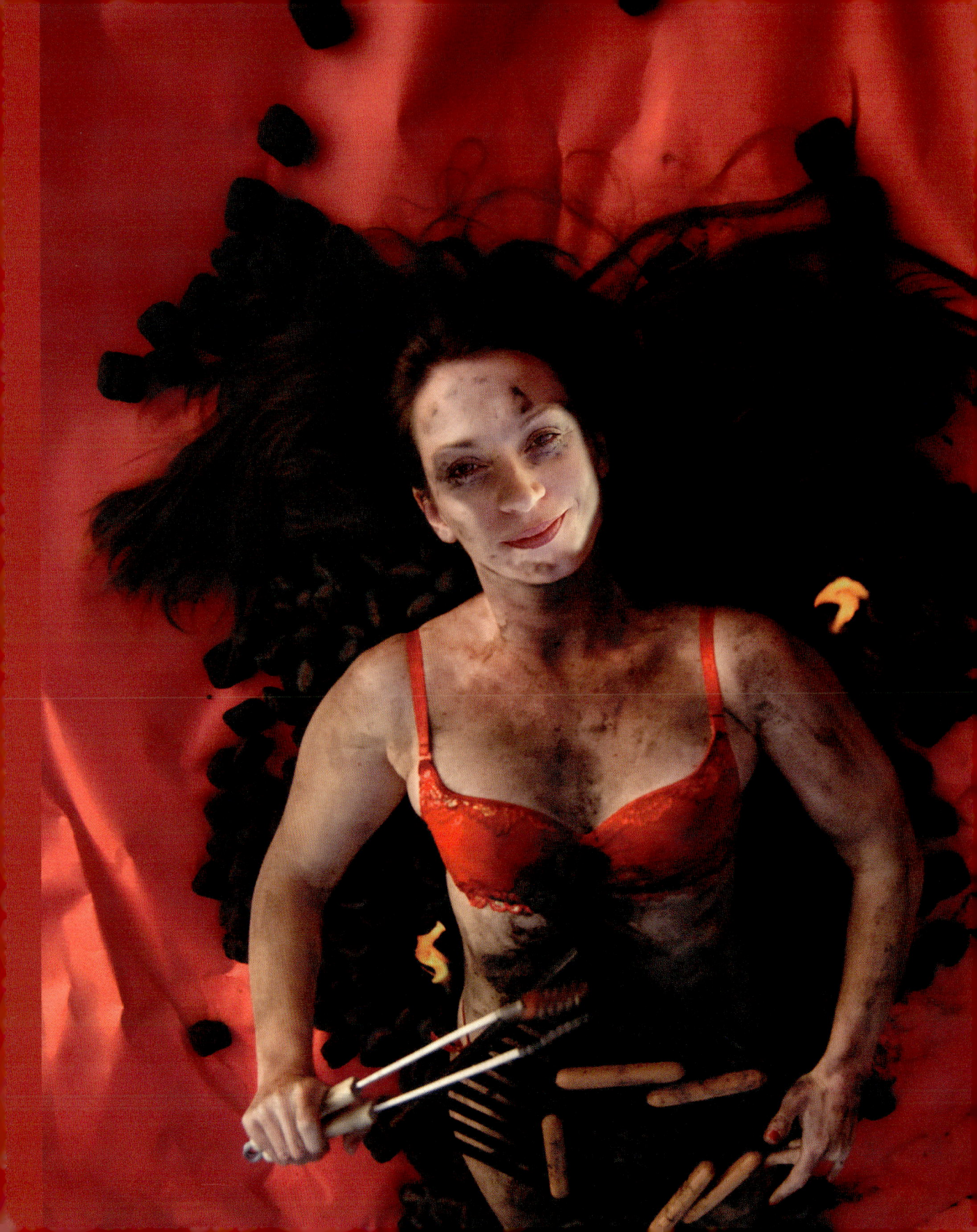

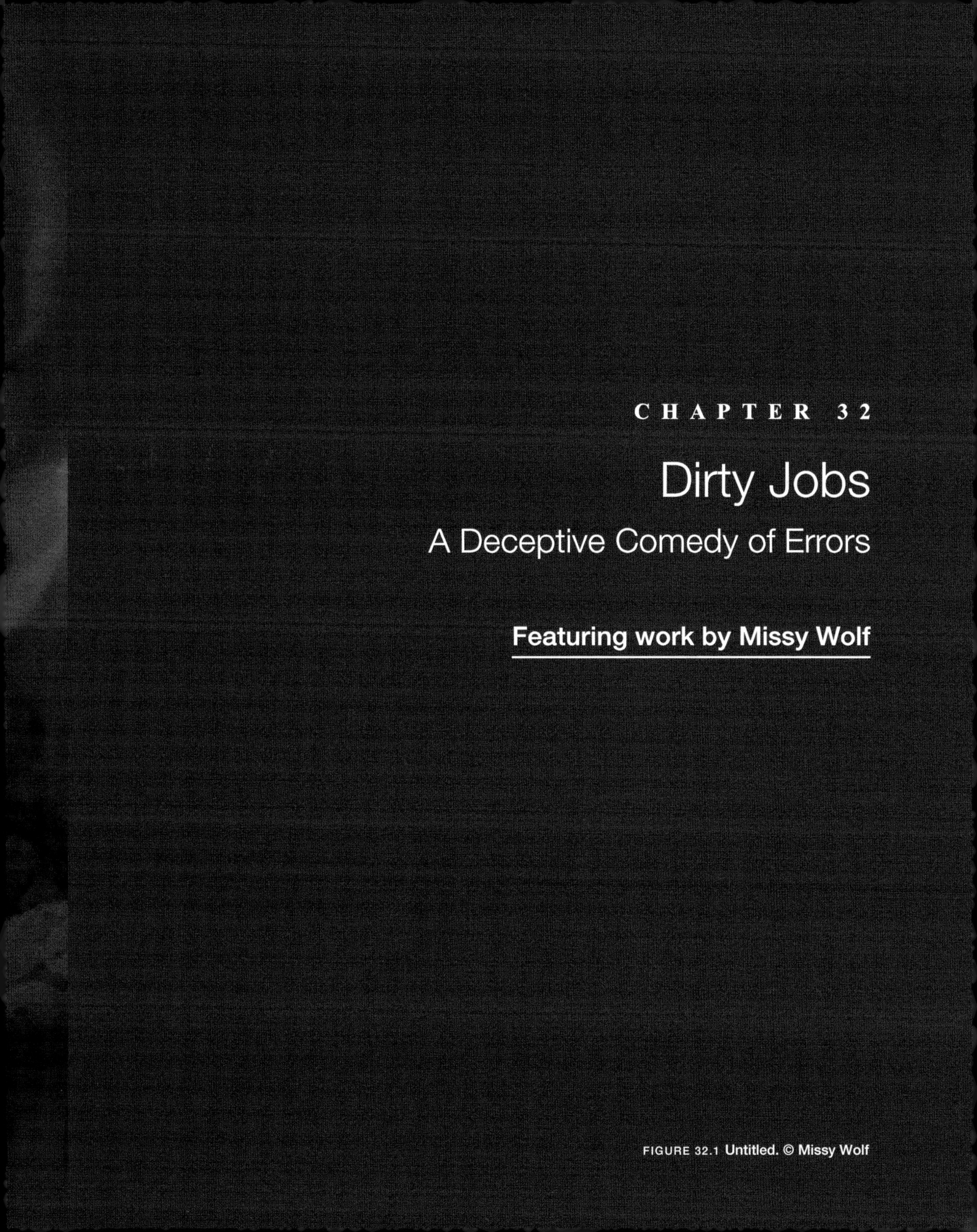

CHAPTER 32

Dirty Jobs
A Deceptive Comedy of Errors

Featuring work by Missy Wolf

FIGURE 32.1 Untitled. © Missy Wolf

THE ALL-AMERICAN backyard barbeque is often portrayed as a quintessentially male pursuit. This may be linked to several factors. First and foremost the indoor kitchen is relatively safe. Whatever is going to catch on fire, set off every last one of the smoke detectors in the house, and turn the floor into a permanent grease pit is safely occurring outside.

Of course the lid to the barbeque may have to be retrieved from a neighbor's yard, lawn turf replaced in large sections, and a home delivery takeout on standby if the meal ends up utterly cremated. All this is more fun than it sounds. The chef is likely to be somewhat hammered by the several beers that traditionally accompany such culinary endeavors and then there are all the toys; heaps of charcoal that can be set aflame with lighter fluid; pressurized propane tanks made to hiss before what is basically liquid napalm takes its toll on the food. In that sense this could be considered to be another American spectator sport.

All of this is performed with great bravado, and the women who are mostly far more experienced and better cooks, bear witness to these debacles with the indulgence one might show a toddler who is teething on the tail of the good-natured family dog. There is always hope. If nobody ends up in the hospital, and we're not talking trivialities like food poisoning, everyone generally considers such cookouts a success, particularly if their gums aren't subsequently bleeding and any previous dental work is still in place.

Wolf's parody admirably lays waste to such institutionalized machismo with devastating effect (Figure 32.1).

By glamourizing a woman who seemingly and, alarmingly, suffers from the same delightful dysfunctionality as many of her traditionally male counterparts when it comes to outdoor cooking, Wolf takes her discourse in an entirely different direction.

What Are We Looking at?

Not only is the charcoal on the ground, the woman is lying on top of it with no distress and it appears to be partially burning. Given that the whole image is staged on crumpled photographic backdrop paper, we are not meant to see this as anything other than a staged setup. It is not meant to be real. So how can we say that Wolf is satirizing a macho activity when in fact she depicts a woman in the context of a barbeque debacle, as opposed to a man?

We haven't yet covered the oversized utensils that are part of the grilling ritual. Forks that might satisfy Poseidon, spatulas the size of small frying pans, and tongs that could be used as forceps to deliver a baby, they are the intermediaries between the hands and the flame.

In Wolf's work the only tools in use are the forceps and they are separating something other than a baby from the womb. The mischievous grin on the model's face in her festive brassiere does not divert us from the fact that she is going to work on the hot dogs. The concentration of them in the vicinity of her own womb and the vice grip on one caught in the serrated tongs suggests frivolous emasculation.

How Can the Image Be Interpreted?

Hot dogs all look the same. Is Wolf implying that men are all the same? Incompetent cooks and self-absorbed lovers? Maybe. Is she asking in this comedy: what if the roles were reversed? Do you really want a sweaty, barbeque-briquette covered, beer-soaked significant other near you? And then a darkness descends that is so terrible and unforgivable that we are reminded that comedy has always been used to speak truth to power, from court jesters to their contemporary equivalents, Jon Stewart, Steven Colbert, and Bill Maher, among others. All is funny until it is not. This is not the velvet hammer we started off with. This is the sledgehammer that only comedy delivers. The least anticipated force hits us before we know it. It might as well be a bullet, because it will have pierced us before we hear the shot. If we survive, we may not even feel the pain at first. Our systems go into shock to protect us, and shocked we should be indeed.

The reverse of Wolf's parody is not the sexy woman who seems to mirror male ineptitude. She is the woman who asks instead, what if this image were reversed in another way. A woman covered in symbols of female genitalia. According to the World Health Organization, WHO, over two hundred million women worldwide, most of whom were minors at the time, have been violated by the practice of female genital mutilation.

This odious practice that mostly women are forced to perform on other women for reasons that are "cultural," and the lifelong physical and psychological conditions this causes are well documented by WHO and UNICEF. I will spare you the details, but encourage you to research this scourge yourself when you feel up to it.

Conclusion

Wolf's photography reminds us again, painfully, that substantive work is often not what it first appears to be. Wolf made this image before she decided to become a nurse and, as part of her career as a humanitarian aid worker, now travels to countries where this practice is common. I am not suggesting that she consciously thought of the link between what she photographed then and what she is doing now. I am however humbly reminded that if we let our own work speak back to us, in relation to the intended and that which was not, we don't just become better artists and communicators. We can help bring awareness and subsequent change to the world. Don't underestimate the value of humor or frivolity. Sometimes we need to be our own jesters to get to an unspeakable truth, the subtext of our own and other's work. If we engage this process it will lead us to where we are meant to be, whether as artists, otherwise, or both.

Assignments You May Want to Challenge Yourself With

- Humor as a lure
- Engaging Human Rights via the familiar
- F.G.M.
- Social justice

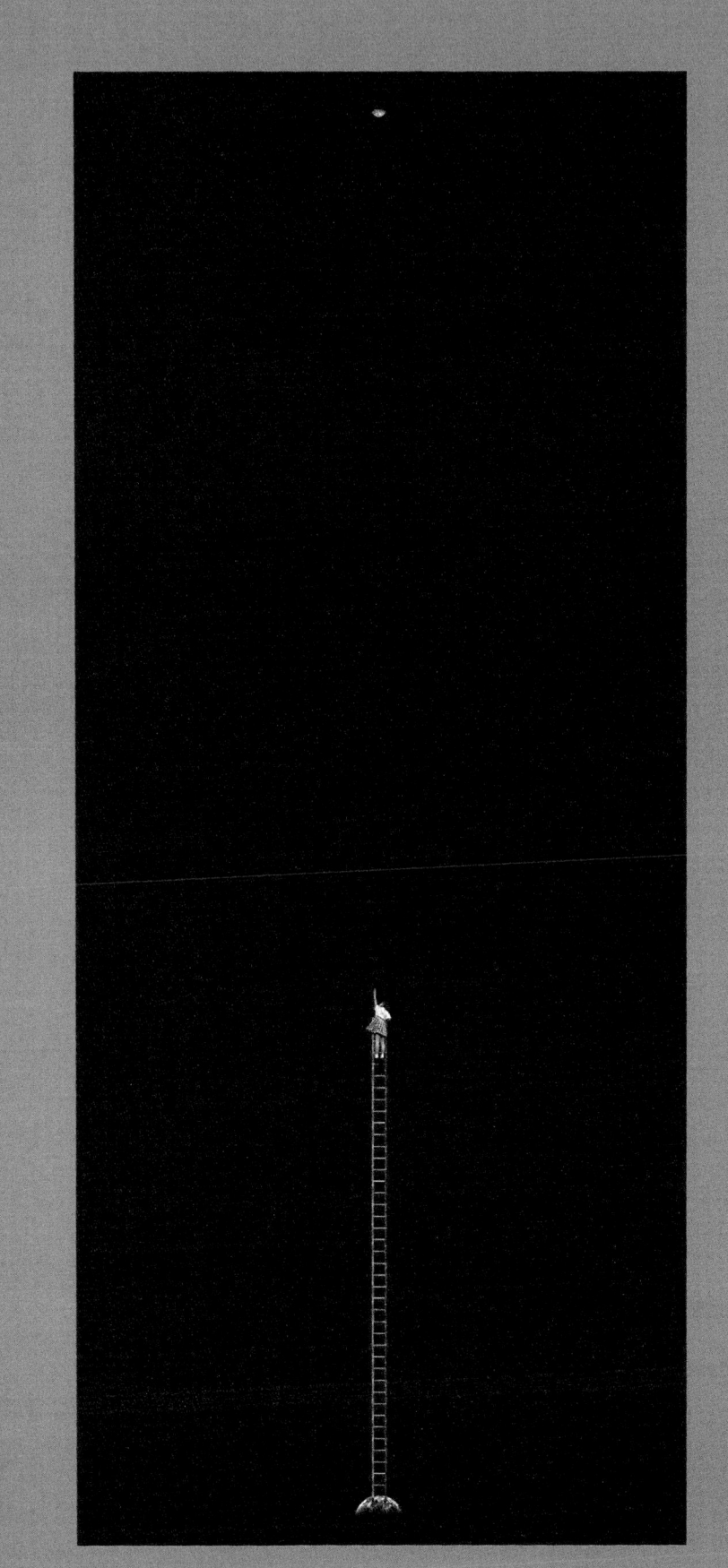

CHAPTER 33

What is to Come
Dreaming

Featuring work by Jon Lewis

FIGURE 33.1 Untitled. © Jon Lewis

From Jules Verne, Gene Roddenberry, to George Lucas we have learned to dream of escaping our earthly boundaries and explore new worlds. Why? We have that other yearning, *Fernweh*, as mentioned earlier. We are explorers and pioneers as much as we are homebodies. Given the chance, I suspect few of us would refuse a seat on a spacecraft to see, experience, and learn more beyond the confines of our troubled planet. In fact, to maintain the numbers in which we exist, we have little chance of so doing unless we colonize other flying rocks. It is a simple enough equation between resources in all their forms and human replication within a limited space. I am reminded of the books by Ben Elton, *Stark* and Mary Doria Russell's, *The Sparrow*. I read them a while ago but the melodies of both still linger.

What Are We Looking at?

Lewis' ladder is firmly planted on our small planet, or is it another apple? That would really take the cake. In terms of scientific fact, it is utterly disproportionate and incorrect. We are taught that science is a matter of provable, repeatable, and demonstrable phenomena. Sir Isaac Newton's apple falls to the ground and presto; there is endlessly repeatable proof of the invisible force of gravity and applesauce.

On a side note, why is it always an apple?! How come the tree of knowledge is no longer the forbidden fruit? This is quite a legitimate question. If we look at all the forbidden foods in many religions, how come Christians eat them by the ton? Why is eating them not taboo in Christianity? Was Eve, the first woman, in fact also our first scientist? Is this the root of the uneasy relationship between religion and science? Are we meant to reconcile it? Yes, I digress, but digression is undervalued as a gateway to discovering new paths to follow. Still, I'll leave it up to you whether you want to follow it further or not.

For all we know, the girl took an apple with her as a snack, though with or without sustenance she has reached the end of her escape. She can climb no further, reaching out as she might. And she is only reaching for the moon, not another solar system or even galaxy. She is not greedy in that sense, but merely looking for the next empty place. Those using public transport do this every workday, trying to find an empty seat. Instead, she has built her own infrastructure to get from A to B, the ladder. Admittedly, this leaves the planet short of a few trees, and yes, if they were apple trees with a degree of irony.

How Can the Image Be Interpreted?

The ladder has thirty-eight rungs and a lot comes up on Google in relation to that number. What I found interesting was on the site affinitynumerology.com: "the essence of the number 38 is a composite containing the ideas of:

- coexistence
- relationships
- creative self-expression
- efficiency
- diplomacy
- optimism."

Since 38 is made up of 3 and 8, the site offers the following equation:

3 + 8 = 11

1 + 1 = 2

"the numerology number 2 represents a composition containing the ideas of:

- relationships
- teamwork
- companionship
- coexistence
- diplomacy."

Like astrology, numerology is not considered to be a hard science. And yet, astrology, numerology, the I Ching (no, not invented by Apple), tarot cards, palm reading, and other systems to create meaning in the chaos we so often can't fathom, have held sway over people in ways that are at times similar to religion. Whether in the stars or in a stack of cards, we keep searching for answers about the future and the past.

Maybe that is why Lewis' image of the girl contains a degree of ambiguity. She looks like a schoolgirl eager to find the answer to a question. Is she in fact bringing knowledge instead of seeking it? Does she have an answer or a question?

Another great science fiction movie, *Contact*, proposed that Nazi Germany's high-frequency broadcast of the 1936 Olympics might have broken through the atmosphere, subsequently sending Hitler's opening speech through space at the speed of light. Though, with any luck, this original hypothesis by astrophysicist Carl Sagan did hopefully not occur. Was Lewis thinking about this when he conceived of this image and is the girl simply performing the Hitler salute as a stark reminder of how atrociously we may have introduced ourselves to the universe?

Somehow I think not. In her reach, to the point where her skirt is hiking up in a way that might make her vulnerable to unwanted attention, she seems to know that she is quite alone. Like Amelia Earhart, she is out there with the tools and wit that she's been given and that's it.

I am reminded of dismissive sayings when someone attempts the seemingly impossible: "Those who reach too high just fall harder" and "S/he is reaching for the stars" as if the absurdity of the attempt needs no further explanation. It is understood to be futile, self-indulgent, stupid, and to demonstrate a host of other deplorable delusions.

Yet, there she stands. Unwavering, determined beyond reason, reaching or greeting, we know not. She uses her left hand in the gesture, is she left-handed? She holds on to the ladder with her right hand, is she right-handed? Is she ambidextrous? Even if we knew, would it help further our understanding?

The words that overlap between the numeral 38 and 2 are:

- coexistence
- relationships
- diplomacy.

Coexistence is a prerequisite for any of us to come into being. Relationships are the ships of relation/relating. Is she exploring disconnect and connectedness? Does our nature require the dualistic experience of both to understand either? Is diplomacy the tool to avoid one and to further the other?

You might wonder why I keep coming back to the incidental, the number of the rungs. In a critique none of us would be able to look up the meaning of 38 and there is plenty to say without any further interpretation of this aspect in the image. Though even in a critique you can count the rungs. You can state that there are 38 of them. You can articulate that 38 is not a prime number but only divisible once, by 2, which equals 19, which is a prime number. In that way the number represents two singularities that together create a plurality. Looking at the numbers visually the number 3 essentially looks like the number 8 split down the middle. A half and a whole. If you are willing to give the visual some latitude the closest resembling letters are a B and an inverted E. BE, "be" (exist) "to be or not to be," we might as well throw in Shakespeare, everyone else does too.

The point is, we can react on the spot and sometimes the incidental is a great key. The thing we pay least attention to is likely to be the least conscious decision, even for the maker. Whatever conscious or unconscious decision prompted Lewis to create 38 rungs is now part of the image. In (19)38 the Nazis destroyed hundreds of synagogues and thousands of Jewish businesses during *Kristallnacht*. What led us to Hitler by studying the girl's gesture in space now leads us back by the ladder.

Conclusion

Possibly, what Lewis suggests to us at the deepest level is that isolation is not the answer but togetherness is, but only if we exclude no one. If we fail to do that, a sense of togetherness defined by what we exclude becomes the opposite, potentially something as hateful as what the Nazis espoused.

So let us hope the girl wakes up from her dream. Let us hope that her dream was beautiful, empowering, and that it spurred her imagination and hopes into a future that is worth dreaming of and working for, together.

> **Assignments You May Want to Challenge Yourself With**
>
> - Dreaming (day or night)
> - Gravity
> - Apples
> - Fascism
> - Alphanumeric symbolism

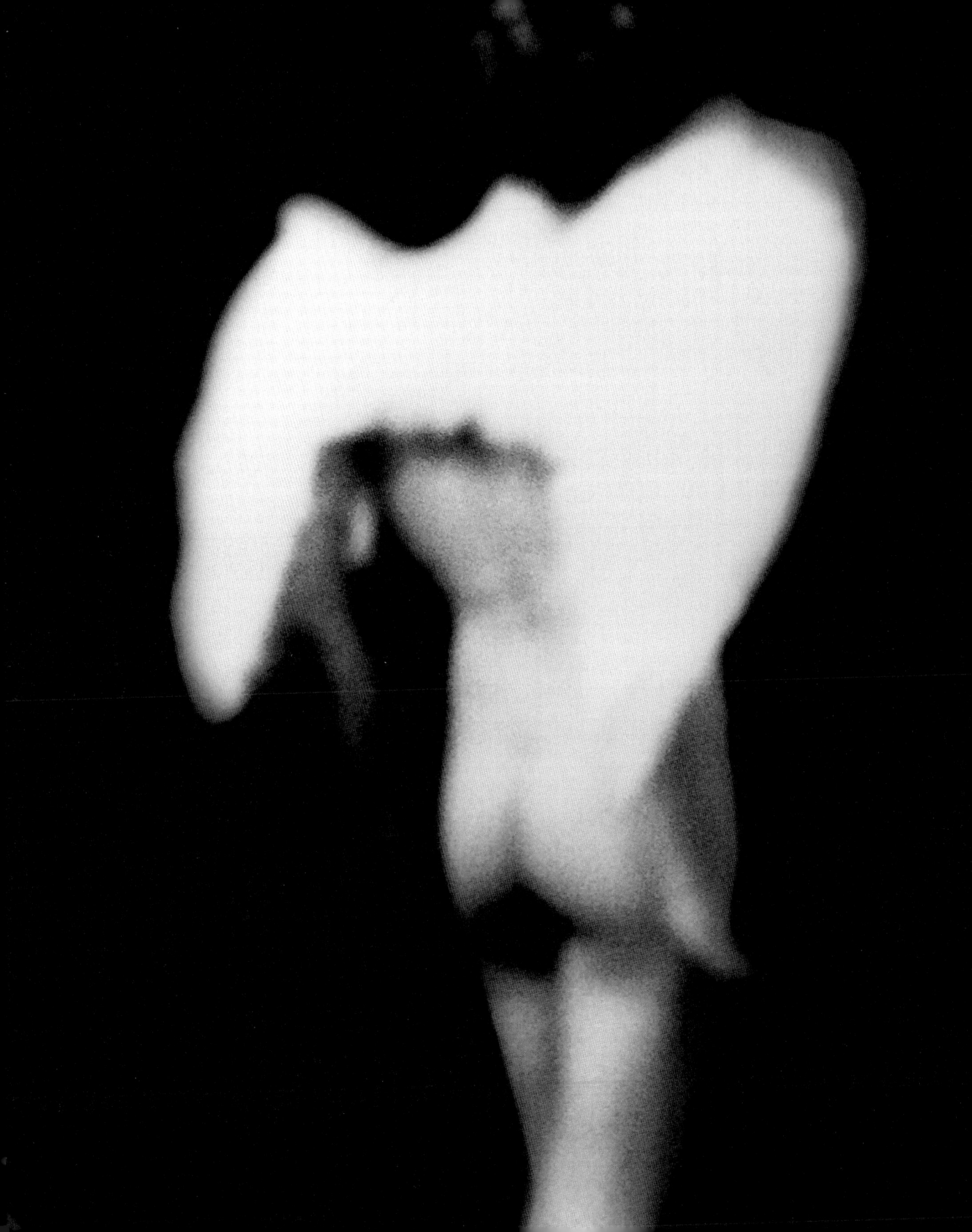

CHAPTER 34

The Angel and the Wasp
The Order of the Elements

Featuring work by Jennifer Edwards

FIGURE 34.1 One. © Jennifer Edwards

WHILE WE HAVE TOUCHED on the composition of the elements, what is included in the ingredients, even how they might be stirred, we have not really explored the order in which the ingredients are added.

In pictorial language, this is simply the order in which images are presented: the sequence, the beginning, the middle, and the end, if we are inclined to look at them linearly.

This can consist of a portfolio, usually twelve to twenty-four images; the current measure of proof of a sustained inquiry, the visual essay for lack of a better word, something that tells the story. Storytelling, as we think of it in "picture books."

This is important, because a sustained inquiry and the subsequent ordering of the sequence is the stuff of monographs, exhibitions, magazine publications, and the somewhat elusive idea of rigor. Since we are living in the paradigm of this perception, it merits attention.

I thank Edwards for sending me a number of images to play with. She did not send them in any order, or as a sequenced sustained inquiry. Instead, I got to choose as I pleased from several bodies of work—a menu consisting of unrelated courses. This, after all, is to indulge the magic of curating. She sent me eleven images, in all, from the years she was my student.

I also want to acknowledge that since I chose to write about more than the obviously connected images she sent, she surrendered her images to this fate. I am intent to put together a narrative that will render the trove of individual images subservient to the meaning of the whole, based on something which grabbed me while clicking through the "buffet." Before we get to that, let me also mention that the stylistic consistency made wandering between distinct bodies of work so inviting.

This is the second level of subtext. If you remember the prologue, now we are playing chess on a three-dimensional, instead of a two-dimensional, board.

What Are We Looking at?

We already know how far the subtext of one or several closely related images can lead, and arguably each of Edwards' images deserves this individual attention. I trust, that at this point in the book, you can determine if and how you connect with them individually.

I now want us to take the additional step of putting them together as a sequence. As such, we will consider them not once, but reordered four times to examine the varied experiences and responses this can yield.

For argument's sake, let's call her untitled images One, Two, and Three. Version 1 is the order that immediately worked for me most deeply (Figures 34.1, 34.2 and 34.3).

How Can the Image Be Interpreted, Version 1?

Image order One, Two, and Three: the angel, the insect, and the thousand-mile stare.

The ethereal nature of the angel photograph, with its lack of focus stands visually apart from the in-focus images in a substantive way. Why? Because the winged beings are next to each other and the difference in visual treatment between them and the third image is pronounced. The angel and the wasp are immediate neighbors, not separated by the stare but instead punctuated by it.

This opens up a direct discourse between the angel and the wasp—or, between religion and nature. We have already visited this theme. But it did not so obviously lead to an acronym. Wasp plus a sprinkle of angelic dust inevitably leads us to WASP, White Anglo-Saxon Protestant. Image number Three may well ask the question, "Am I that?"

Okay, so what happens when we change the order?

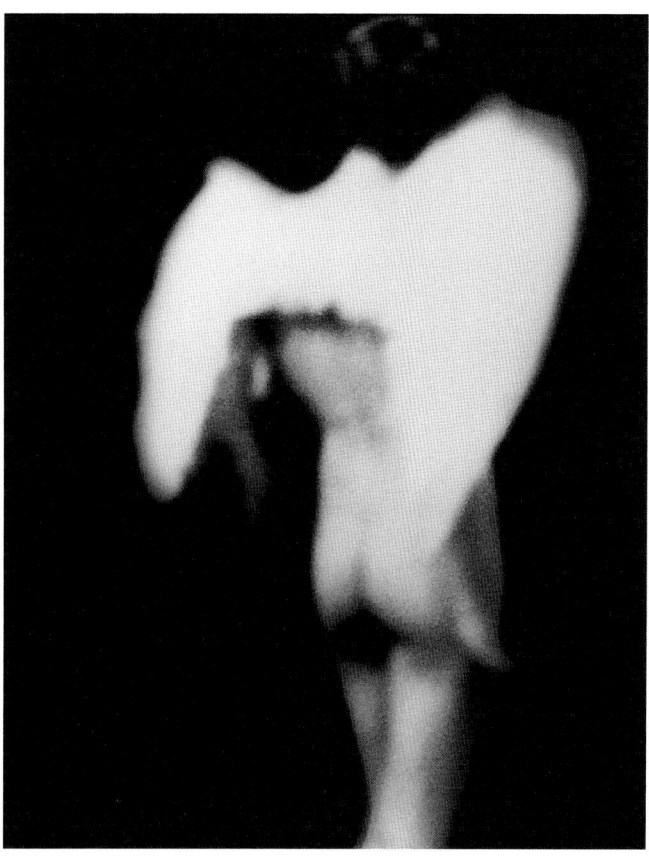

FIGURE 34.1 One. © Jennifer Edwards

How Can the Image Be Interpreted, Version 2?

Image order Two, One, and Three: the insect, the angel, and the thousand-mile stare.

The angelic quality in the wasp: this can be considered as such because the angel is trapped by the two in-focus images, immediately following the wasp. Now we are back to empathy—the dying insect. We may be reminded of the Jains, who brush the ground so as to not crush another living being, the Indian sect that sweeps a path of non-destruction. At their end, they offer themselves in a sky burial to carrion eating birds. So closes the circle of sustenance among those that lived and those that are still living.

The thousand-mile stare now is a meditation on the worth of a life, any life. The insignificant insect and icon of another religion are suddenly conflated into an unseen bird. A raptor, a relative of something so much more ancient than us, it is a dinosaur that will take the meat from a corpse. An arguable salute to the meteor that wiped them out and which we are not likely in need of, for we are doing this job for ourselves. I don't know enough about the Jain religion and assume that if I did, there would be some Jain humor in that.

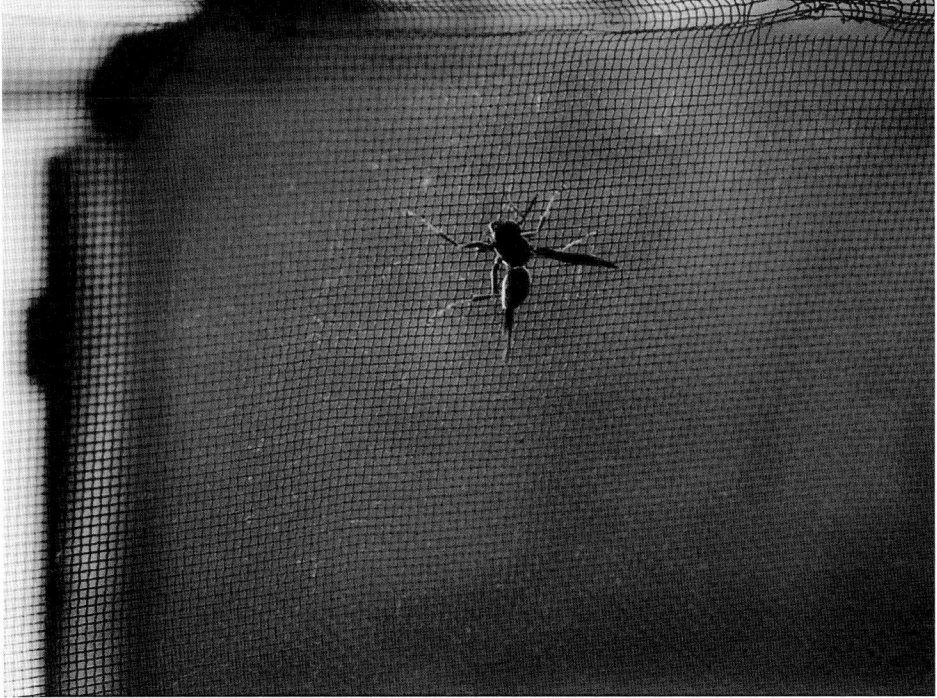

FIGURE 34.2
Two.
© Jennifer Edwards

How Can the Image Be Interpreted, Version 3?

Image order Three, One, and Two: the thousand-mile stare, the angel, and insect.

Again, the in and out-of focus experience is divided. We start with contemplation rather than conclusion. We now realize the two are not only interchangeable but, in fact, we may have confused them from the start. Does contemplation result in conclusion or is it the other way around? Does conclusion result in contemplation?

The first seems to linearly make more sense, yet it is our conclusions and associated decisions that often lead to genuine contemplation, particularly if we determine that we have made a mistake. I don't mean Monday morning quarterbacking or all that rearview mirror stuff. Rather, what if the wasp is the angel? The inventor of the polio vaccine, Jonas Salk, has often been referenced for saying, "If all insects on Earth disappeared, within fifty years all life on Earth would end. If all human beings disappeared from the Earth, within fifty years all forms of life would flourish." Who is the angel now?

Edwards, I now suspect, threw us all a challenge. "Do what you want." What a gift and what a burden. To me it also represents artistic courage.

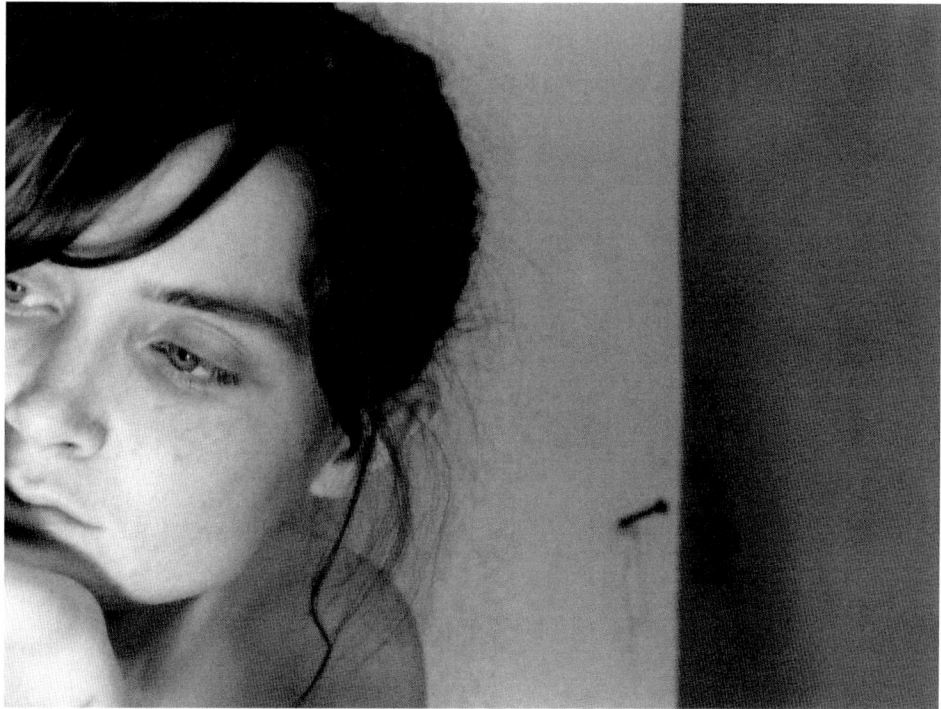

FIGURE 34.3
Three.
© Jennifer Edwards

Conclusion

This is the gift all artists share—with themselves, each other, and anyone and everyone who cares to look. As previously mentioned in "art-speak," the reciprocal relationship between the artist and her or his work, the reciprocal relationship between the artist and viewer, increases across centuries, millennia, and ever growing populations. We are again visited by time.

We must remember to play, as all animals do. This is the gift of everyone who so generously agreed to contribute to this book. Edwards added the additional element of eloquent delivery, "Do what you want." Don't forget that.

Only after writing this chapter am I struck by how long it's been since I've heard this sentiment, "Do what you want" expressed with positive intentions. When exactly did "Do what you want" become so charged with disapproval?

We have examined three out of six possible combinations.

You may want to consider: image order One, Three, and Two—the insect, the thousand-mile stare, and the angel; image order Two, Three, and One—the thousand-mile stare, the insect, and the angel.

How Can the Image Be Interpreted, Version 4?

Image order Three, Two, and One: the insect, the thousand-mile stare, and the angel.

At some point we have to acknowledge that the wasp, to most not an endearing creature, is nevertheless trapped. What if the woman is contemplating the insect, its fate? What if she has control over so little that suddenly this realization becomes important? The angel image may ultimately lead the way though last in the sequence. Something may spurn the unforgiving stair into lifting the screen and let the confused insect go free.

Assignments You May Want to Challenge Yourself With

- Do what you want
- Image sequencing, re-sequencing
- Try to discover a story instead of creating one
- Explore acronyms visually

A woman lies on her back with her feet up in the air.

A man stands on the soles of her feet above her.

A deluge of milk pours over them both.

CHAPTER 35

In the End
Censorship

Featuring work by "John Smith"

FIGURE 35.1 Redacted. © John Smith

THIS LAST CHAPTER is dedicated to "John Smith." John was an extremely gifted student and dear friend who died very tragically. Let's take a moment to acknowledge that negotiating one's artistic gifts is not always easy. John was not only extremely talented; he was empathetic, sensitive, and highly intelligent. I think these are not necessarily exceptional traits among artists, but they were extraordinarily pronounced in John. Managing such gifts can be challenging, even painful, and as a result, I start each critique seminar by showing two TED talks.

Ms. Elizabeth Gilbert's *Your Elusive Creative Genius*, and Sir Ken Robinson's *Do Schools Kill Creativity*?

I recommend both of these talks to you. They have stood the test of time, during a period where the drive and purpose of creative engagement and the value of so doing, even of the teaching of art in schools, continue to be questioned on the most fundamental level. Is it beneficial for students and society to learn and teach art? What once may have seemed like a ludicrous question in terms of supporting deep individual growth and a profound enrichment of society, the vaunted legacy of each generation and what culture leaves behind, is now the subject of increasing cuts, to the point where many schools can't offer any art education at all.

This is not only a huge loss for each person's holistic development but arguably a profound disadvantage in navigating pictorial and other creative manipulation at the dawn of what has already been termed the visual century. Visual literacy empowers through the understanding of how visual information increasingly informs and influences us; both in terms of what we are seeing and what is behind it, the subtext. It seems counterintuitive to undervalue the skills we need most, to be informed consumers of an increasing avalanche of visual information that greets us every day, everywhere we look.

It won't be possible for you to see John Smith's amazingly well-crafted and impacting work. Those holding the rights to his work did not want it to be published. To respect their wishes I have redacted both images with vague descriptions of the images. Instead of seeing them you have to imagine them. John Smith is a fictitious name and any resemblance to any real or imagined person or work is purely coincidental. Let this be a reminder to you though. Always get a model release and assign your work to someone you trust as its custodian in the event something should happen to you.

What Are We Not Looking at?

A picture of a man standing on top of a woman. This is an acrobatic balancing act against a deluge of torrential milk rain. Milk is the elemental initial nourishment each mammalian mother produces for her babies. Right here we must pause. We must at least admit that we steal this milk from the babies for whom it was meant by separating them from their mothers, causing each deep pain, and replacing the babies with suction machines that continue to stimulate cows, producing milk on an industrial scale. Milk is the lifeblood for the young to grow and survive. Yet we know how much of it gets spoiled, along with so much other food in the fridge, to the point where we are conditioned to take a quick sniff of the milk carton before trusting that we can pour ourselves a refreshing glass. Whatever the questions are that this conditioning raises and however we may choose to answer these questions, Smith makes them part of his discourse. Milk flows over the man, back to the woman, the one who can lactate (Figure 35.1).

How Can the Image Be Interpreted?

Is Smith questioning whether we do stand on the shoulders of giants (our forefathers) as the idiom goes, rather than standing on the feet of our mothers and grandmothers? It is a valid question for mothers and fathers, daughters and sons. Each female child is born with all of the eggs she'll ever have during her lifetime. When a mother is pregnant with a daughter she contains not only her own eggs but also eventually all those of her daughter, which potentially may develop into her grandchildren. Put another way, each grandchild develops not only in the womb of her or his mother but in that of his or her maternal grandmother, too. In that context does the milky deluge address our generational interconnection, genetically, psychologically, and physiologically?

The milk does not fall like rain on our protagonists. Rather, it originates from a single invisible source. They are being hosed down with it. Are we being directed back to Adam and Eve? That post-apocalyptic moment in Eden, which gave birth to humanity? Was the snake merely a long fuse line that ignited the bomb, shaped like an apple, that shattered it all and made the heavens weep?

Unlike our relatives, the apes and monkeys, we humans have lost dexterity in our feet. Most of us can barely pick up a pencil with our toes. Had we not lost our prehensile feet and even tails to pull ourselves up by the proverbial bootstrap, in all likelihood our lives would not be easier. Axioms of how we are meant to better ourselves are often foolishly impossible. If you don't believe me, get out a pair of boots, sneakers will do in a pinch, and try to pull yourself up. If you are strong, one of two things is likely to occur. You will tear your shoelaces or cut off the blood supply to your fingers, but you will still find yourself firmly planted on the ground. For those with a persistent nature the most likely outcome will be that they will eventually fall over.

What has this to do with the image we are looking at? I see rebirth. Maybe we are looking at Jesus and Mary. The impossible sacrifice expected of a mother. To see her child tortured and killed. Still she attempts to save him. Given the choice, that is what most parents would do. She is the one who is visually crucified, though bent to ninety degrees at the intersection of Immaculate Conception. The son looks down at her with determination. He is an adult and while his hands are not raised, he may be attempting to explain his sacrifice.

When this image was made, the longest war in US history had just started. How many mothers have hoped and prayed and are still hoping and praying that their sons, despite their determination to follow through with the ultimate sacrifice if necessary, will return home, whole in mind and body; that their sons' and now also daughters' fate will ultimately allow them to keep their arms by their sides? How many mothers and fathers of soldiers, of civilians, of inner-city kids dread that phone call, dread that knock on the door, that death certificate, which is the final bureaucratic insult to their unspeakable loss with its appearance barely more substantive than that of a parking ticket. Not to speak of those with no closure, with no knowledge of their child's fate, forever suspended in limbo between ever decreasing hope and ever increasing despair. Again, we see the balancing act in a deluge of tears.

Much of what has been said here has already been touched upon in previous chapters. That there is the potential for so much reiteration makes this image so powerful and appropriate for the last chapter of this book. As we have probed and explored the relational meaning in various works, the subtext appears to emerge. Buried within all subject matter that viscerally impacts us are great questions, the meaning of life, love, hate, suffering, joy, and existence itself.

It is this interrogation of the work, and by extension interrogation of ourselves, that Smith engenders and what also makes his work such a lasting legacy. The spilled milk and, by implication, the lack of rain where it is needed and the devastating flooding where it is not— impacting the planet and so many individual lives—are alluded to in the image as well. The lack of sustenance, often right from the start that we all need to sustain us. The abundance of so much that goes to waste and the simultaneous inaccessibility of it for so many, are also suggested.

Smith connects his characters by the soles of their feet. Neither their hands nor their heads. Feet intersect with the earth, and are the point of closest contact that connects every single thing to each of us who are lucky enough to have them.

Conclusion

The journey into the heart of images should be an adventure for both maker and viewer. Each time we set sail we can't know where it will lead us. Like most adventures this can be perilous and enchanting and probably both. As we set sail to shores unknown at the beginning of a semester or whenever we pick up the tools of our trade and engage the process, the reciprocal dynamic of impulse and feedback, intuition and rationalization will be different for each person, each cohort, and each viewer. Really all that is required is an open mind and heart. This is the currency that makes life worth living; it is what gives life its true meaning. But unfortunately, to protect ourselves, we shut it off more often than not. When art teachers tell their students to take a risk that can mean many things. For me it is the willingness to take that risk, which makes you vulnerable. That is the price. A leap of faith, which, at times can be painful, is essential to pursue. If the passion and courage of the images we have explored throughout this text have taught you anything, it should be that the alternative of not taking a risk is worse. Sometimes, it is worth crying over spilled milk and then to make art about it.

Assignments You May Want to Challenge Yourself With

- Collaboration
- Spilled milk
- Rebirth
- Friendship

A few years before we elected the first African American President, before the nasty underbelly of racism reasserted itself more openly than it had in decades, leading to the advocacy movement of Black Lives Matter, Smith's empathy and awareness seemed eerily fine-tuned and prescient.

I leave you with this image, without further comment, to connect with, experience, and question (Figure 35.2). I hope this book has helped you to feel more confident in so doing and, in the face of censorship, imagine what I was forced to redact. No matter what, photography will no doubt chronicle and co-create our individual and collective journey towards demise or reason.

FIGURE 35.2 Redacted. © John Smith

A man has black paint poured over his head and torso.

The white man looks now like a black man.

The transformation is convincing and impactful.

VIII

If Lost or Lonely
Get Your Work Out There

They say that the answer in life is always no, unless you ask. Asking can be hard because it requires the very opposite of what this book is about. In the case of presenting your work at a portfolio review, submitting it to a jury, entering it in a competition, or otherwise getting it out there you have to establish a degree of separation between your work and yourself.

I've heard many students say, "I have been rejected." The fact is your work was not included in a show or publication, because it likely had a certain theme or other conceptual focus that someone determined and your work did not fit into it. Your work may have been truly appreciated but deemed to be outside of the thematic constraints. I say someone because in most cases they don't know you. Remember that they don't know you and therefore did not reject you. They simply did not find a fit for your work.

You have to develop this thick skin and learn to differentiate responses to your work from responses to you. They are not the same thing. Even in life, when you feel personally rejected this is, in actuality, rarely the case. Very few interactions or reactions are truly personal. You must develop the capacity to have your work rejected without feeling personally dismissed.

This can be challenging for many of us, particularly if we pour our deepest feelings into the work and put ourselves out there. To add insult to injury, these submissions are often associated with a non-refundable fee.

The more you do this, the more inoculated against rejection you will become and the more used to how the "game" is played. You will recognize the capriciousness in responses for what they often are. These responses are arbitrary, based on criteria you may not be aware of, and the personal biases of how certain work ought to look, feel, and what it says to those "someones" who are doing the deciding.

There are some tricks (techniques) to help yourself. First, read exactly how the work is to be submitted and follow the process to the letter. If you don't do that, much like at the Department of Motor Vehicles, your application will be rejected for being incomplete, incorrectly filled out, and you will have to go back even if that puts you at risk of a ticket for driving around with expired plates.

While frustrating, few people would say that they were rejected by the DMV. Instead there will be some grumbling about the bureaucracy that everyone is caught up in, and that you just have to provide what they need in order to process your case. So, think that you are applying to the DMV, and don't trip yourself up by being sloppy about it in any way.

This means that your work has to be equally and consistently sized in relation to the number of pixels on the longest axis or length in inches, along with the required dpi, file format, usually TIFF or JPEG, color space, RGB Adobe 98, CMYK, or sRGB. The date of each work, its printed size, and type of print, are often additional requirements along with an artist's statement and consistent labeling of each file down to the underline dashes. Hand-signed model releases will often also be a prerequisite for the publication of your work. Don't forget to secure these for every model you photograph at the time of doing so. Even if they are your personal friends, this should offend no one because you are dependent on these releases in order to legally publish your work.

If you submit your work exactly as required you have already won the first part of the battle. Imagine the frustration of receiving inconsistently labeled, sized, or otherwise incomplete applications. If you think of the volume of submissions that are processed, you can understand why this can lead to a rejection of your work because it did not conform to the submissions' guidelines, long before it actually ever gets in front of a jury.

The second piece of important advice is to sequence your work as compellingly as possible. This includes conceptual, compositional, color complementary, and narrative considerations, whether you put three or thirty images forward. Think of your sustained visual inquiry as an essay, a story. This story can unfold in a linear or in a circular way. It can be tangible or totally abstract and everything in between. What matters most is that it holds together and is readable in a way that keeps the viewer engaged. This may require the sacrifice of a great image because it doesn't fit as part of your sequence. While it may be hard to take out a favorite image, it shouldn't feel personal, just as the acceptance or rejection of work in a particular instance is not.

Third, do your research. What work does a particular gallery or publication showcase? Be prepared to speak to other work in that forum and how your work complements it, relates to it. As you experience your first successes and they may be modest, you nevertheless are starting to build a network. People become aware of your work and eventually one thing will lead to another. I recommend you build a web presence allowing you to direct interested parties to a well-organized repository of your work for reference and further dialogue. You can do the same with social media, such as dedicating a Facebook page to your work under the same name as your website. Finally, see if you can get accepted to online galleries with search engines by key word. You never know when an editor is looking for a particular theme that, if your image is correctly tagged, may lead them straight to you.

By creating your initial luck, by taking the risk to ask, the answer may eventually be yes and that one yes can lead to others where eventually people may seek you out rather than the other way around. The easier and more likely it is that they find you, the more likely you are to lay the foundation for visibility and a growing community where you can find invaluable advice.

Use that advice in many ways. For instance, make small work prints of a big project, mix them all up, and let others sequence them and see what happens. Write down the sequence on the back with the initials of that series and repeat. Then repeat again. Find the most diverse group of people you trust. More often than not, two or three images are consistently sorted in the same order and eventually a pattern of consensus emerges on how certain images grab an audience in a certain way.

At some point you have to cut the cord, take everything you have learned into consideration and construct a more cohesive series that is speaking back to you and your audience. If possible repeat the process that should now lead to more nuanced responses and then fine-tune your sequence until you are happy with it and it makes sense to you. This should also inform your artist's statement.

As with your work, less is sometimes more, and a sparse, short, and enticing statement of intent is again more likely to engage someone as opposed to some generic, non-committal statement that sounds like the ten previous ones they just read. Tie your work to larger issues than what might have driven the initial creative engagement on your part. Find a way to tether your personal impulse to bigger questions. The reason for this is simple. The more room you leave for others to find their own access and connection to the work, the easier it will be for them to do so. This is the fourth skill to develop in promoting your work.

The fifth is to try and try again. For some people your work may resonate with them but they want to see commitment and growth. If the work gets rejected one year, come back better and stronger the next year. If you receive feedback about why your work did not make it into the final round, see whether you can enter into a conversation that will help you to understand what was considered to be lacking. If you disagree with that assessment, this may simply mean that there is nothing wrong with your work but the outlet you have been pursuing is the wrong one. Instead of dismissing the response, thank the person who took the trouble to give you feedback and don't be shy to ask where in their opinion your work might fit better. Sometimes such rejections lead you to the right place by the simple process of elimination. You started somewhere and the relationships that you build in so doing lead you somewhere unanticipated.

So don't take a rejection as a personal judgment on the worth of your work or, even worse, your own self-worth. Instead look at it as an opportunity to find the right place. A closed door can be as much of a signpost as an open door if you look at them in a dispassionate way.

Ultimately you are trying to establish a mutually beneficial, professional, business relationship. As antithetical as that may sound this is the reality for most artists who are starting out.

Like finding a job or a partner or a place to live, multiple elements have to click and it is no different with your work and the career you have decided to embark on.

So go for it. The answer will always be no until it is yes! Since you already have that experience in other interpersonal situations, rely on your knowledge, hone it, and make it part of your way to negotiate the art world and/or academia.

IX

Epilogue
Florence + The Machine

As a non-native English speaker who grew up in Switzerland, I have a difficult time understanding English lyrics in songs. To this day, unless it's Leonard Cohen or Bob Dylan, I rarely understand the lyrics correctly. Growing up, English was just another sound, for the greatest part, in music. This influenced how I came to look at art.

I've heard people actually complain that they can't understand Michael Stipe of R.E.M. either because of his lack of supposed enunciation or his stream of non-sequiturs. To argue that he is a musical surrealist may be too much to ask. This only came as a surprise to me because I never actually expect to understand what is sung or to think of music as something other than surreal. One only has to think of Pink Floyd's trip to the dark side of the moon.

For me the human voice has merely represented another infinite variation of a musical score used to support the melody.

While I am a predominantly visual person, throughout the process of writing this book I've become more interested in words again. I'm constantly amazed at the way in which some words and phrases of the songs I listen to over and again are misheard. I think we all have this experience, often we feel incredulous when we find out what we should have heard. Listening to music and not hearing the words correctly suggests to me that this arguable deficit of understanding is not a deficit in the way we conventionally think of it.

This is where my interest in visual literacy intersects with linguistic literacy.

Where the musical voice ultimately transports me, is less connected to the actual words than to the feeling, the melody, and the tone. So often it is particularly the pathos of the song that transports me.

Where the visual voice ultimately takes me is equally less connected to the actual subject matter than to the feeling it elicits, the subtext, where I hope you will in your own way, intensely connect.

I hope the visual connection in the thirty-five preceding examples will help you to listen to your own voice and empower you to determine how you individually connect with what you visually encounter.

I am willing to bet that you already do this with music even when you understand the words perfectly. To read the lyrics is not the same as to hear them. To read the information in a photograph (or any other piece of art) is not the same as feeling how and where it moves you. To read a movie script is not the same as the intangible suspension of disbelief, resulting from a combination of great directing, acting, filming, and editing. Finishing a great book can be profoundly sad: we say goodbye to characters we imagined to be a certain way, and no two readers will ever have imagined the characters the same way. One of the reasons people who loved a book often don't like the movie is because they feel the casting director miscast and misinterpreted "their" characters.

If you are still in doubt, think of an operatic performance. Even if you speak the language perfectly it can be impossible to understand what is sung. However, the sound can move us to tears.

With the foregoing in mind, I would like to thank a band called Florence + The Machine. I listened to their album, "How Big, How Blue, How Beautiful" over and over while writing this book. It created a tonal space of focus and creativity where I would no longer consciously hear the music but remained suspended in its embrace. Thank you Ms. Florence, Ms. Ester, and the band, for your songs and inspiration. Thank you also to those who are living with me for not freaking out upon hearing me repeat-play this album.

It is never the actual thing I see or hear, even if I understand it, but rather the inflection in how it is conveyed.

Quick Reference Index
Featured Artists in Alphabetical Order

Artist	* Medium	Chapter		Page
ABBRUZZESE ANNI	SGP	4	Nike and the Butterfly	p. 19
ANSTETT CHAI	SGP/APP	25	Hypnagogia	p. 131
ARAGONCILLO HENRY	APP	18	Recycling	p. 93
CARSON ELAINE	APP	27	Snap	p. 143
DELAY CHRISTINE	APP	7	Henry's Tale	p. 35
EDWARDS JENNIFER	SGP	34	The Angel and the Wasp	p. 183
ELLENWOOD LIZ	SGP	5	Staying in Line	p. 23
FAY D. ROBERTSON	APP	3	Just Fashion	p. 13
FLECKENSTEIN JORDAN	SGP	17	Lady Like	p. 89
JANSSON JOHAN	APP	15	A Conversation with God	p. 79
JONES ANDREA	APP	8	Moment by Moment	p. 41
JUTTA ANOUK	APP	24	Blood is Blood	p. 127
KELLY RIGBY	SGP	1	The Velvet Hammer	p. 1
KRAVITS ELLIOTT	APP	22	Reflection	p. 117
LEROY VANESSA	APP	2	The Personal Galaxy	p. 7
LEVESQUE TYLA	SGP	13	The Tyranny of Borders	p. 69
LEWIS JON	APP	33	What Is to Come	p. 177
LEWIS PAUL	APP	29	Big and Small	p. 155
MAEZ MAX	APP	14	The Holy Rosary	p. 75
MAINHART HANNAH	APP	26	Harmonia	p. 137
PLUM SARA	APP	20	Dad	p. 107

continued

Artist	*Medium	Chapter	Page
RAPPE ELEANOR	APP	19 Appropriation	p. 101
REEVES-HENNING JACKSON	SGP/APP	12 The Original	p. 61
REYES-NEWELL ADRIANA	APP	11 The Other Half	p. 57
RILEY KAREN	APP	6 Politics	p. 29
SAENGSOURIYHETH THAP	APP	28 Recognition	p. 149
SANCHEZ MARCOS	APP	23 Sky View	p.121
SAUNIER RICHARD	APP	21 Speed and Stoicism	p. 111
SELAVY SHERRY	APP	30 Ammo and a Happy Meal	p. 159
SIKORA STEVE	SGP	16 Superstructure	p. 85
SMITH JOHN	APP	35 In the End	p. 191
TEIWES MARK	APP	9 The Drowned Gun	p. 46
VU TRANG	APP	31 The Spider and the Net	p. 165
WHITNEY MEGAN	APP	10 Split Again	p. 53
WOLF MISSY	APP	32 Dirty Jobs	p. 173

* Media: SGP—silver gelatin print; APP—archival pigment print